ESTATE PUBLICATIONS

SURREY

Street maps with index
Administrative Districts
Population Gazetteer
Road Map with index

Street plans prepared and published by ESTATE PUBLICATIONS, BRIDEWELL HOUSE, TENTERDEN, KENT and based upon the ORDNANCE SURVEY maps with the sanction of the controller of H.M. Stationery Office.

Every effort has been made to verify the accuracy of information in this book but the publishers cannot accept responsibility for expense or loss caused by any error or omission. Information that will be of assistance to the user of the maps will be welcomed.

The Publishers acknowledge the co-operation of the local authorities of towns represented in this atlas

CONTENTS

SURREY ADMINISTRATIVE DISTRICTS: page 4

GAZETTEER INDEX TO ROAD MAP page 5
(with populations)

SURREY ROAD MAP: pages 6-7
(Scale: 4 miles to 1 inch)

TOWN CENTRE STREET MAPS:

Scale of street plans: 4 inches to 1 mile (unless otherwise stated on map)

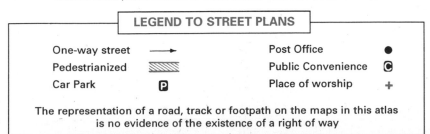

LEGEND TO STREET PLANS

One-way street	→	Post Office	●
Pedestrianized	(hatched)	Public Convenience	Ⓒ
Car Park	Ⓟ	Place of worship	+

The representation of a road, track or footpath on the maps in this atlas
is no evidence of the existence of a right of way

ADMINISTRATIVE DISTRICTS

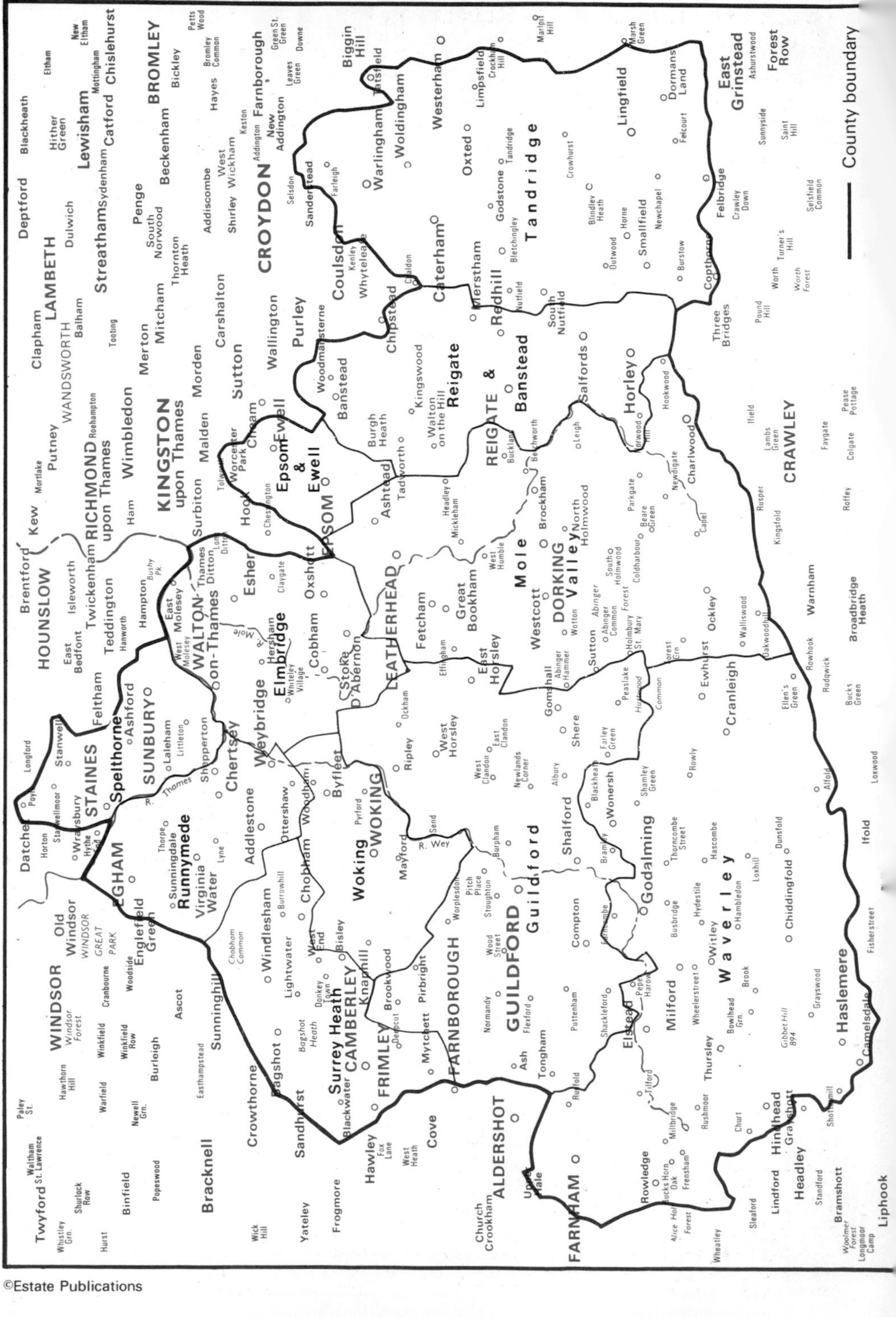
County boundary
HOUNSLOW
RICHMOND upon Thames
KINGSTON upon Thames
LAMBETH
WANDSWORTH
BROMLEY
CROYDON
Sutton
SPELTHORNE
STAINES
SUNBURY
Runnymede
EGHAM
WALTON-on-Thames
Elmbridge
Epsom & Ewell
EPSOM
Reigate & Banstead
REIGATE
Tandridge
Mole Valley
DORKING
LEATHERHEAD
Woking
WOKING
Surrey Heath
CAMBERLEY
FRIMLEY
Guildford
GUILDFORD
Waverley
Godalming
FARNBOROUGH
ALDERSHOT
FARNHAM
CRAWLEY
WINDSOR
Bracknell
Haslemere
East Grinstead

GAZETTEER INDEX TO ROAD MAP

with Populations

County of Surrey population **1,018,003**

SURREY Districts:

Elmbridge	**114,479**
Epsom and Ewell	**67,007**
Guildford	**122,378**
Mole Valley	**79,220**
Reigate & Banstead	**117,777**
Runnymede	**71,789**
Spelthorne	**89,987**
Surrey Heath	**79,073**
Tandridge	**76,316**
Waverley	**110,212**
Woking	**86,765**

Abinger Common	7 E5
Abinger Hammer **1,780**	6 D4
Addlestone	6 C2
Albury **1,188**	6 D4
Alfold **1,086**	6 D6
Artington **370**	*
Ash, **15,519**	6 B4
Ashford, **25,739**	6 D1
Ashstead, **13,363**	7 E3
Bagshot (& Windlesham) **16,147**	6 B2
Banstead, **43,404**	7 F3
Beare Green	7 E5
Betchworth **937**	7 F4
Bisley **3,542**	6 C3
Blackheath	6 C4
Blackwater	6 A3
Bletchingley **2,858**	7 G4
Blindley Heath	7 G4
Bowlhead Green	6 B5
Bramley **3,163**	
Brockham **2,669**	7 E4
Brook	6 B5
Brookwood	6 B3
Buckland **584**	7 F4
Bucks Horn Oak	6 A5
Burgh Heath with Kingswood, **6,340**	7 F3
Burnham	6 C4
Burrowhill	6 C2
Burstow, E.C. Wed. **4,591**	7 G5
Busbridge **892**	6 C5
Byfleet **7,120**	6 D3
Camberley (& Frimley) **51,894**	6 B3
Camelsdale	6 B6
Capel **3,481**	7 E5
Caterham (& Warlingham), **32,782**	7 G3
Charlwood **1.969**	7 F5
Chelsham & Farleigh **576**	7 G3
Chertsey **43,067**	6 D2
Chiddingfold **2,852**	6 C6
Chipstead, (with Woodmansterne and Hooley **6,319**	7 F3
Chobham **4,144**	6 C2
Churt (with Hindhead)	6 A5
Claygate **6,495**	7 E2
Cobham **10,252**	6 D3
Coldharbour	7 E5
Compton **964**	6 C4
Copthorne	7 G5
Cranleigh **11,479**	6 D5
Crowhurst **2,907**	7 H4
Croydon (Gtr. Ln.)	7 G2
Deepcut	6 B3
Dockenfield **405**	*
Donkey Town	6 B3
Dorking **24003**	7 E4
Dormans land	7 H5
Dunsfold **1,066**	6 C6
East Clandon **283**	6 D4
East Horsley **4,081**	6 D4
East Molesey **5,613**	7 E2
Effingham **2,499**	6 D3
Egham **28,722**	6 C1
Ellen's Green	6 D6
Elstead **2,436**	6 B5
Englefield Green **7,118**	6 C1

Epsom (with Ewell) **67,007**	7 E3
Esher **62,559**	7 E2
Ewell (with Epsom) **67,007**	7 F2
Ewhurst **2,369**	6 D5
Farleigh & Chelsham **576**	7 G3
Farley Green	6 D5
Farncombe	6 C5
Farnham **36,284**	6 A4
Felbridge **1,916**	7 G5
Felcourt	7 H5
Fetcham **8,317**	7 E3
Flexford	6 B4
Forest Green	6 D5
Frensham **2,740**	6 A5
Frimley (with Camberley) **51,894**	6 B3
Godalming **20,086**	6 C5
Godstone **5,515**	7 G4
Gomshall	6 D4
Grayshott	6 B6
Grayswood	6 B6
Great Bookham (with Little Bookham) **10.421**	7 E3
Guildford **59,976**	6 C4
Hambledon **664**	6 C5
Hascombe **292**	6 C5
Haslemere **15,235**	6 B6
Headley **709**	7 E3
Hersham **11,853**	6 D2
Hindhead (with Churt)	6 B6
Holmbury St Mary	6 D5
Holmwood **892**	*
Hookwood	7 F5
Horley **19,267**	7 F5
Horne **895**	7 G5
Hydestile	6 C5
Kingston upon Thames (Gtr.Ln.)	7 E1
Kingswood with Burgh Heath **6,340**	7 F3
Knaphill	6 B3
Laleham **7,330**	6 D2
Leatherhead **41.819**	7 E3
Leigh **944**	7 F4
Lightwater	6 B2
Limpsfield **3,456**	7 H4
Lingfield **8,161**	7 H5
Littleton	6 D2
Long Ditton **3,998**	7 E2
Loxhill	6 C6
Lyne	6 C2
Mayford	6 C3
Merstham	7 G4
Mickleham **484**	7 E3
Milford	6 B5
Millbridge	6 A5
Mytchett	6 B3
Newchapel	7 G5
Newdigate **1,499**	7 E5
Newlands Corner	6 D4
Normandy **2,499**	6 B4
North Holmwood **5,427**	7 E4
Norwood Hill	7 F5
Nutfield **2,682**	7 G4
Oakwoodhill	6 D6
Ockham **407**	6 D3
Ockley **864**	7 E5
Ottershaw	6 C2
Outwood	7 G5
Oxshott (with Stoke) **5,708**	7 E2
Oxted **10,063**	7 H4
Parkgate	7 E5
Peaslake	6 D5
Peper Harow **164**	6 B5
Pirbright 3,862	6 B3
Pitch Place	6 C4
Poyle	6 C1

Puttenham **532**	6 B4
Pyrford	6 C3
Reigate (with Redhill) **52,007**	7 G4
Richmond (Gtr. Ln.)	7 E1
Ripley **1,697**	6 D3
Rowledge	6 A5
Rowly	6 D5
Runfold	6 B4
Rushmoor	6 A5
St Martha **674**	*
Salfords and Sidlow **3,099**	6 C3
Seal & Sands **851**	*
Send **3,975**	6 C3
Shackleford **650**	6 B5
Shalford **3,781**	6 C4
Shamley Green	6 D5
Shepperton **11,589**	6 D2
Shere **3,373**	6 D4
Shottermill	6 B6
Smallfield	7 G5
South Holmwood	7 E5
South Nutfield	7 F4
Staines **54,254**	6 D1
Stanwell **9,317**	6 D1
Stanwell Moor	6 D1
Stoke D'Abernon (with Oxshott) **5,708**	6 D3
Stoughton	6 C4
Sunbury **50308**	6 D1
Sunningdale	6 C2
Sutton	6 D4
Sutton (Gtr. Ln.)	7 F2
Tadworth and Walton on the Hill **6,370**	7 F3
Tandridge **678**	7 H4
Tatsfield **1,816**	7 H3
Thames Ditton **5,000**	7 E2
Thorncombe Street	6 C5
Thorpe **5,182**	6 C1
Thursley **635**	6 B5
Tilford **742**	6 B5
Titsey **94**	*
Tongham (with Seale) **2,073**	6 B4
Virginia Water **4,120**	6 C2
Wallswood	6 E5
Walton-on-Thames and Weybridge **51,920**	6 D2
Walton on the Hill and Tadworth **6,370**	7 F3
Wanborough **301**	*
Warlingham (with Caterham) **32.725**	7 G3
West Clandon **1,309**	6 D4
West End **3,346**	6 C2
West Horsley **2,728**	6 D3
West Humble	7 E4
West Molesey	6 D2
Westcott **2,118**	7 E4
Weybridge and Walton-on-Thames **51,920**	6 D2
Wheelerstreet	6 B5
Whiteley Village	6 D2
Whiteley Village	6 D2
Whyteleafe **3,166**	7 G3
Windlesham (with Bagshott) **16,147**	6 B2
Wisley **171**	*
Witley **7,290**	6 B5
Woking **86,765**	6 C3
Woldingham **1,993**	7 H3
Wonersh **3,332**	6 C5
Woodham	6 C2
Woodmansterne, with Chipstead and Hooley **6,319**	7 F3
Wood Street	6 C4
Worcester Park	7 F2
Worplesdon **8,175**	6 C3
Wotton **578**	7 E4

Population figures are based upon the 1991 census and relate to the local authority or parish as constituted at that date. Places with no popoulation figure form part of a larger local authority area or parish. Boundaries of local authority areas are shown on page 4.

Population figures in bold type.

*Places not included on map due to limitation of space.

ROAD MAP

Scale 4 miles to 1 inch

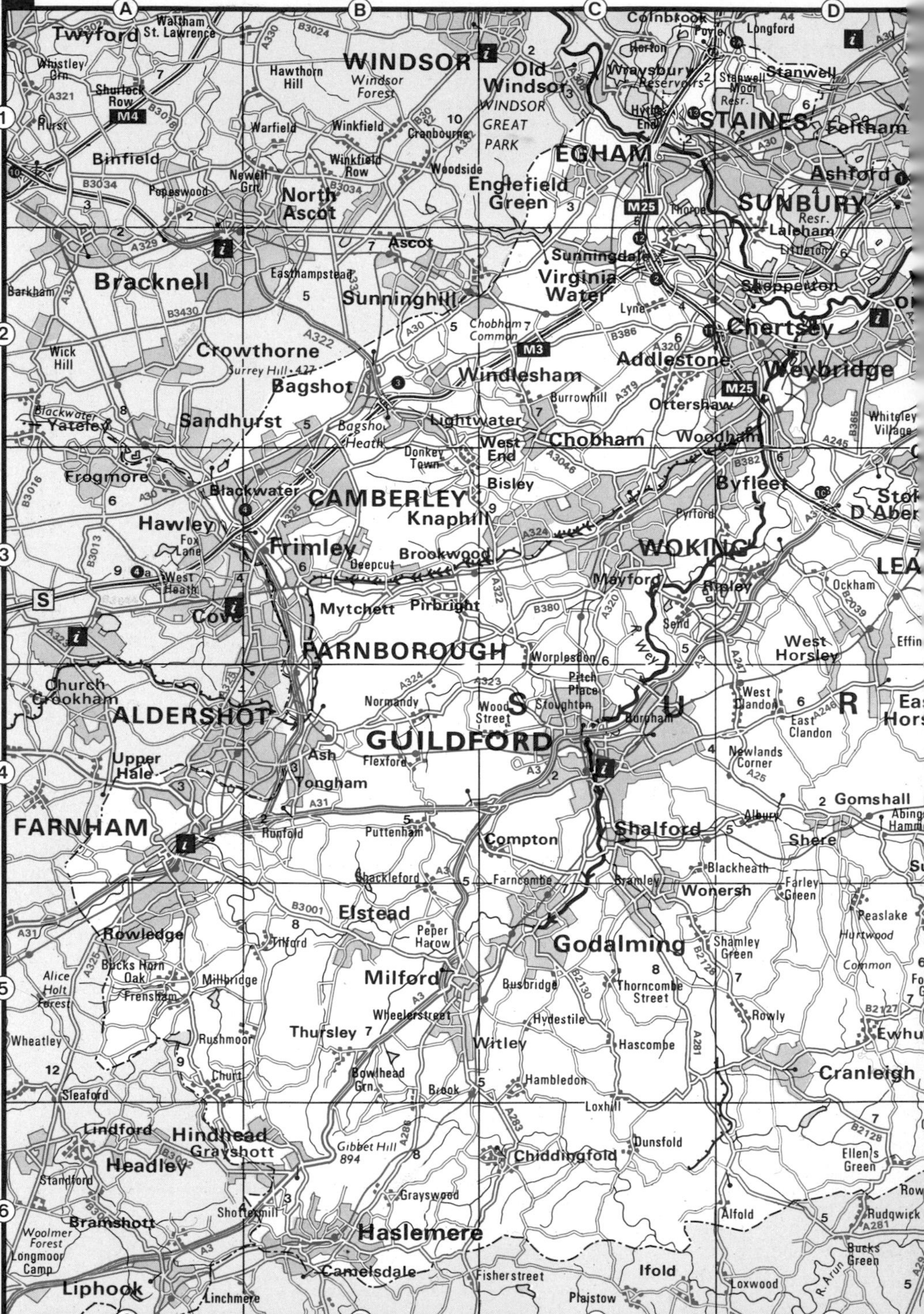
A
B
C
D
1
2
3
4
5
6
Twyford
Waltham St. Lawrence
WINDSOR
Windsor Forest
Old Windsor
WINDSOR GREAT PARK
Colnbrook
Poyle
Longford
Horton
Wraysbury
Reservoirs
Stanwell
Stanwell Moor
Resr.
Whistley Grn.
Hawthorn Hill
Shurlock Row
Hurst
M4
Warfield
Winkfield
Cranbourne
Hythe End
STAINES
Feltham
Binfield
Winkfield Row
Woodside
EGHAM
Ashford
Newell Grn.
Popeswood
North Ascot
Englefield Green
Thorpe
M25
SUNBURY
Resr.
Laleham
Littleton
Ascot
Sunningdale
Bracknell
Easthampstead
Virginia Water
Shepperton
Barkham
Sunninghill
Lyne
Chertsey
Chobham Common
M3
Addlestone
Wick Hill
Crowthorne
Surrey Hill · 427
Windlesham
Weybridge
Bagshot
Burrowhill
Ottershaw
Blackwater
Yateley
Sandhurst
Bagshot Heath
Lightwater
Whiteley Village
Donkey Town
West End
Chobham
Woodham
Frogmore
Blackwater
CAMBERLEY
Bisley
Byfleet
Hawley
Knaphill
Pyrford
Stoke D'Abernon
Fox Lane
Frimley
WOKING
West Heath
Deepcut
Brookwood
Mayford
Ripley
Ockham
Cove
Mytchett
Pirbright
Send
R. Wey
FARNBOROUGH
Worplesdon
West Horsley
Effingham
Church Crookham
Pitch Place
Stoughton
West Clandon
ALDERSHOT
Normandy
Wood Street
Burpham
East Clandon
S
U
R
GUILDFORD
Newlands Corner
Upper Hale
Ash
Flexford
Tongham
Gomshall
FARNHAM
Runfold
Puttenham
Albury
Abinger Hammer
Compton
Shalford
Shere
Shackleford
Farncombe
Bramley
Blackheath
Wonersh
Farley Green
Elstead
Peper Harow
Peaslake
Rowledge
Tilford
Godalming
Shamley Green
Hurtwood
Common
Bucks Horn Oak
Millbridge
Milford
Busbridge
Thorncombe Street
Alice Holt Forest
Frensham
Wheelerstreet
Hydestile
Rowly
Ewhurst
Wheatley
Thursley
Rushmoor
Witley
Hascombe
Cranleigh
Churt
Bowlhead Grn.
Brook
Hambledon
Sleaford
Loxhill
Lindford
Hindhead
Grayshott
Gibbet Hill 894
Chiddingfold
Dunsfold
Ellen's Green
Headley
Standford
Grayswood
Shottermill
Bramshott
Alfold
Rudgwick
Woolmer Forest
Longmoor Camp
Haslemere
Bucks Green
Camelsdale
Fisherstreet
Ifold
Liphook
Linchmere
Plaistow
Loxwood
R. Arun

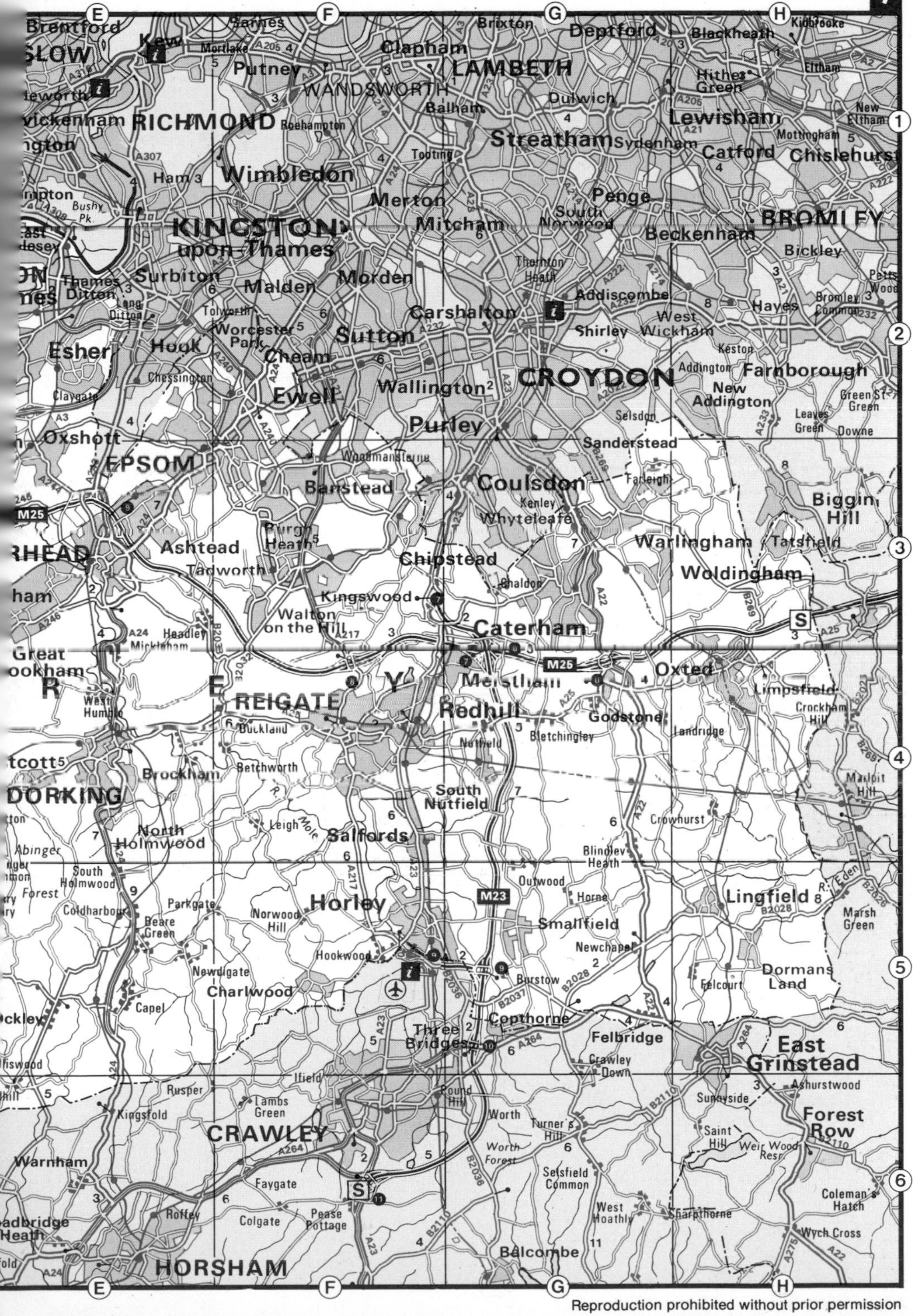

E
F
G
H
1
2
3
4
5
6
Brentford
Kew
Barnes
Mortlake
Putney
Clapham
Brixton
LAMBETH
WANDSWORTH
Deptford
Blackheath
Kidbrooke
Eltham
Hither Green
Balham
Dulwich
Lewisham
New Eltham
RICHMOND
Roehampton
Streatham
Sydenham
Mottingham
Catford
Chislehurst
Tooting
Ham
Wimbledon
Merton
Penge
South Norwood
Mitcham
BROMLEY
Bushy Pk.
KINGSTON upon Thames
Beckenham
Bickley
Thornton Heath
Surbiton
Thames Ditton
Long Ditton
Malden
Morden
Addiscombe
Hayes
Bromley Common
Tolworth
Worcester Park
Carshalton
West Wickham
Shirley
Keston
Esher
Hook
Sutton
Cheam
Chessington
Claygate
Ewell
Wallington
CROYDON
Addington
Farnborough
New Addington
Green Street Green
Selsdon
Leaves Green
Downe
Purley
Oxshott
Sanderstead
EPSOM
Woodmansterne
Banstead
Coulsdon
Farleigh
Kenley
Whyteleafe
Biggin Hill
M25
Ashtead
Burgh Heath
Tadworth
Chipstead
Warlingham
Tatsfield
Woldingham
Kingswood
Chaldon
Walton on the Hill
Headley
Mickleham
Caterham
Great Bookham
Oxted
REIGATE
Merstham
Redhill
Limpsfield
West Humble
Buckland
Godstone
Bletchingley
Tandridge
Crockham Hill
Nutfield
Brockham
Betchworth
DORKING
South Nutfield
Mole
Leigh
Salfords
Crowhurst
North Holmwood
Abinger
Blindley Heath
South Holmwood
Outwood
Lingfield
Forest
Horne
M23
Coldharbour
Parkgate
Horley
Beare Green
Norwood Hill
Smallfield
Marsh Green
Newchapel
Hookwood
Newdigate
Dormans Land
Burstow
Charlwood
Felcourt
Capel
Copthorne
Three Bridges
Felbridge
East Grinstead
Crawley Down
Ifield
Ashurstwood
Rusper
Pound Hill
Sunnyside
Kingsfold
Lambs Green
Worth
Forest Row
Turner's Hill
CRAWLEY
Saint Hill
Weir Wood Resr.
Worth Forest
Warnham
Selsfield Common
Faygate
Coleman's Hatch
West Hoathly
Roffey
Colgate
Pease Pottage
Sharpthorne
Wych Cross
Balcombe
HORSHAM

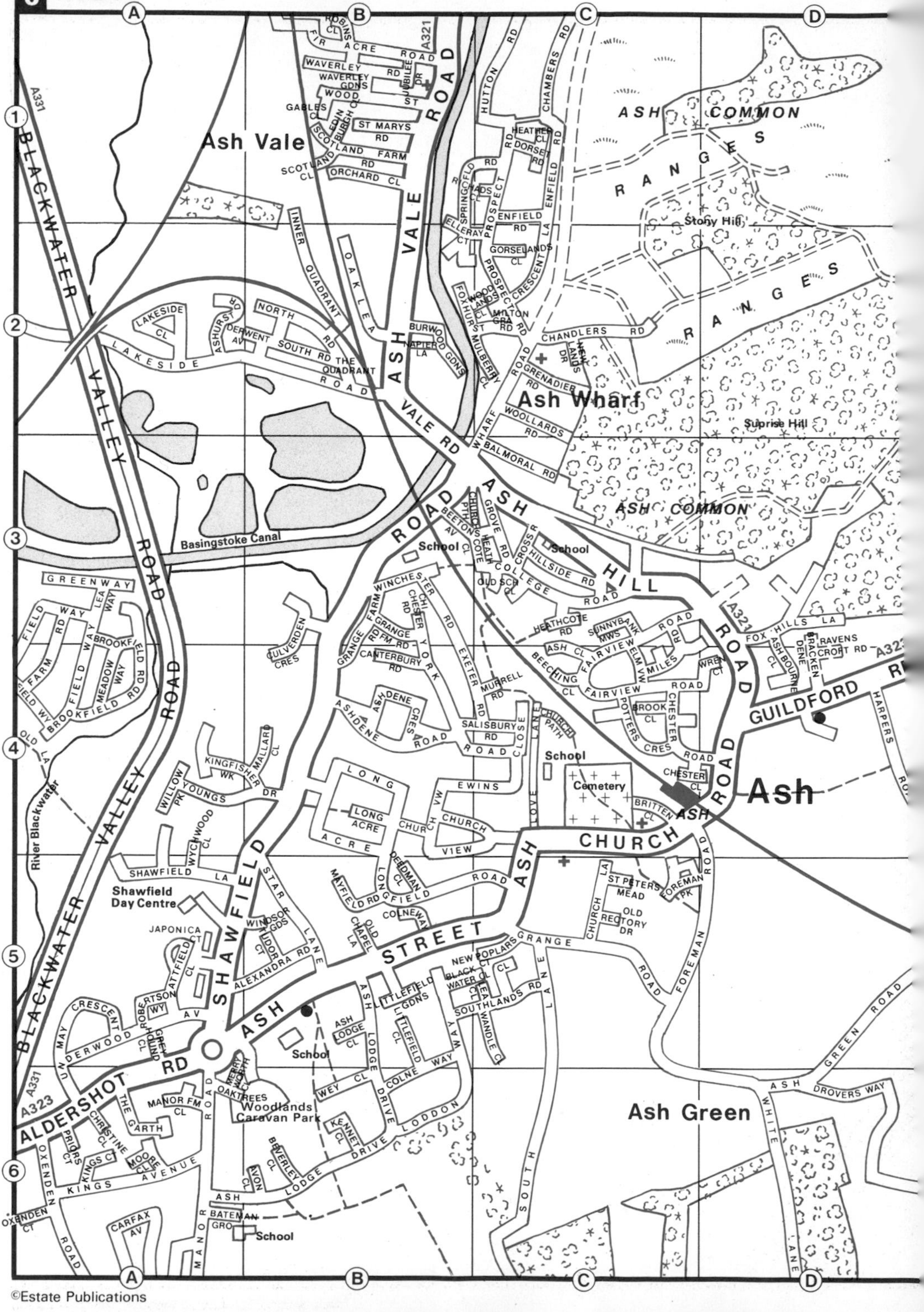

A
B
C
D
1
2
3
4
5
6
Ash Vale
Ash Wharf
Ash
Ash Green
ASH COMMON
RANGES
Stony Hill
Suprise Hill
Basingstoke Canal
River Blackwater
BLACKWATER VALLEY ROAD
A331
A321
A323
ROBINS
FIR ACRE ROAD
WAVERLEY RD
WAVERLEY GDNS
JUBILEE DR
WOOD ST
GABLES CL
EDINBURGH CL
ST MARYS RD
SCOTLAND FARM RD
SCOTLAND CL
ORCHARD CL
ASH VALE ROAD
HUTTON RD
CHAMBERS RD
HEATHER CL
DORSET RD
ENFIELD RD
ENFIELD LA
SPRINGFIELD RD
ST CHADS CL
PROSPECT RD
PROSPECT CRESCENT
ELLERAY CT
GORSELANDS CL
WOODLANDS CL
FOXHURST
MILTON GRA
MULBERRY CL
BURWOOD GDNS
NAPIER LA
OAKLEA
INNER QUADRANT
THE QUADRANT
NORTH RD
SOUTH RD
LAKESIDE CL
LAKESIDE ROAD
ASHURST DR
DERWENT AV
CHANDLERS RD
NEWLANDS DR
WHARF ROAD
GRENADIER RD
WOOLLARDS RD
BALMORAL RD
VALE RD
ASH HILL ROAD
BEETONS AV
CHURCH PATH
HEATH COTE
GROVE RD
CROSS RD
HILLSIDE RD
COLLEGE ROAD
OLD SCH CL
School
WINCHESTER CL
CHICHESTER RD
GRANGE FARM RD
GRANGE RD
CANTERBURY RD
YORK
EXETER RD
HEATHCOTE RD
SUNNYBANK MWS
ASH CL
FAIRVIEW
ELM VW
MILES RD
WREN CT
BEECHING CL
BROOK CL
POTTERS CRES
CHESTER ROAD
CHESTER CL
FOX HILLS LA
ASHBOURNE
BRACKEN DENE
RAVENSCROFT RD
GUILDFORD RD
HARPERS RD
GREENWAY
LEA WAY
FIELD WAY
FARM RD
BROOKFIELD RD
MEADOW WAY
FIELD WY
CULVERDEN CRES
ASHDENE CRES
ASHDENE ROAD
MURRELL RD
SALISBURY RD
ROAD CLOSE
LOVE LANE
Cemetery
BRITTEN CL
KINGFISHER WK
MALLARD CL
WILLOW PK
YOUNGS DR
WYCHWOOD CL
LONG ACRE
EWINS
CHURCH VW
CHURCH VIEW
ASH CHURCH ROAD
OLD LA
SHAWFIELD LA
SHAWFIELD ROAD
Shawfield Day Centre
STAR LANE
MAYFIELD RD
LONGFIELD RD
DEEDMAN CL
COLNE WAY
ST PETERS MEAD
FOREMAN PK
FOREMAN ROAD
OLD RECTORY DR
CHURCH LA
JAPONICA CT
WINDSOR GDS
TUDOR CT
ALEXANDRA RD
CHAPEL LA
ASH STREET
NEW POPLARS CT
GRANGE ROAD
BLACKWATER CL
LITTLEFIELD GDNS
LITTLEFIELD CL
SOUTHLANDS RD
WANDLE CL
ATTFIELD CL
ROBERTSON WY
MAY CRESCENT
UNDERWOOD AV
HOLLIS GREEN CL
ALDERSHOT RD
ASH LODGE CL
ASH LODGE DRIVE
COLNE WAY
WEY CL
MERRYWORTH
OAKTREES
MANOR FM CL
MANOR ROAD
THE GARTH
CHRISTINE CL
PRIORS CT
KINGS CT
MOORE CL
KINGS AVENUE
OXENDEN ROAD
OXENDEN CT
Woodlands Caravan Park
KENNET CL
LODDON
BEVERLEY CL
AVON CL
ASH LODGE
BATEMAN GRO
CARFAX AV
SOUTH LANE
WHITE LANE
ASH GREEN ROAD
DROVERS WAY

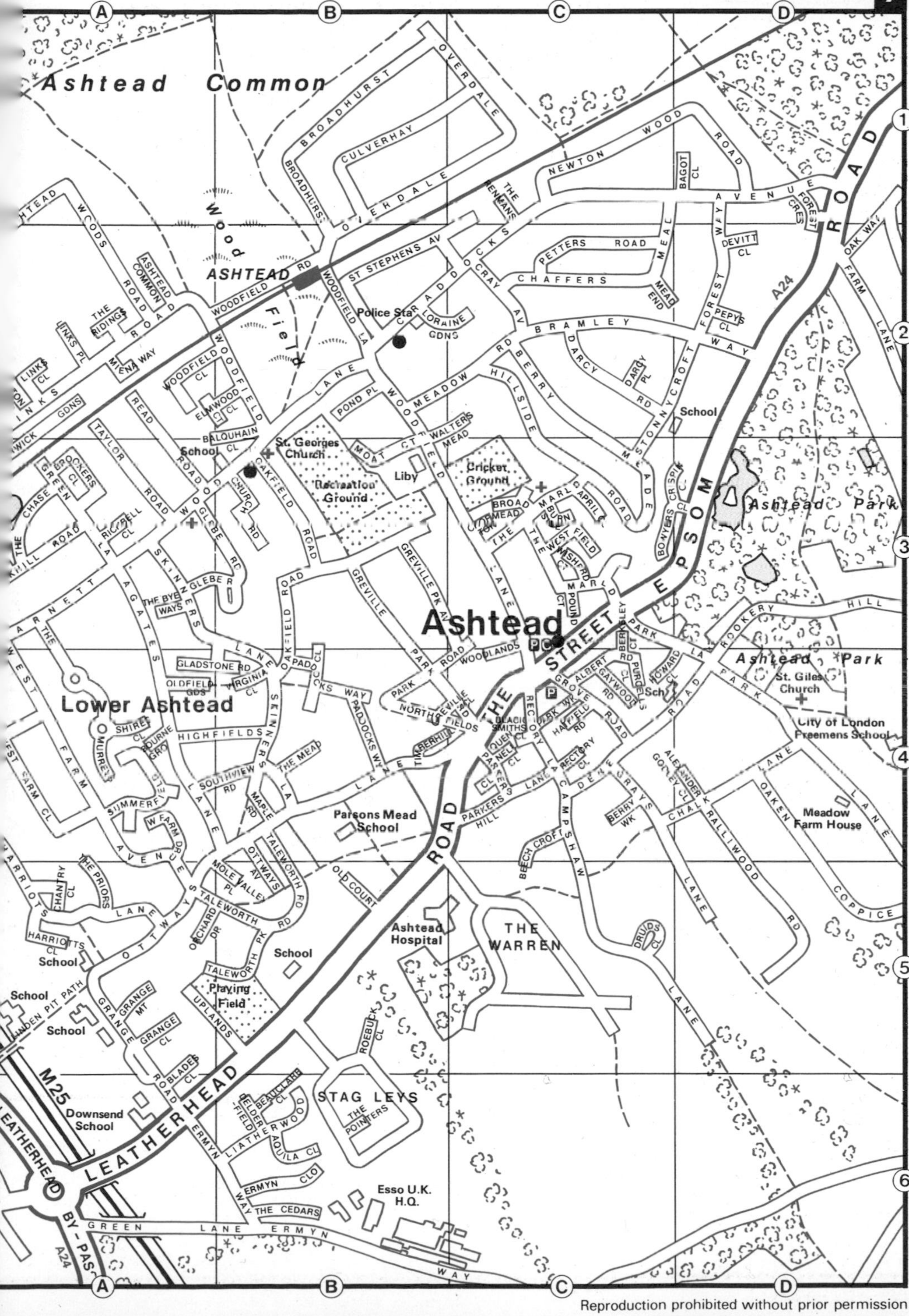
Ashtead Common
Wood Field
ASHTEAD
Ashtead
Lower Ashtead
Ashtead Park
Police Sta
St. Georges Church
Recreation Ground
Liby
Cricket Ground
School
St. Giles Church
City of London Freemens School
Parsons Mead School
Meadow Farm House
Ashtead Hospital
THE WARREN
Playing Field
Downsend School
STAG LEYS
Esso U.K. H.Q.
EPSOM ROAD
A24
THE STREET
LEATHERHEAD ROAD
LEATHERHEAD BY-PASS
M25
WOODFIELD RD
WOODS
OVERDALE
BROADHURST
CULVERHAY
NEWTON WOOD ROAD
AVENUE
FOREST CRES
OAK WAY
FARM LANE
BAGOT CL
THE MARLINS
ST STEPHENS AV
PETTERS ROAD
CHAFFERS MEAD
MEAD END
DEVITT CL
PEPYS CL
FOREST WAY
BRAMLEY WAY
CRADDOCKS AV
LORAINE GDNS
DARCY RD
DARCY PL
STONNYCROFT
ASHTEAD COMMON
THE RIDINGS
LINKS PL
LINKS CL
LINKS GDNS
MIENA WAY
WOODFIELD CL
ELMWOOD CL
BALQUHAIN CL
READ RD
TAYLOR ROAD
BROCKERS CL
GREEN CHASE
RICHBELL CL
GLEBE RD
CHURCH RD
OAKFIELD ROAD
WOODFIELD LA
POND PL
MEADOW RD
HILLSIDE
BERRY
MOAT CT
WALTERS MEAD
MEADE
CRISPIN CL
BONYERS CL
BROADMEAD
THE MARLING
APRIL CL
WEST FIELD
MARY ROAD
POUND CT
GREVILLE PK AV
GREVILLE
SKINNERS LANE
AGATES LANE
THE BYE WAYS
GLADSTONE RD
OLDFIELD GDNS
VIRGINIA CL
PADDOCKS WAY
PARK ROAD
WOODLANDS
BERKELEY PARK
ROOKERY HILL
PARK LANE
NORTHFIELDS
GREVILLE CL
GROVE RD
ALBERT RD
GAYWOOD RD
PURCELLS CL
HOWARD CL
RECTORY LANE
PARK LA
HAYFIELD RD
BLACKSMITHS
QUENNELL CL
PARKERS CL
RECTORY CL
DENE RD
GRAYS LA
ALEXANDER GODLEY CL
ALEXANDER WALK
OAKEN LANE
CHALK LANE
RALLIWOOD ROAD
COPPICE LANE
HIGHFIELDS
SHIRES CL
MURREYS
BOURNE GRO
FARM CL
FARM
SOUTHVIEW RD
THE MEAD
MAPLE RD
TIMBERHILL
SUMMERFIELD
BARNETT
THE WEST
PARKERS HILL
CAMPSHAW
BERRY WK
BEECH CROFT
DRUIDS CL
MARRIOTTS
CHANTRY CL
THE PRIORS
HARRIOTTS CL
OTTWAYS LANE
MOLE VALLEY PL
OTTWAYS AV
TALEWORTH RD
TALEWORTH CL
TALEWORTH PK
ORCHARD DR
OLD COURT
UPLANDS
GRANGE RD
GRANGE MT
GRANGE CL
LINDEN PIT PATH
BLADES CL
ROEBUCK CL
BELDERFIELD
BEAUCLARE CL
LIATHERWOOD
AQUILA CL
THE POINTERS
ERMYN CLO
ERMYN WAY
THE CEDARS
GREEN LANE
A
B
C
D
1
2
3
4
5
6

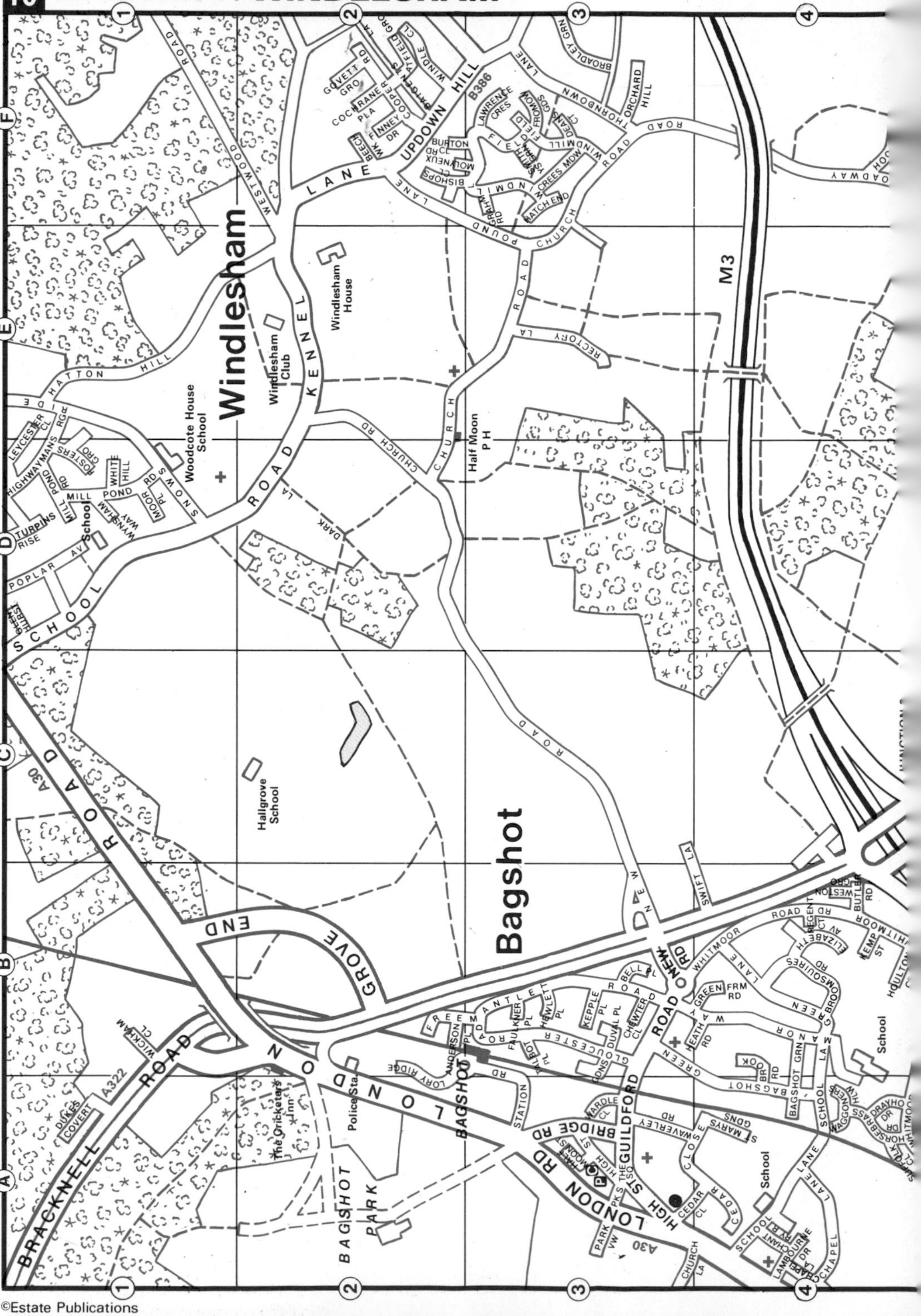
Windlesham
Bagshot
Windlesham House
Windlesham Club
Woodcote House School
Half Moon PH
Hallgrove School
Police Sta.
The Cricketers Inn
School
M3
A30
A322
B386
BRACKNELL ROAD
LONDON ROAD
KENNEL ROAD
UPDOWN HILL
LANE
HATTON HILL
SCHOOL ROAD
WESTWOOD ROAD
CHURCH RD
DARK LA
POUND LANE
CHURCH ROAD
RECTORY LA
THORNDOWN LANE
ORCHARD HILL
BROADLEY GRN
WINDMILL ROAD
LAWRENCE CRES
BURTON CL
MOLYNEUX RD
BISHOPS CL
HATCH END
GOVETT GRO
COCHRANE PLA
FINNEY DR
BEECH WK
POPLAR AV
TURPINS RISE
HIGHWAYMANS RGE
LEYCESTER CL
FOSTERS GRO
MILL POND RD
WHITE HILL
MOOR PL
WYNSHAM WAY
SNOWS RD
GROVE END
NEW RD
SWIFT LA
BAGSHOT PARK
BRIDGE RD
GUILDFORD ROAD
HIGH ST
STATION RD
LORY RIDGE
WICKHAM CL
DUKES COVERT
FREEMANTLE ROAD
FAULKNER PL
HEWLETT PL
KEPPLE PL
DUVAL PL
CHEWTER CL
GLOUCESTER GDNS
TALBOT PL
ANDERSON PL
BELL PL
WHITMOOR ROAD
HEATH RD
GREEN LANE
WAVERLEY RD
ST MARYS GDNS
CEDAR CL
CLOSE
PARK VW
CHURCH LA
LAMBOURNE DR
CHAPEL LANE
SCHOOL LANE
MANOR WAY
BAGSHOT GRN
WAGGONERS HOLLOW
KEMP ST
REGENT CT
ELIZABETH AV
BUTLER RD
WESTON GRO
SQUIRES RD
BROOK RD
HOULTON CT

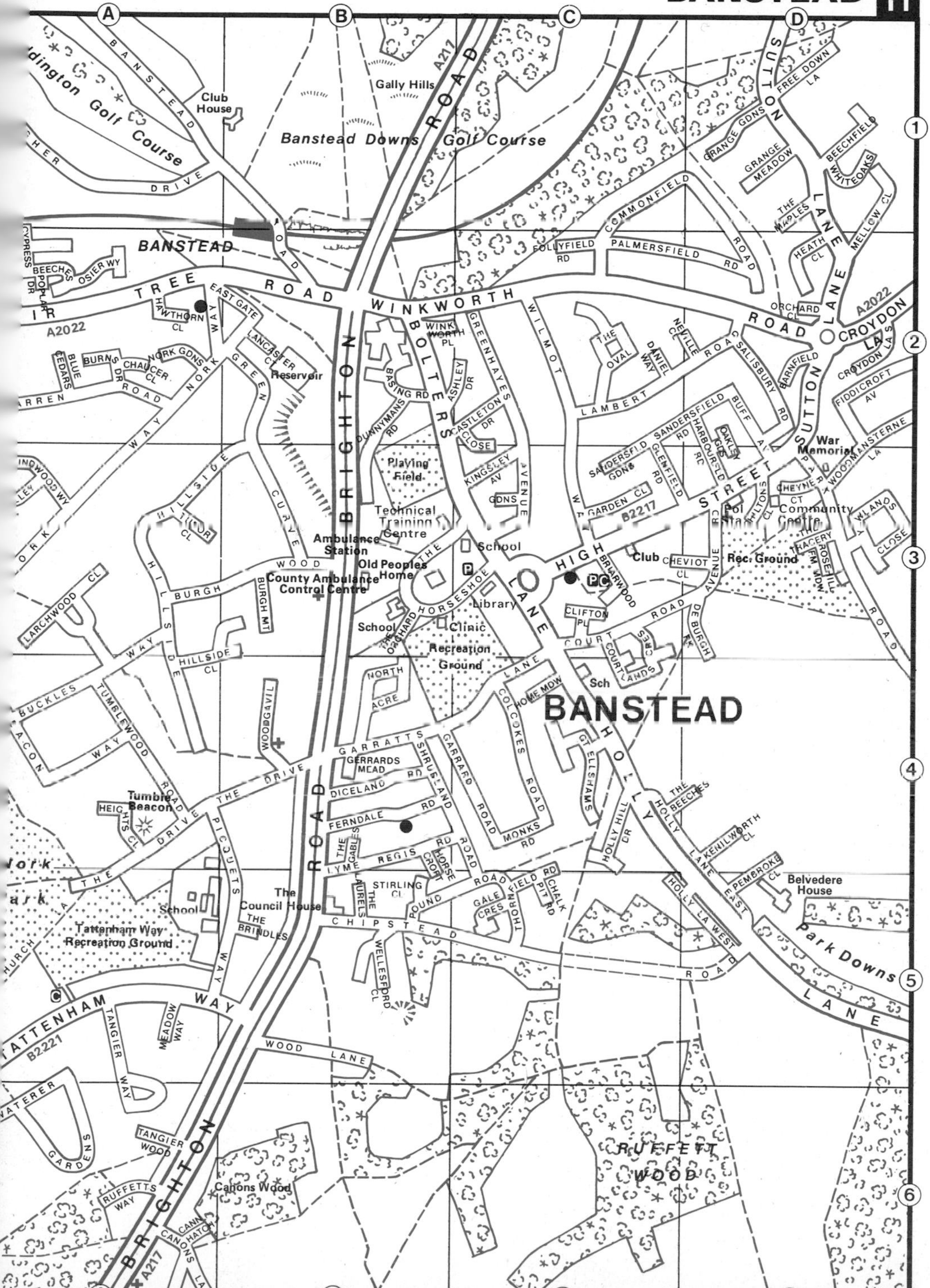
A
B
C
D
1
2
3
4
5
6
Banstead Downs Golf Course
Gally Hills
Club House
BANSTEAD
BRIGHTON ROAD
A217
WINKWORTH ROAD
A2022
CROYDON LA
SUTTON LANE
COMMONFIELD ROAD
PALMERSFIELD RD
FOLLYFIELD RD
BOLTERS LANE
GREENHAYES AVENUE
WILMOT WAY
LAMBERT ROAD
HIGH STREET
B2217
Reservoir
Playing Field
Technical Training Centre
Ambulance Station
Old Peoples Home
County Ambulance Control Centre
School
Library
Clinic
Recreation Ground
Club
Rec. Ground
War Memorial
Community Centre
Pol Sta
BANSTEAD
HIGH LANE
HOLLY LANE
GARRATTS LANE
THE DRIVE
Tumble Beacon
The Council House
CHIPSTEAD ROAD
TATTENHAM WAY
B2221
Tattenham Way Recreation Ground
Park Downs
PARK DOWNS LANE
Belvedere House
WOOD LANE
RUFFETT WOOD
Canons Wood
NORK WAY
Sch

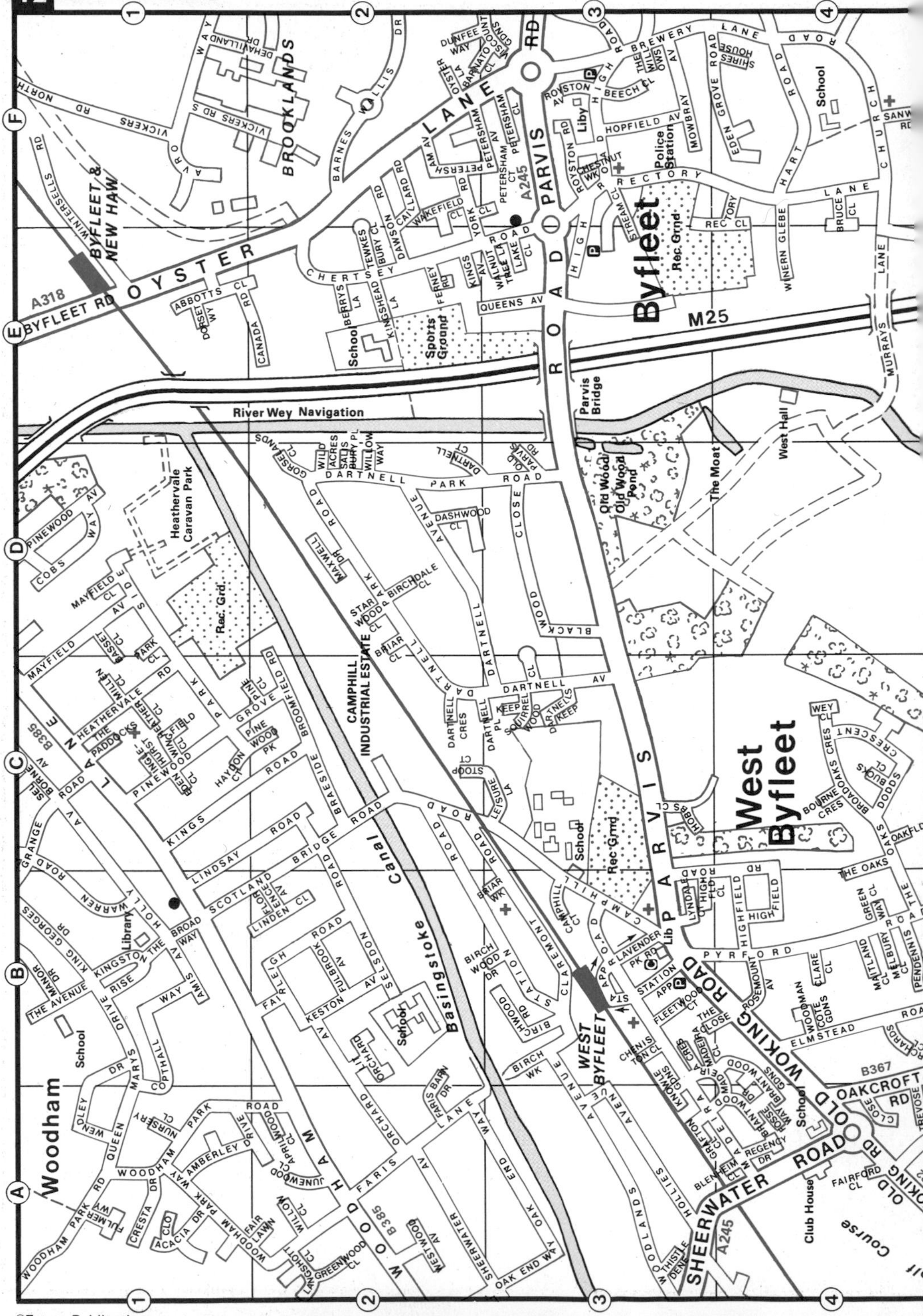
Byfleet
West Byfleet
Woodham
BROOKLANDS
BYFLEET & NEW HAW
WEST BYFLEET
OYSTER LANE
PARVIS ROAD
A245
A318
BYFLEET RD
M25
River Wey Navigation
Basingstoke Canal
CAMPHILL INDUSTRIAL ESTATE
Heathervale Caravan Park
Parvis Bridge
Old Wood Pond
The Moat
West Hall
Police Station
Liby
Library
School
Sports Ground
Rec. Grd.
Club House
Golf Course
HIGH ROAD
RECTORY LANE
CHURCH LANE
HART ROAD
BREWERY LANE
CHERTSEY ROAD
QUEENS AV
DARTNELL PARK ROAD
DARTNELL AV
BLACKWOOD CLOSE
PYRFORD ROAD
WOKING ROAD
OLD WOKING RD
SHEERWATER ROAD
OAKCROFT RD
B367
B385
B382
WOODHAM LANE
WOODHAM PARK ROAD
CAMPHILL ROAD
STATION APP
MADEIRA ROAD
ELMSTEAD ROAD
HIGHFIELD RD
SELDON ROAD
FAIRLEIGH ROAD
HOLLY WARREN
KINGS ROAD
SCOTLAND BRIDGE ROAD
LINDSAY ROAD
BROOMFIELD RD
HEATHERVALE RD
MAYFIELD AV
VICKERS RD
NORTH RD
WINTERSELLS RD
BARNES WALLIS DR
CANADA RD
OAK END WAY
WOODLANDS AV
FARIS LANE
ORCHARD AV
SHEERWATER AV
CLAREMONT AV
BIRCHWOOD DR
HOLLIES AV

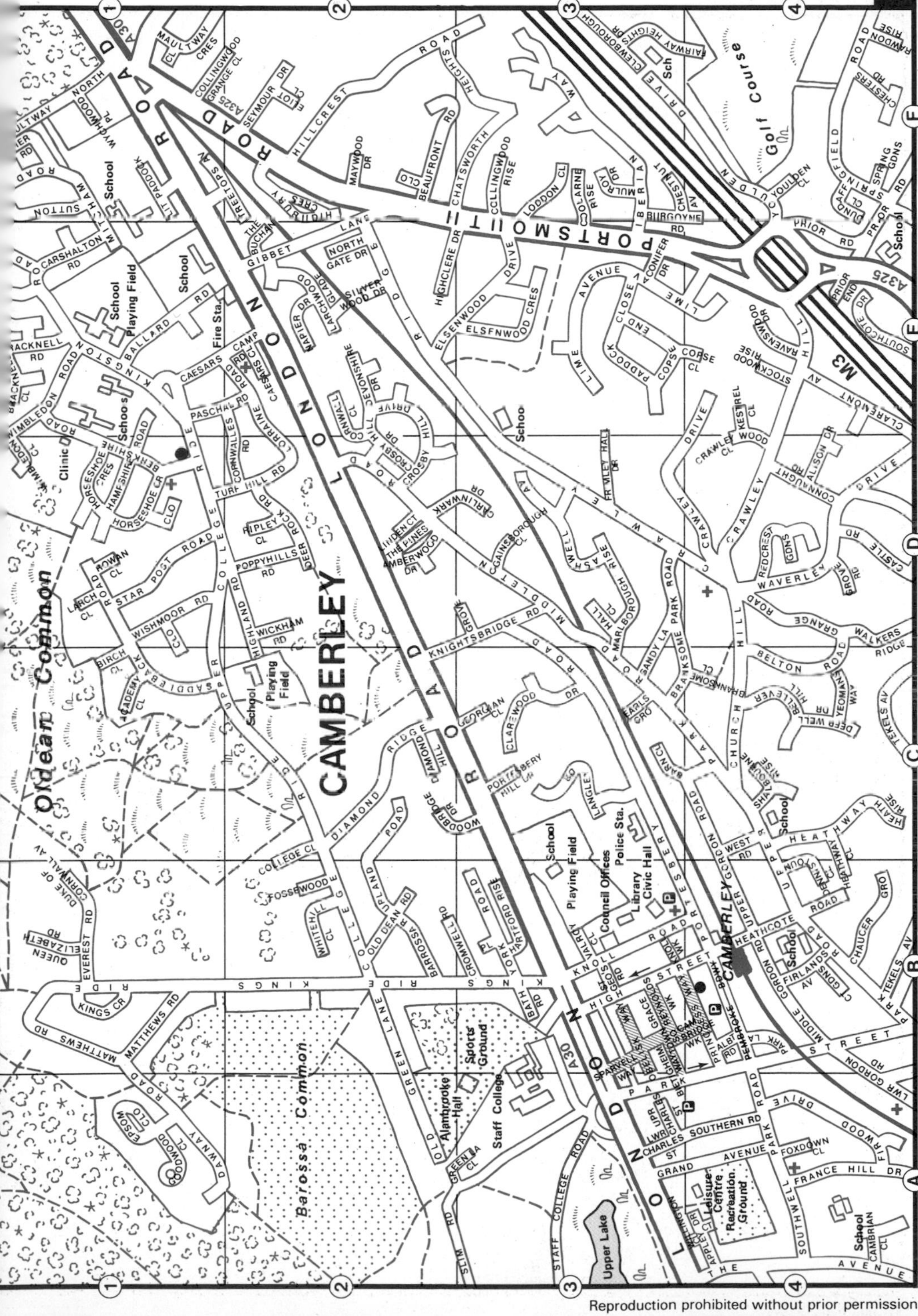
CAMBERLEY
Oldean Common
Barossa Common
Golf Course
Upper Lake
LONDON ROAD
PORTSMOUTH RD
KINGS RIDE
M3
A30
A325
Staff College
Sports Ground
Alanbrooke Hall
Leisure Centre
Recreation Ground
Council Offices
Library
Civic Hall
Police Sta.
Fire Sta.
Clinic
School
Playing Field

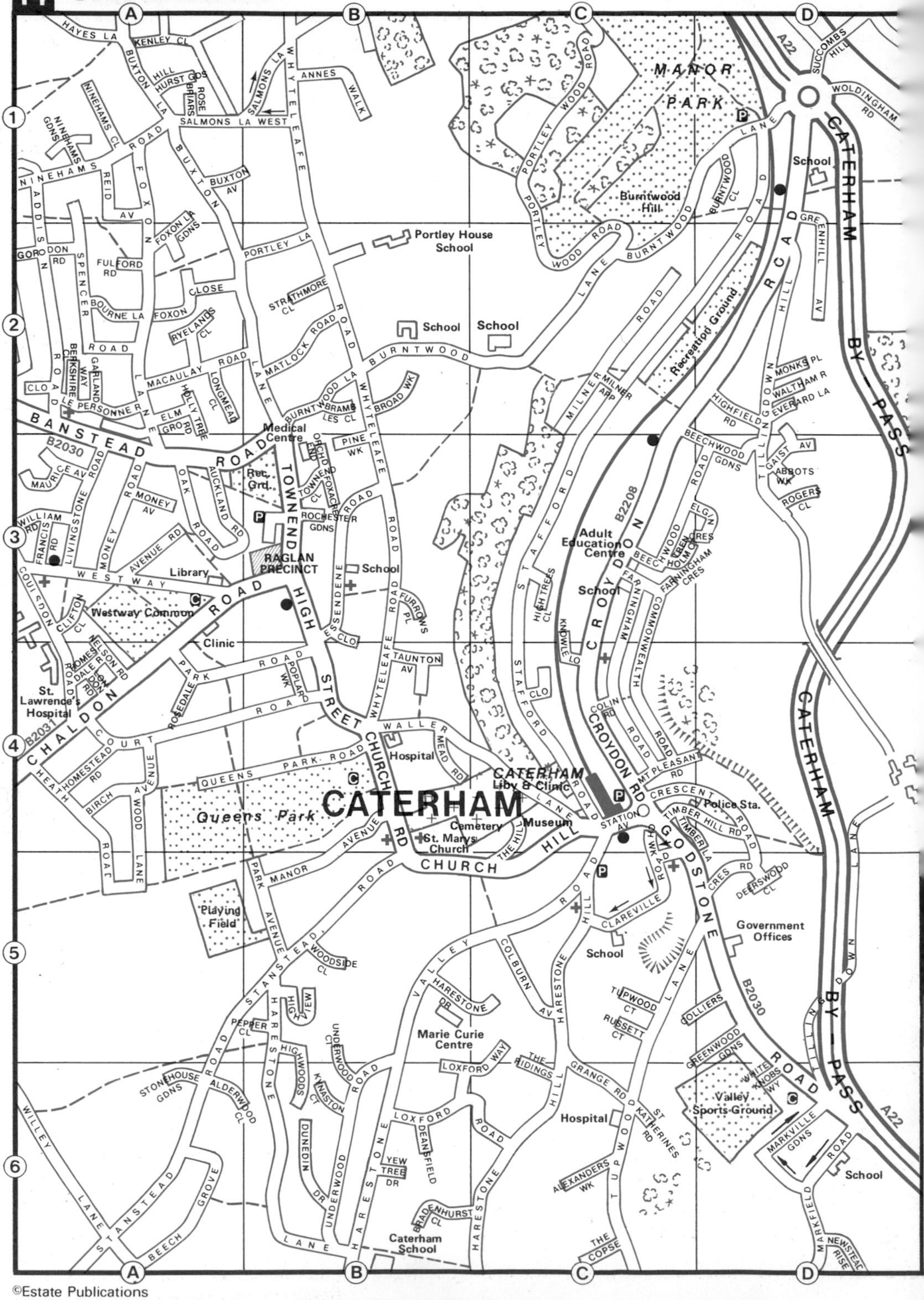

A
B
C
D
1
2
3
4
5
6
HAYES LA
KENLEY CL
BUXTON
HILL
HURST GDS
ROSE
BRIARS
SALMONS LA
SALMONS LA WEST
ANNES
WALK
WHYTELEAFE
NINEHAMS
GDNS
NINEHAMS CL
NINEHAMS
ROAD
REID
AV
FOXON
BUXTON
BUXTON AV
ADDISON
GORDON RD
SPENCER
FULFORD RD
FOXON LA GDNS
PORTLEY LA
Portley House School
STRATHMORE CL
CLOSE
BOURNE LA
FOXON
RYELANDS CL
MATLOCK ROAD
ROAD
School
School
BURNTWOOD
BERKSHIRE CL
GARLAND WAY
MACAULAY
LONGMEAD
HOLLY TREE
CLO
LE PERSONNE
ELM GRO
RD
LANE
BURNTWOOD LA
BRAMBLES CL
BROAD WK
PINE WK
BANSTEAD
ROAD
B2030
Medical Centre
ORCHID END
TOWNEND
FOXACRE
Rec. Grd.
MAURICE AV
MONEY AV
OAK
AUCKLAND RD
ROCHESTER GDNS
WILLIAM RD
FRANCIS RD
LIVINGSTONE
MONEY
AVENUE RD
RAGLAN PRECINCT
School
WESTWAY
Library
COULSDON
CLIFTON CL
Westway Common
ROAD
HIGH
STREET
ESSENDENE
CLO
FURROWS PL
Clinic
NELSON RD
HOMES DALE RD
LONDON RD
St. Lawrence's Hospital
PARK
POPLAR WK
ROSEDALE
TAUNTON AV
B2031
CHALDON
COURT
ROAD
WALLER
MEAD RD
CHURCH
Hospital
HEATH
HOMESTEAD RD
QUEENS PARK ROAD
QUEENS
AVENUE
BIRCH
WOOD
LANE
ROAD
Queens Park
CATERHAM
Cemetery
St. Marys Church
Museum
THE HILL
CATERHAM
Liby & Clinic
MANOR
AVENUE
RD
CHURCH
HILL
STATION AV
PARK
AVENUE
Playing Field
STANSTEAD
WOODSIDE CL
HIGH VIEW
HARESTONE
PEPPER CL
HIGHWOODS
UNDERWOOD CT
KYNASTON CT
UNDERWOOD ROAD
VALLEY
HARESTONE DR
Marie Curie Centre
LOXFORD WAY
COLBURN AV
HARESTONE
THE RIDINGS
GRANGE RD
HILL
Hospital
ST KATHERINES RD
STONEHOUSE GDNS
ALDERWOOD CL
DUNEDIN DR
LOXFORD
DEANSFIELD
YEW TREE DR
BRADENHURST CL
Caterham School
TUPWOOD
ALEXANDERS WK
THE COPSE
WILLEY
LANE
STANSTEAD
GROVE
BEECH
LANE
MANOR PARK
PORTLEY WOOD ROAD
Burntwood Hill
BURNTWOOD CL
BURNTWOOD
LANE
ROAD
MILNER ROAD
MILNER APP
Recreation Ground
STAFFORD
HIGH TREES CL
KNOWLE LO
CLO
Adult Education Centre
School
B2208
CROYDON
ROAD
CROYDON RD
BEECHWOOD
BEN HOLME
ELGIN CRES
FARNINGHAM CRES
FARNINGHAM
COMMONWEALTH
COLIN RD
ROAD
MT PLEASANT RD
CRESCENT
Police Sta.
TIMBER HILL RD
TIMBERLA
HAWK RD
GODSTONE
CLAREVILLE
School
Government Offices
DEERSWOOD CL
CRES
TUPWOOD CT
RUSSETT CT
LANE
COLLIERS
GREENWOOD GDNS
WHITE KNOBS WY
Valley Sports Ground
ROAD
B2030
MARKVILLE GDNS
ROAD
School
MARKFIELD
NEWSTEAD RISE
A22
SUCCOMBS HILL
WOLDINGHAM RD
School
GREENHILL AV
HILL
ROAD
TILLINGDOWN
MONKS PL
WALTHAM R
EVERARD LA
HIGHFIELD RD
BEECHWOOD GDNS
ROAD
GAIST AV
ABBOTS WK
ROGERS CL
CATERHAM
BY-PASS
CATERHAM
BY-PASS
TILLINGDOWN LANE
A22

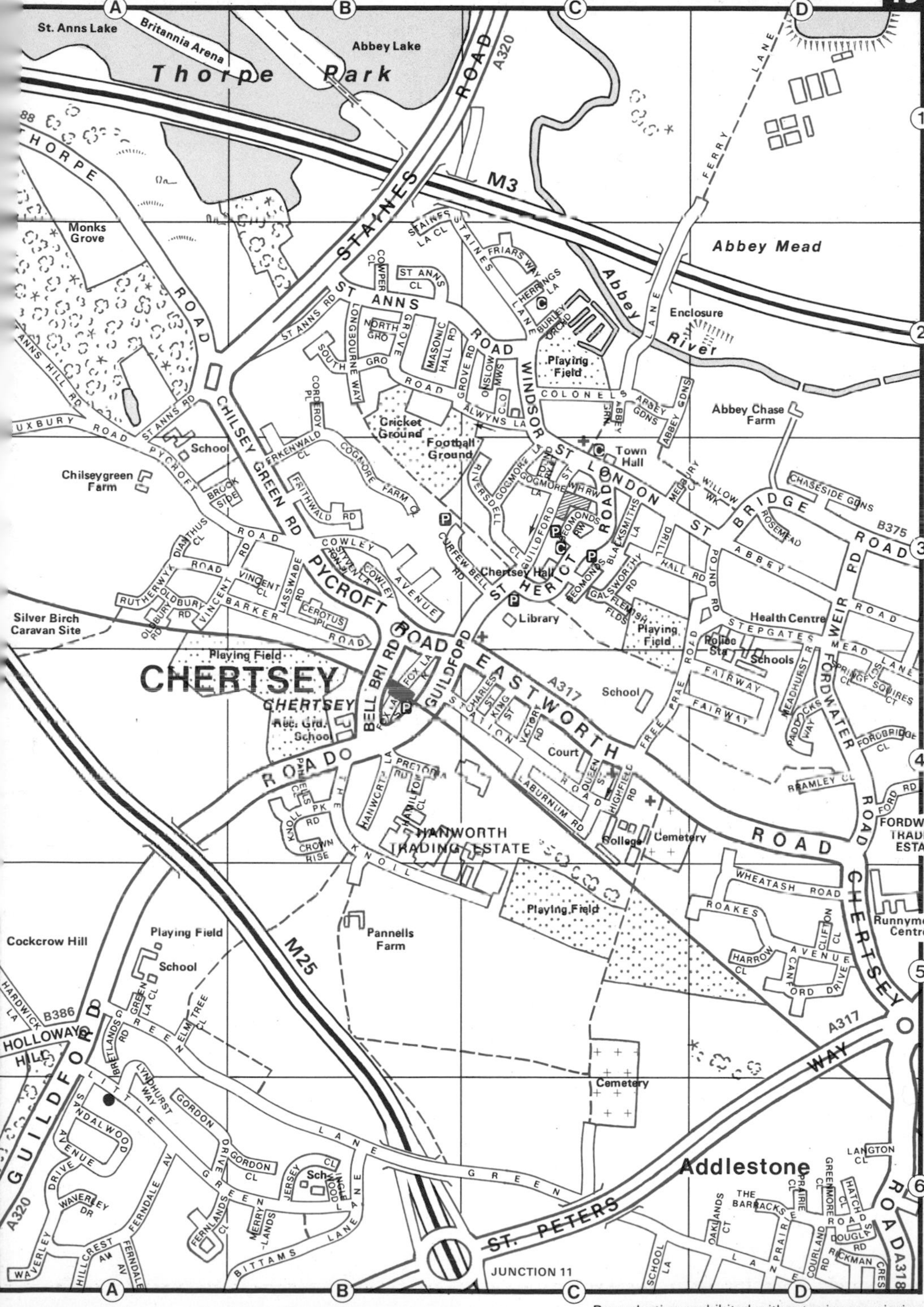

St. Anns Lake
Britannia Arena
Abbey Lake
Thorpe Park
STAINES ROAD
A320
M3
FERRY LANE
THORPE ROAD
Monks Grove
Abbey Mead
ST ANNS ROAD
ST ANNS CL
COWPER CL
LONGBOURNE WAY
NORTH GRO
SOUTH GRO
MASONIC HALL RD
GROVE RD
ONSLOW MWS
FRIARS WAY
HERRINGS LA
BURLEY ORCH
Abbey River
Enclosure
Playing Field
WINDSOR ST
COLONELS LA
ABBEY GDNS
ALWYNS LA
Abbey Chase Farm
CHILSEY GREEN RD
LUXBURY ROAD
ST ANNS HILL RD
School
Cricket Ground
Football Ground
Town Hall
LONDON ST
BRIDGE ROAD
CHASESIDE GDNS
B375
ROSEMEAD
WILLOW WK
ABBEY RD
Chilseygreen Farm
PYCROFT ROAD
BROOK SIDE
FRITHWALD RD
COGMORE FARM CL
CURFEW BELL RD
GOGMORE LA
HERIOT ROAD
BLACKSMITHS LA
HALL RD
DRILL
POUND RD
WEIR RD
DIANTHUS CL
COWLEY AVENUE
SYLVENTA
Chertsey Hall
Library
Health Centre
STEPGATES
Police Sta
Schools
MEAD LANE
SPRINGFIELD CL
SQUIRES CT
Silver Birch Caravan Site
RUTHERWYK
OLDBURY RD
VINCENT RD
BARKER ROAD
LASSWADE RD
CEROTUS PL
GALSWORTHY RD
FLEMISH FLDS
Playing Field
FAIRWAY
MEADHURST RD
PADDOCKS WAY
FORDWATER RD
FORDBRIDGE CL
Playing Field
CHERTSEY
BELL BRI RD
FOX LA
GUILDFORD ST
EASTWORTH ROAD
A317
CHARLES ST
KING ST
STATION RD
VICTORY RD
School
Court
QUEENS RD
HIGHFIELD
FREE PRAE ROAD
BRAMLEY CL
FORD RD
FORDWATER TRADING ESTATE
CHERTSEY
Rec. Grd.
School
GUILDFORD ROAD
PANNELLS CL
PRETORIA RD
HANWORTH LA
HAMILTON CL
KNOLL PK
KNOLL RD
CROWN RISE
HANWORTH TRADING ESTATE
LABURNUM RD
College
Cemetery
WHEATASH ROAD
ROAKES AVENUE
CLIFTON CL
HARROW CL
CANFORD DRIVE
Runnymede Centre
CHERTSEY ROAD
Playing Field
Pannells Farm
Cockcrow Hill
Playing Field
School
M25
HARDWICK LA
B386
HOLLOWAY HILL
GUILDFORD ROAD
A320
GREEN LA CL
BRETLANDS RD
ELM TREE CL
LYNDHURST WAY
LITTLE GREEN LANE
GORDON DRIVE
GORDON CL
SANDALWOOD AVENUE
DRIVE
WAVERLEY DR
FERNDALE AV
FERNLANDS CL
MERRYLANDS
JERSEY CL
Sch
INGLEWOOD
LANE
BITTAMS LANE
WAVERLEY
HILLCREST AV
FERNDALE AV
Cemetery
A317
ST. PETERS WAY
JUNCTION 11
SCHOOL LA
Addlestone
OAKLANDS CT
THE BARRACKS
PRAIRIE CL
PRAIRIE LANE
GREENMORE CT
COURTLAND RD
HATCH CL
DOUGLAS RD
RICKMAN CRES
LANGTON CL
ROAD
A318
A B C D
1 2 3 4 5 6

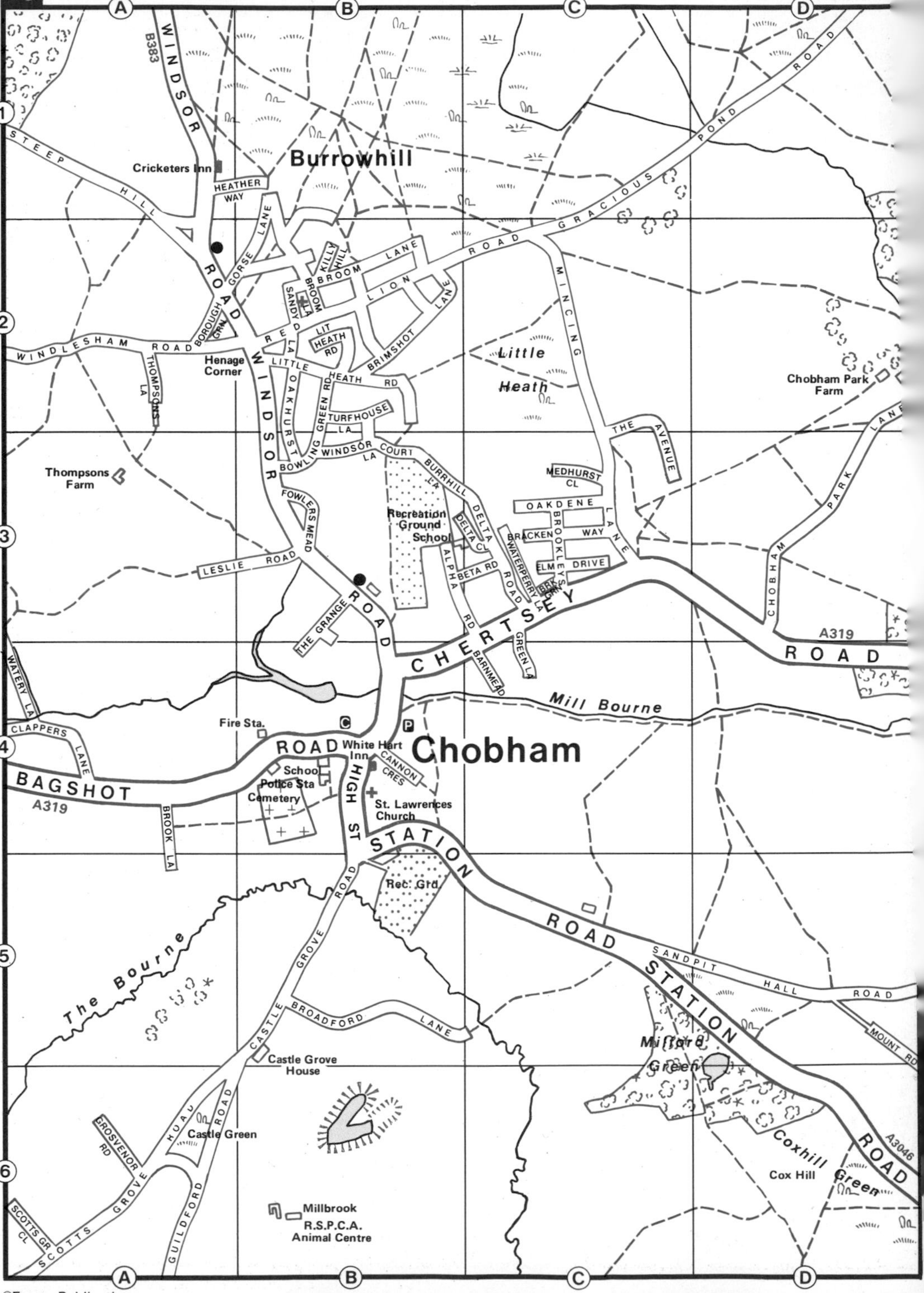
Burrowhill
Cricketers Inn
HEATHER WAY
GORSE LANE
KILLY HILL
BROOM LANE
SANDY LA
BROOM LA
LION LANE
BRIMSHOT LANE
LIT HEATH RD
REDDING
BOROUGH GRN
WINDSOR ROAD
B383
STEEP HILL
WINDLESHAM ROAD
Henage Corner
THOMPSONS LA
LITTLE HEATH RD
OAKHURST
GREEN RD
TURFHOUSE LA
BOWLING
WINDSOR COURT
BURRHILL LA
Thompsons Farm
FOWLERS MEAD
Recreation Ground
School
DELTA CL
DELTA
ALPHA
BETA RD
RD
WATERPERRY
ROAD
BRACKEN WAY
BROOKLEYS
OAKDENE
ELM DRIVE
BRK GRN
MEDHURST CL
THE AVENUE
LANE
MINCING
Little Heath
GRACIOUS POND ROAD
Chobham Park Farm
CHOBHAM PARK LANE
LESLIE ROAD
THE GRANGE
CHERTSEY
A319
ROAD
BARNMEAD
GREEN LA
WATERY LA
Mill Bourne
CLAPPERS LANE
Fire Sta.
White Hart Inn
Chobham
CANNON CRES
School
Police Sta
Cemetery
St. Lawrences Church
HIGH ST
BAGSHOT
BROOK LA
STATION
Rec. Grd
GROVE
The Bourne
SANDPIT HALL ROAD
MOUNT RD
Milford Green
BROADFORD LANE
CASTLE
Castle Grove House
Castle Green
GUILDFORD ROAD
GROSVENOR RD
SCOTTS GROVE
SCOTTS GR CL
Coxhill Green
Cox Hill
A3046
Millbrook
R.S.P.C.A.
Animal Centre
A B C D
1 2 3 4 5 6

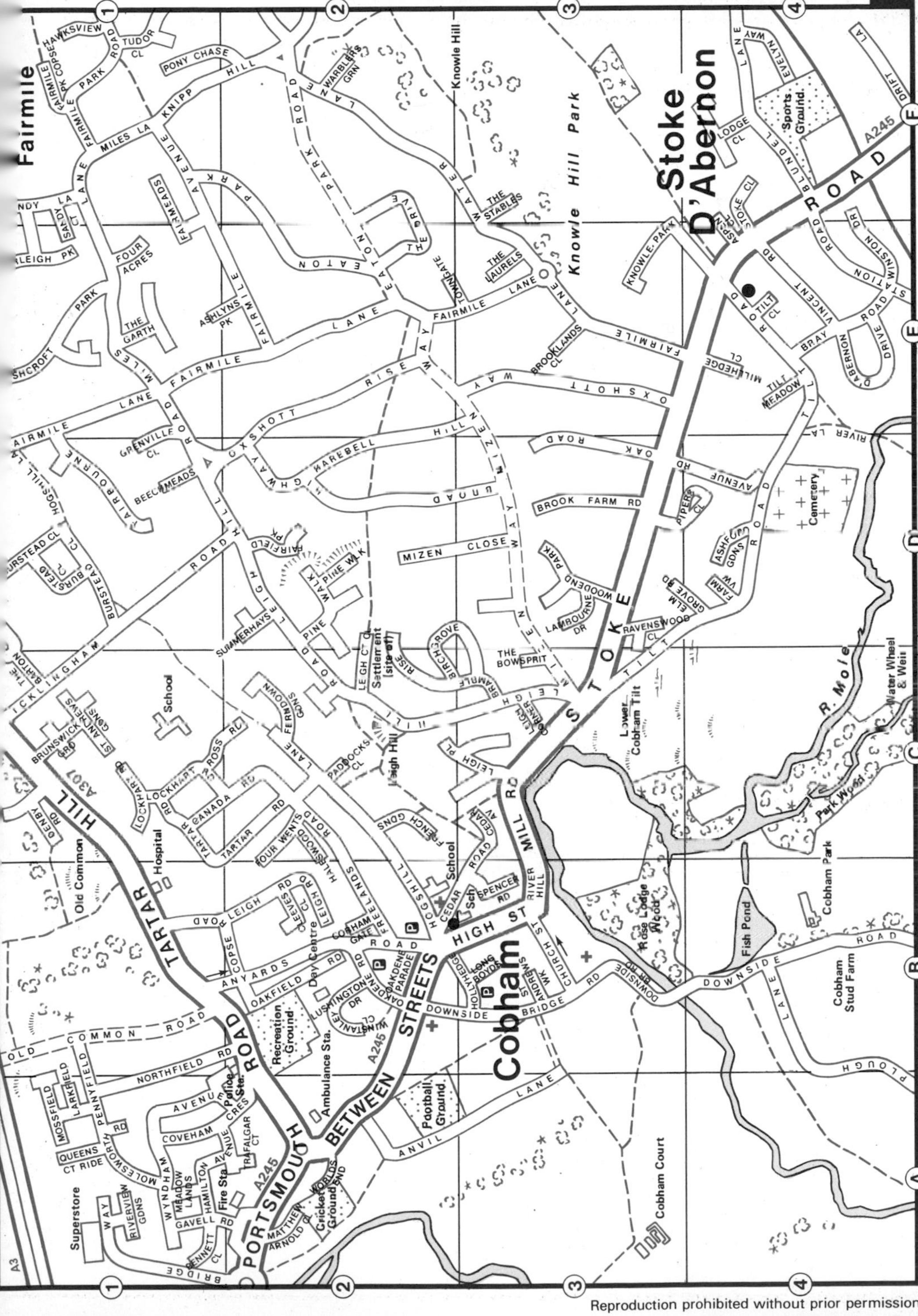
Fairmile
Stoke D'Abernon
Cobham
Knowle Hill Park
Knowle Hill
Hawksview
Tudor Cl
Pony Chase
Fairmile Pk Copse
Park Road
Knipp Hill
Miles La
Fairmile Lane
Sandy La
Sandy Ct
Four Acres
The Garth
Ashlyns Pk
Fairmeads
Park Avenue
Eaton Park Road
Warblers Grn
Water Lane
The Stables
The Drive
The Laurels
Tovngate
Brooklands Cl
Oxshott Way
Oxshott Rise
Grenville Cl
Beechmeads
Harebell Hill
Highway
Round
Mizen Way
Mizen Close
Brook Farm Rd
Oak Road
Avenue Rd
Pipers Cl
Fairfield Pk
Pine Walk
Pine Road
Burstead Cl
Cricklingham
Barton
Summerhays
Leigh Hill Road
Leigh Ct Cl
Settlement (site of)
Birchgrove
Bramble Rise
The Bowsprit
Lambourne Dr
Woodend Park
Ravenswood Cl
Elm Grove Rd
Farm Vw
Ashford Gdns
Cemetery
Knowle Park
Aspen Cl
Stoke Cl
Tilt Cl
Lodge Cl
Evelyn Way
Sports Ground
Blundel Lane
Drift
Station Road
Winston Dr
Vincent Road
Bray Road
D'Abernon Drive
Tilt Meadow
Tilt Road
Millhedge Cl
River La
Stoke Road
A245
Lower Cobham Tilt
R. Mole
Water Wheel & Weir
Park Wood
Cobham Park
Brunswick Grd
St Andrews Gdns
School
Ross Rd
Lockhart Rd
Ferndown Gdns
Paddocks Cl
Leigh Hill
Leigh Pl
Cedar Avenue
Mill Road
A307
Tartar Hill
Denby Rd
Old Common
Hospital
Canada Rd
Tartar Rd
Four Wents
Hallwood Road
French Gdns
Hogshill Lane
School
Cedar Road
Sch
Spencer Rd
River Hill
Freelands
Leigh Rd
Cleeves Rd
Day Centre
Cobham Gate
Road
High St
Long Boyds
Hollyhedge
St Andrews Wk
Church St
Rose Lodge Wood
Fish Pond
Cobham Park
Downside Br Rd
Downside Road
Cobham Stud Farm
Plough Lane
Copse Road
Anyards Rd
Oakfield Rd
Oakdene Parade
Oakdene Rd
Lushington Dr
Winstanley Cl
Downside Bridge Rd
Between Streets
Recreation Ground
Ambulance Sta.
Old Common Road
Northfield Rd
Portsmouth Road
Police Sta.
Avenue Cres
Mossfield
Larkfield
Pennyfield
Coveham Avenue
Trafalgar Ct
Queens Ct Ride
Molesworth Rd
Wyndham
Meadow Lands
Hamilton Avenue
Fire Sta
Gavell Rd
Bennett Cl
Riverview Gdns
Way
Superstore
A3
Bridge
Matthew Arnold Cl
Cricket Ground
Worlds End
Football Ground
Anvil Lane
Cobham Court
1
2
3
4
A
B
C
D
E
F

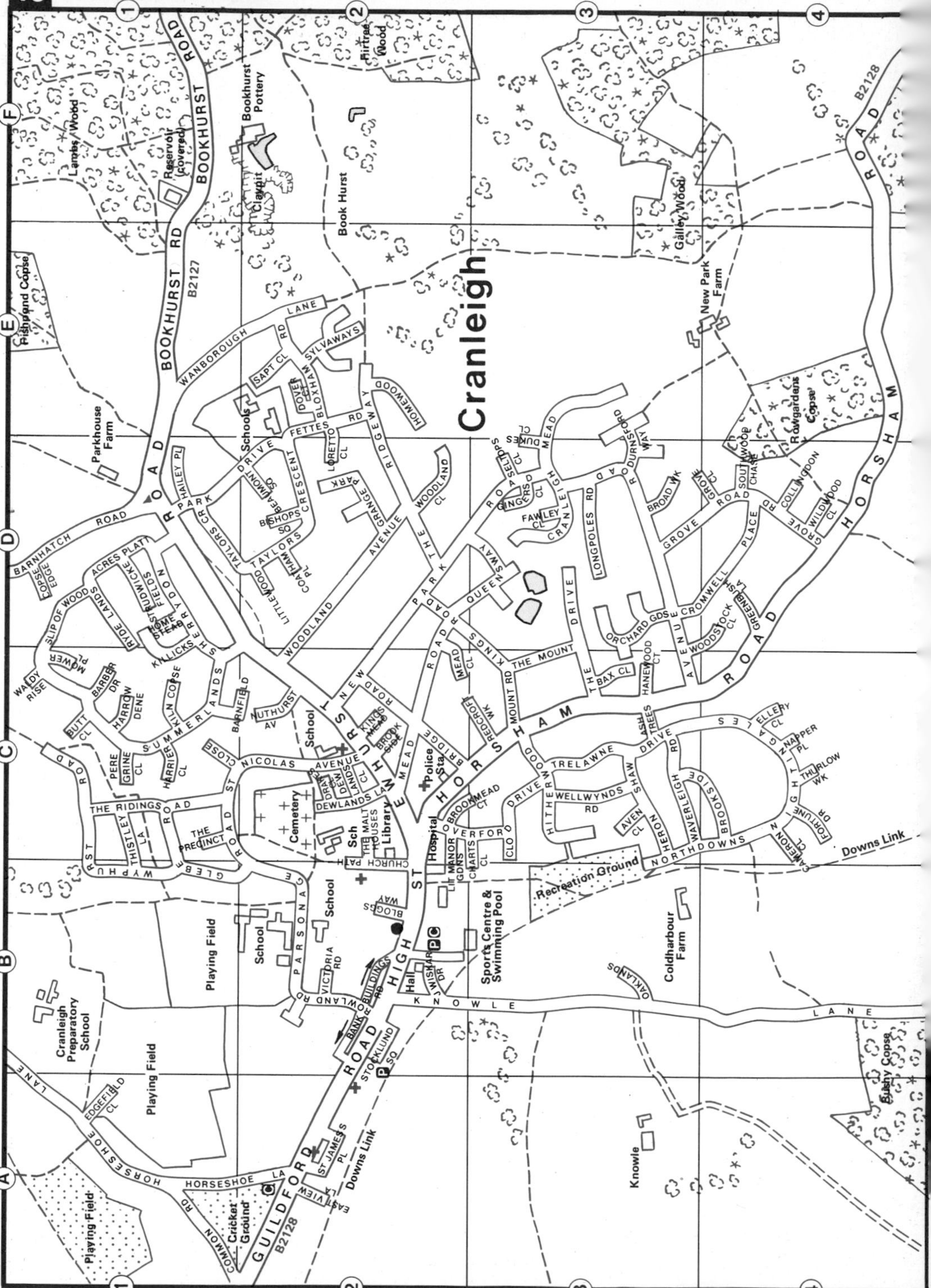
Cranleigh
Lambs Wood
Reservoir (covered)
Bookhurst Pottery
Claypit
Firtree Wood
Book Hurst
Galley Wood
New Park Farm
Rowgardens Copse
Fishpond Copse
Parkhouse Farm
BOOKHURST ROAD
BOOKHURST RD
B2127
B2128
WANBOROUGH LANE
SAPT CL
SYLVAWAYS
DOVER
BLOXHAM
HOMEWOOD
Schools
FETTES RD
LORETTO CL
RIDGEWAY
PARK DRIVE
HAILEY PL
BARNHATCH ROAD
COPSE EDGE
ACRES PLATT
STRUDWICKE FIELDS
RYDON
TAYLORS CR
TAYLORS SQ
BISHOPS SQ
CRESCENT
BEAUMONT
GRANGE PARK
AVENUE
WOODLAND AVENUE
THE WOODLAND CL
LITTLEWOOD
COAL HAM PL
SLIP OF WOOD
RYDE LANDS
HOME STEAD
KILLICKS
MOWER PL
WALDY RISE
BARBER DR
HARROW DENE
BUTT CL
KILN COPSE
SUMMERLANDS
BARNFIELD
NUTHURST AV
School
NEW PARK ROAD
KINGS MEAD
BROOK SIDE
EWHURST
ROAD
PERE
GRINE CL
HARRIER CL
CLOSE
ST NICOLAS AVENUE
Cemetery
DEWLANDS LA
Police Sta
MEAD
BRIDGE
THE RIDINGS ROAD
THISTLEY LA
THE PRECINCT
ROAD
GLEBE
WYPHURST
Sch
THE MALT HOUSES
Library
CHURCH PATH
Hospital
HIGH ST
MANOR GDNS
CHARTS CL
BLOGGS WAY
School
PARSONAGE
VICTORIA RD
Playing Field
School
Hall
WISKAR DR
ROWLAND RD
BUILDINGS
BANK
KNOWLE LANE
Cranleigh Preparatory School
Playing Field
EDGEFIELD CL
HORSESHOE LANE
HORSESHOE LA
ST JAMES PL
STOCKLUND SQ
ROAD
GUILDFORD
EAST VIEW
Downs Link
Cricket Ground
COMMON RD
Playing Field
Sports Centre & Swimming Pool
Recreation Ground
Coldharbour Farm
OAKLANDS
Knowle
Bushy Copse
Downs Link
DUKES CL
MEAD
ASELTOPS
GINGERS CL
FAWLEY CL
CRANLEIGH ROAD
DURNSFORD WAY
LONGPOLES RD
BROAD WK
QUEENSWAY
PARK ROAD
KINGS ROAD
MEAD CL
THE MOUNT
MOUNT RD
DRIVE
THE BAX CL
HANEWOOD CT
ORCHARD GDS
CROMWELL
AVENUE
WOODSTOCK CL
GREENBUSH LA
GROVE ROAD
SOUTHWOOD CHASE
COLLINGDON
GROVE CL
WILDWOOD CL
PLACE
HORSHAM ROAD
REDCROFT WK
BROOKMEAD CT
OVERFORD CLOSE
TRELAWNE
HITHERWOOD DRIVE
WELLWYNDS RD
ASH TREES
SHAW DRIVE
AVEN CL
HERON
WAVERLEIGH RD
BROOKSIDE
NORTHDOWNS
CAMERON CL
FORTUNE DR
THURLOW WK
NAPPER PL
ELLERY CL
NIGHTINGALES
1
2
3
4
A
B
C
D
E
F

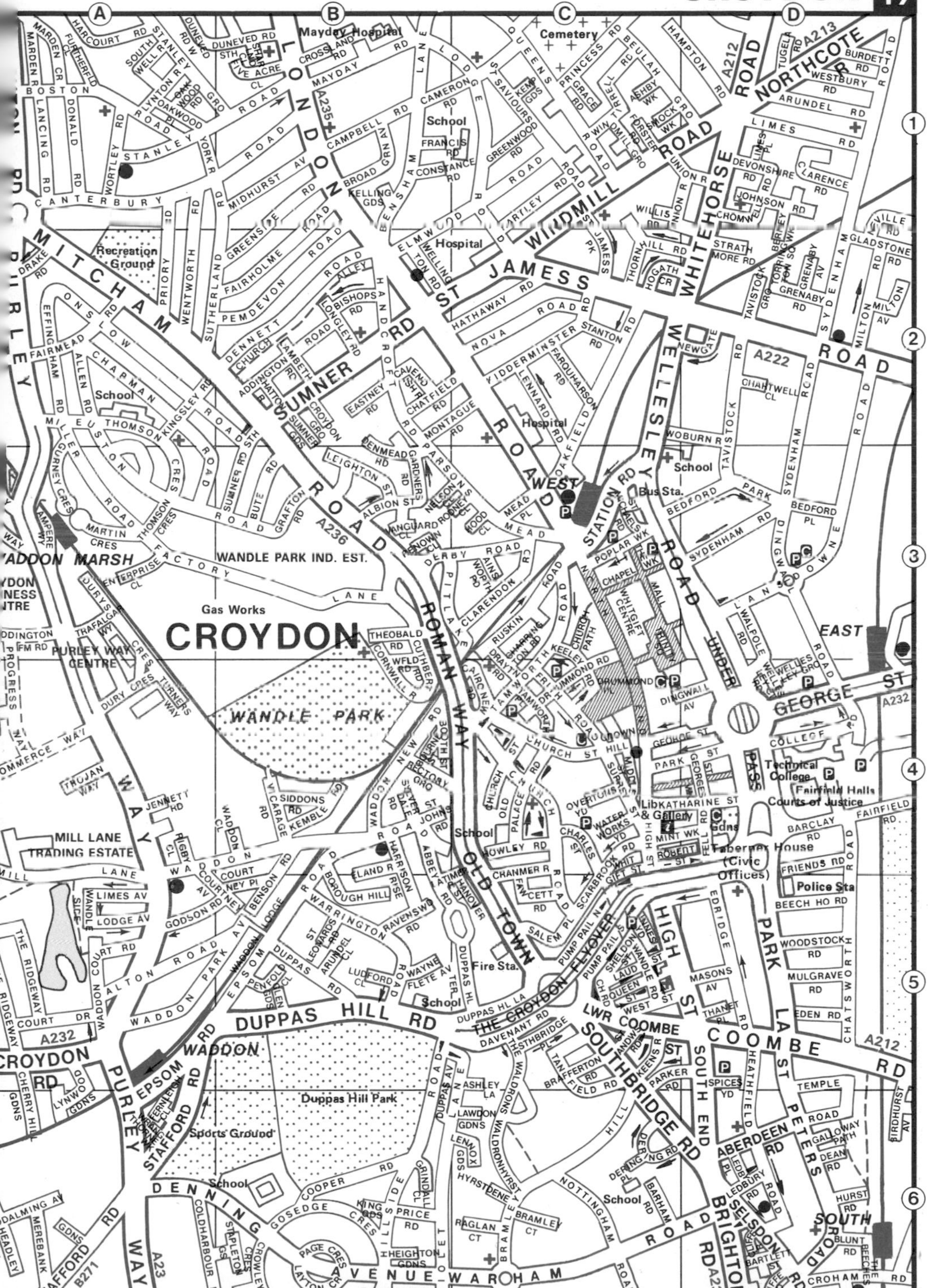
A
B
C
D
1
2
3
4
5
6
Mayday Hospital
Cemetery
HARCOURT RD
MARDEN RD
MARDEN CR
FURTHERFIELD
SOUTH WELL RD
STANLEY GRO
DUNEVED RD
CROSSLAND RD
MAYDAY RD
FIVE ACRE CL
LONDON
A235
QUEENS RD
PRINCESS RD
BEULAH GRO
HAMPTON RD
A212
ROAD
NORTHCOTE
A213
TUGELA RD
BURDETT RD
WESTBURY RD
ARUNDEL RD
BOSTON
LANCING RD
DONALD RD
LYNTON RD
OAK WOOD RD
OAKWOOD PL
STANLEY RD
WORTLEY RD
YORK RD
CAMERON RD
CAMPBELL RD
School
FRANCIS RD
CONSTANCE RD
GREENWOOD RD
ST SAVIOURS RD
KEMP GDS
GRACE RD
ASHBY WK
MOCK WK
WINDMILL GRO
LIMES RD
DEVONSHIRE RD
CLARENCE RD
JOHNSON RD
CHOMWELL
CANTERBURY RD
MIDHURST AV
BROAD GRN AV
KELLING GDS
BENSHAM LANE
ARTLEY RD
WINDMILL
ROAD
UNION RD
WHITEHORSE
WILLIS RD
MITCHAM
Recreation Ground
PRIORY
WENTWORTH RD
SUTHERLAND RD
GREENSIDE RD
FAIRHOLME RD
PEMDEVON RD
BISHOPS RD
ELMWOOD RD
WELLINGTON RD
Hospital
ST JAMESS
ST JAMES PK
THORNHILL RD
HOGATH CR
STRATH MORE RD
TAVISTOCK GRO
GRENABY AV
GRENABY RD
SYDENHAM
GLADSTONE RD
MILTON AV
DRAKE RD
PURLEY
ONSLOW
EFFINGHAM RD
FAIRMEAD RD
ALLEN RD
CHAPMAN RD
School
HATHAWAY RD
NOVA RD
KIDDERMINSTER RD
STANTON RD
FARQUHARSON RD
WELLESLEY
NEWGATE
A222
ROAD
CHARTWELL CL
SUMNER
DENNETT RD
CHURCH RD
ADDINGTON RD
LAMBETH RD
EASTNEY RD
CAVENDISH RD
CHATFIELD RD
MONTAGUE RD
LENNARD RD
ROAD
Hospital
THOMSON CRES
KINGSLEY RD
EUSTON RD
MILLER RD
GURNEY CRES
SUMNER GDS
CROYDON GRO
DENMEAD RD
LEIGHTON ST
GARDNERS RD
PARSONS MEAD
OAKFIELD RD
WOBURN RD
School
TAVISTOCK RD
SYDENHAM RD
MARTIN CRES
BUTE RD
GRAFTON RD
ALBION ST
NELSON RD
ROD
MEAD PL
WEST
STATION RD
Bus Sta.
BEDFORD PARK
BEDFORD PL
DINGWALL RD
WADDON MARSH
AMPERE WY
A236
WANDLE PARK IND. EST.
FACTORY LANE
ENTERPRISE CL
VANGUARD CL
RENOWN CL
DERBY ROAD
AINSWORTH RD
SYDENHAM RD
POPLAR WK
CHAPEL WK
MALL
LANSDOWNE
CROYDON BUSINESS CENTRE
DURY ST
THAFALGAR WY
Gas Works
CROYDON
PITLAKE
CLARENDON RD
RUSKIN
WHITGIFT CENTRE
CHURCH PATH
WALFOLE RD
EAST
ADDINGTON
FM RD
PURLEY WAY CENTRE
THEOBALD RD
CUTHBERT RD
CORNWALL RD
WFLD RD
ROMAN WAY
CAIRO RD
CHARRINGTON RD
TAMWORTH RD
KEELEY RD
DRUMMOND RD
DRUMMOND PL
UNDER
WELLESLEY GRO
GEORGE ST
A232
DINGWALL AV
PROGRESS
DURY CRES
TURNERS WAY
WANDLE PARK
CROWN HILL
CHURCH ST
GEORGE ST
PARK ST
COLLEGE
COMMERCE WAY
TROJAN WAY
JENNETT RD
WAY
SIDDONS RD
KEMBLE RD
VICARAGE RD
WADDON NEW RD
RECTORY GRO
ST JOHNS
OLD PALACE RD
SURREY ST
KATHARINE ST
Lib & Gallery
Technical College
Fairfield Halls
Courts of Justice
PASS
FAIRFIELD
BARCLAY RD
MILL LANE TRADING ESTATE
RIGBY CL
WADDON CL
School
HOWLEY RD
OVERTONS YD
WATER WORKS YD
CHARLES ST
MINT WK
ROBERT ST
Taberner House (Civic Offices)
FRIENDS RD
Police Sta
MILL LANE
WADDON COURT
COURTNEY PL
BENSON RD
HARRISON RISE
ELAND RD
ABBEY RD
HANOVER ST
OLD TOWN
CRANMER RD
FAWCETT RD
SCARBROOK RD
WHITGIFT ST
EDRIDGE RD
BEECH HO RD
WANDLE SIDE
LIMES AV
LODGE AV
GODSON RD
WADDON PARK AV
EPSOM RD
WARRINGTON RD
BOROUGH HILL
RAVENSWOOD
ST LEONARDS RD
ARUNDEL CL
SALEM PL
PUMP PAIL N
PUMP PAIL S
SHELDON ST
LAUD ST
WANDLE RD
HIGH ST
PARK LA
WOODSTOCK RD
MULGRAVE RD
THE RIDGEWAY
COURT DR
ALTON ROAD
DUPPAS RD
PENFOLD CL
LUDFORD CL
WAYNE CL
FLETE AV
Fire Sta.
THE CROYDON FLYOVER
QUEEN ST
WEST ST
MASONS AV
THANET PL
CHATSWORTH
EDEN RD
A232
WADDON COURT RD
DUPPAS HILL RD
School
DUPPAS HL LA
DAVENANT RD
LWR COOMBE
COOMBE
A212
CROYDON RD
PURLEY
EPSOM
WADDON
STAFFORD RD
Duppas Hill Park
DUPPAS AV
ASHLEY LA
LAWDON GDNS
WALDRONS
SOUTHBRIDGE PL
BRAFFERTON RD
TANFIELD RD
KEENS RD
ST
PARKER RD
SOUTH END
SPICES YD
HEATHFIELD
TEMPLE RD
BIRDHURST AV
CHERRY HILL GDNS
LYNWOOD
WESTERNLEIGH CL
Sports Ground
LENNOX GDS
WALDRONHYRST
HILL
SOUTHBRIDGE RD
ABERDEEN RD
GALLOWAY PATH
DEAN RD
DERING PL
School
HYRSTDENE
ST PETERS
GODALMING AV
MEREBANK
HEADLEY AV
DENNING
School
COOPER RD
GRINDALL CL
NOTTINGHAM
LEDBURY RD
HURST RD
SOUTH
STAFFORD RD
B271
GOSEDGE CRES
KING GDS
PRICE RD
RAGLAN CT
BRAMLEY CT
ROAD
SELSDON
BRIGHTON
BLUNT RD
WAY
A23
COLDHARBOUR RD
STAPLETON GDS
CROWLEY CRES
PAGE CRES
LAYTON CRES
HEIGHTON GDNS
AVENUE
WARHAM
VIOLET
BARHAM
BARTLETT ST
RD A235
ROAD
CROHAM RD
THE BEECHES
School

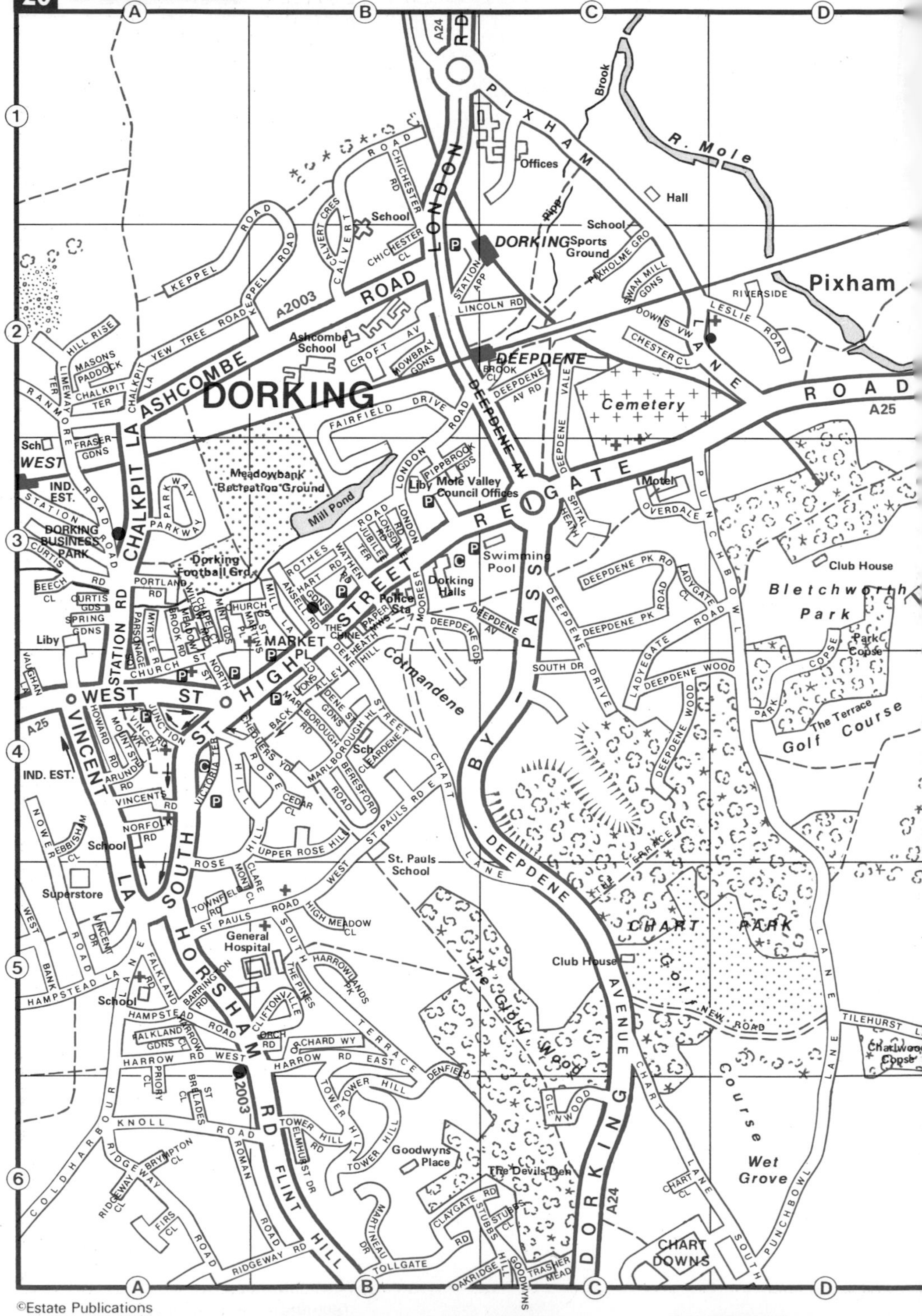
A
B
C
D
1
2
3
4
5
6
DORKING
Pixham
R. Mole
Brook
Ripp
PIXHAM LANE
Offices
Hall
School
DORKING
Sports Ground
LONDON RD
A24
A2003
ROAD
KEPPEL ROAD
CALVERT CRES
CALVERT
CHICHESTER RD
CHICHESTER CL
STATION APP
LINCOLN RD
PIXHOLME GRO
SWAN MILL GDNS
RIVERSIDE
LESLIE ROAD
DOWNS VW
CHESTER CL
YEW TREE ROAD
ASHCOMBE
Ashcombe School
CROFT AV
MOWBRAY GDNS
DEEPDENE
BROOK CL
DEEPDENE AV RD
VALE
Cemetery
ROAD
A25
HILL RISE
MASONS PADDOCK
LIMEWAY TER
CHALKPIT TER
CHALKPIT LA
RANMORE
FRASER GDNS
Sch
WEST
IND. EST.
FAIRFIELD DRIVE
Meadowbank Recreation Ground
Mill Pond
PIPPBROOK GDS
Liby
Mole Valley Council Offices
REIGATE
Motel
OVERDALE
PUNCHBOWL
SPITAL HEATH
STATION ROAD
DORKING BUSINESS PARK
CURTIS RD
BEECH CL
CURTIS GDS
SPRING GDNS
PARK WAY
PARKWAY
Dorking Football Grd
PORTLAND RD
ROTHES
HART RD
ANSELL RD
JUBILEE TER
LONSDALE
WATHEN
Swimming Pool
Dorking Halls
DEEPDENE PK RD
LADYGATE CL
Club House
Bletchworth Park
Park Copse
STATION RD
PARSONAGE
MYRTLE RD
BROOK RD
WILLOW
MEADOW
CHAPEL CT
MINT GDS
CHURCH GS
MARTINS PL
MILL LA
MARKET
STREET
HIGH
Police Sta
THE CHINE
PAPER MWS
HEATH HILL
DENE
MOORES RD
DEEPDENE AV
DEEPDENE GDS
Cotmandene
SOUTH DR
DEEPDENE DRIVE
DEEPDENE PK RD
LADYGATE ROAD
DEEPDENE WOOD
COPSE
PARK
The Terrace
Golf Course
Liby
VAUGHAN LA
CHURCH ST
NORTH
WEST ST
ST
JUNCTION
A25
VINCENT
HOWARD RD
MOUNT ST
VINCENT WK
ARUNDEL RD
IND. EST.
LYONS CT
ALLEY
DENE ST
DENE GDNS
BACK
MARLBOROUGH RD
MARLBOROUGH HL
CHEQUERS YD
ROSE HILL
Sch
CLEARDENE
STREET
BERESFORD ROAD
VICTORIA TER
BY-PASS
CHART
VINCENTS RD
NORFOLK RD
School
NOWER
EBBISHAM CL
SOUTH
LA
CEDAR CL
UPPER ROSE HILL
ROSE
CLARE MONT CL
ST PAULS RD E
WEST
ST. Pauls School
LANE
DEEPDENE
Superstore
TOWNFIELD RD
ST PAULS ROAD
HIGH MEADOW CL
General Hospital
HORSHAM
SOUTH TERRACE
HARROWLANDS PK
THE PINES
CLIFTONVILLE
CHART PARK
Golf
Club House
The Glory Wood
AVENUE
NEW ROAD
TILEHURST LA
Chalwood Copse
WEST
BANK
ROAD
VINCENT DR
HAMPSTEAD LANE
School
FALKLAND
BARRINGTON RD
HAMPSTEAD ROAD
FALKLAND GDNS
FARROW CL
ORCH RD
ORCHARD WY
HARROW RD WEST
HARROW RD EAST
DENFIELD
PRIORY CL
ST BRELADES CL
A2003
TOWER HILL
GLENWOOD
DORKING
Course
KNOLL ROAD
TOWER HILL RD
ELMHURST DR
TOWER HILL
Goodwyns Place
The Devils Den
Wet Grove
COLDHARBOUR
RIDGEWAY CL
BRYMPTON CL
ROMAN ROAD
FLINT HILL
MARTINEAU DR
CLAYGATE RD
STUBBS CL
A24
CHART CL
PUNCHBOWL LANE
FIRS CL
ROAD
RIDGEWAY RD
TOLLGATE
OAKRIDGE
HILL
GOODWYNS
TRASHER MEAD
CHART DOWNS
SOUTH

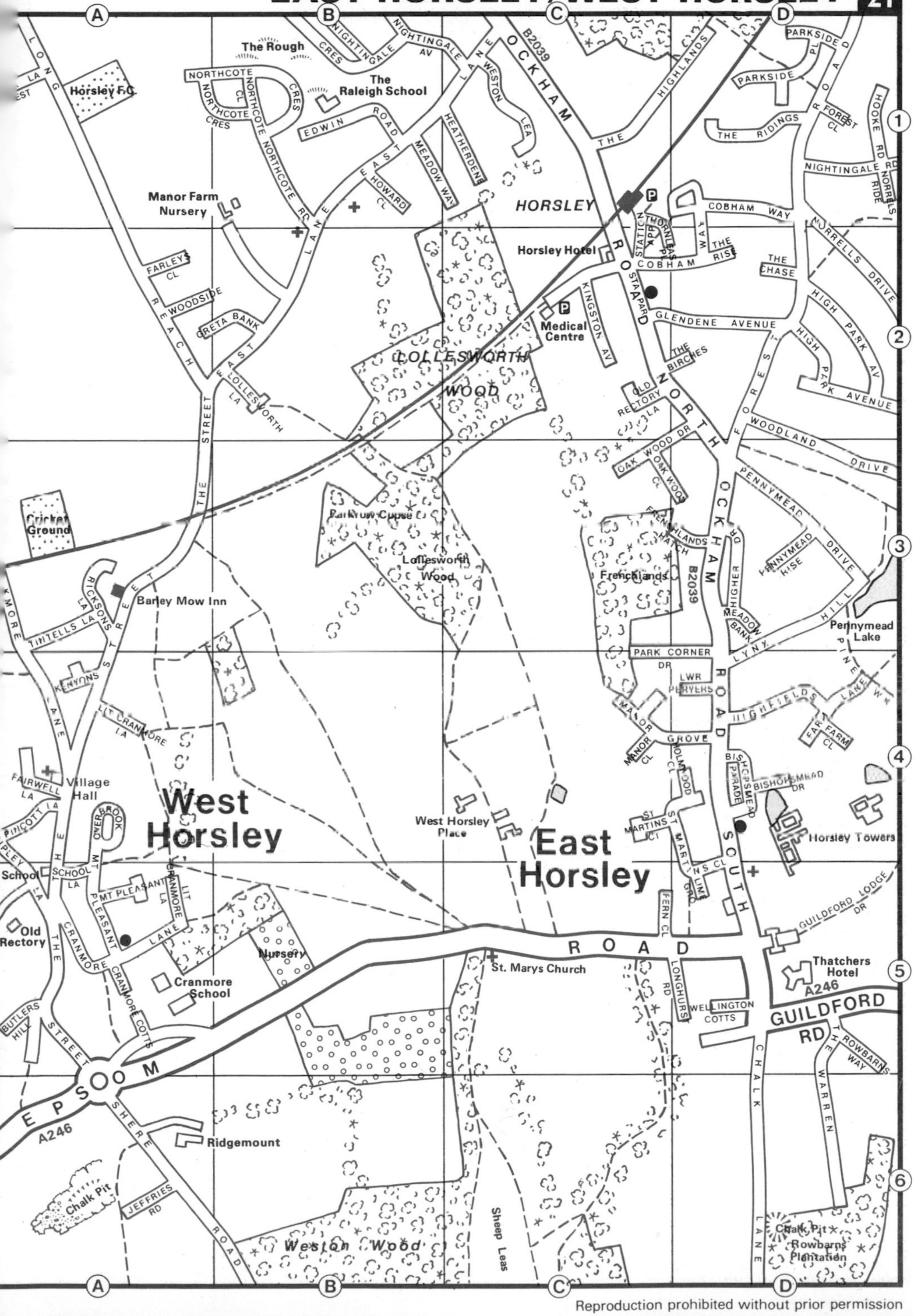

A
B
C
D
1
2
3
4
5
6
The Rough
Horsley F.C.
The Raleigh School
NORTHCOTE CRES
NORTHCOTE CL
NORTHCOTE RD
NIGHTINGALE CRES
NIGHTINGALE AV
EDWIN ROAD
WESTON LEA
HEATHERDENE
MEADOW WAY
HOWARD CL
EAST LANE
OCKHAM ROAD
B2039
THE HIGHLANDS
PARKSIDE PL
PARKSIDE
THE RIDINGS
FOREST CL
HOOKE RD
NIGHTINGALE RD
NORRELS RIDE
Manor Farm Nursery
HORSLEY
COBHAM WAY
STATION APPR
THORNLEAS PL
THE RISE
COBHAM RISE
THE CHASE
NORRELLS DRIVE
Horsley Hotel
FARLEYS CL
WOODSIDE
GRETA BANK
REACH LANE
LONG REACH
KINGSTON AV
Medical Centre
GLENDENE AVENUE
HIGH PARK AV
HIGH PARK AVENUE
THE BIRCHES
FOREST ROAD
LOLLESWORTH WOOD
LOLLESWORTH LA
OLD RECTORY LA
NORTH
WOODLAND DRIVE
OAK WOOD DR
OAK WOOD
PENNYMEAD DRIVE
PENNYMEAD RISE
THE STREET
Cricket Ground
Parkrow Copse
FRENCHLANDS HATCH
Lollesworth Wood
Frenchlands
HIGHER ORCHARD
MEADOW BANK
LYNX HILL
Pennymead Lake
PINE
RICKSONS LA
Barley Mow Inn
TINTELLS LA
PARK CORNER DR
LWR PERRYERS
KENYONS
HIGHFIELDS
LANE
MANOR GROVE
MANOR CL
LIT CRANMORE LA
FAR FARM CL
OCKHAM ROAD SOUTH
HOLMWOOD CL
BISHOPSMEAD PARADE
BISHOPSMEAD DR
FAIRWELL LA
Village Hall
OVERBROOK
PINCOTT LA
West Horsley
West Horsley Place
ST MARTINS CL
ST MARTINS CL
East Horsley
Horsley Towers
School
SCHOOL LA
MT PLEASANT
LIT CRANMORE LA
Old Rectory
CRANMORE LANE
FERN CL
LIME GR
GUILDFORD LODGE DR
ROAD
Nursery
St. Marys Church
LONGHURST RD
Thatchers Hotel
A246
Cranmore School
CRANMORE COTTS
WELLINGTON COTTS
GUILDFORD RD
THE ROWBARNS WAY
BUTLERS HILL
THE STREET
EPSOM
A246
SHERE ROAD
CHALK LANE
THE WARREN
Ridgemount
Chalk Pit
JEFFRIES RD
Sheep Leas
Weston Wood
Chalk Pit
Rowbarns Plantation

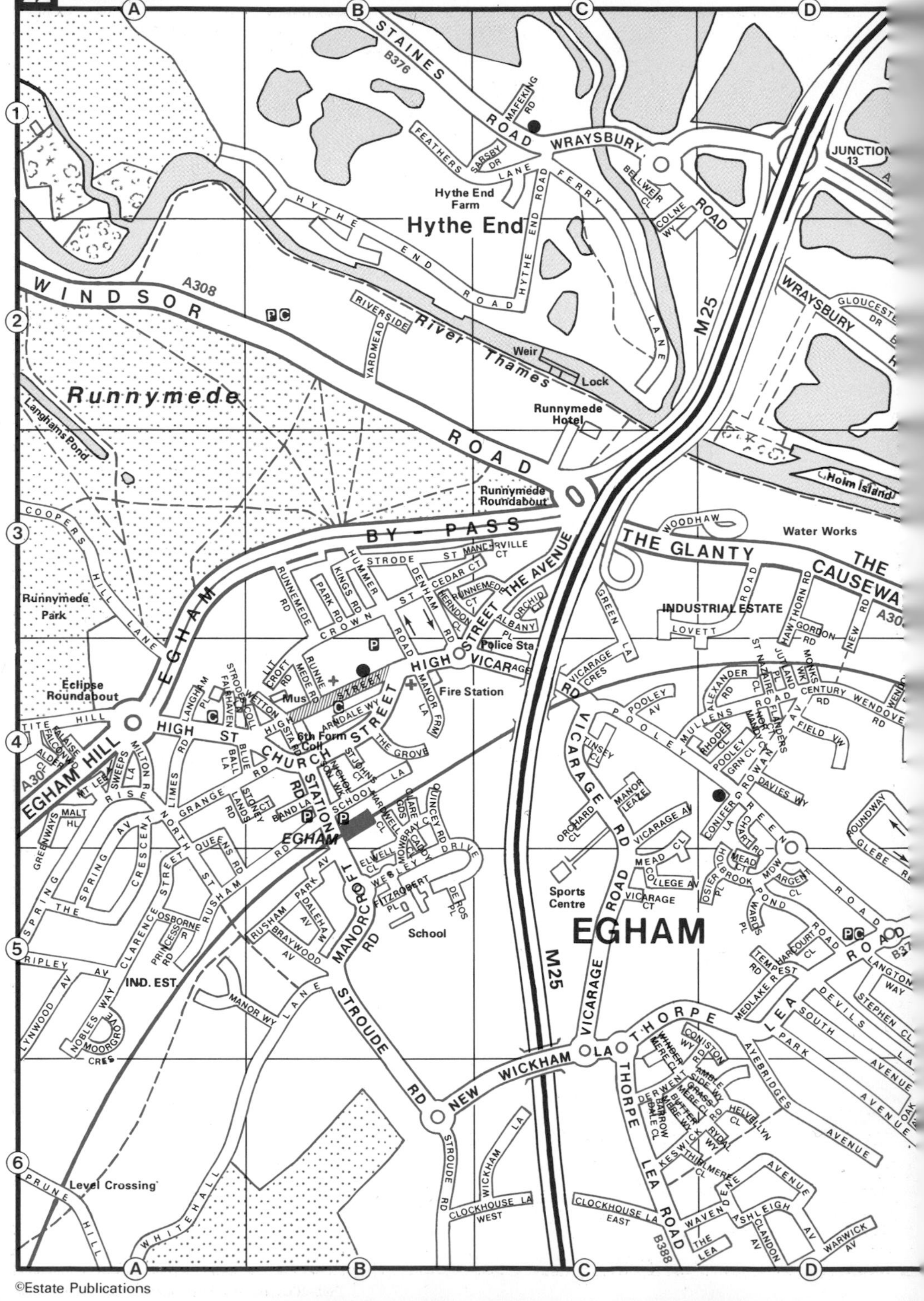

A
B
C
D
1
2
3
4
5
6
STAINES ROAD
B376
MAFEKING RD
FEATHERS LANE
SARSBY DR
WRAYSBURY ROAD
BELLWEIR CL
COLNE WY
JUNCTION 13
Hythe End Farm
Hythe End
HYTHE END ROAD
FERRY LANE
M25
WRAYSBURY
GLOUCESTER DR
WINDSOR ROAD
A308
RIVERSIDE
YARDMEAD
River Thames
Weir
Lock
Runnymede
Langhams Pond
Runnymede Hotel
Holm Island
Runnymede Roundabout
COOPERS HILL LANE
BY-PASS
WOODHAW
THE GLANTY
Water Works
THE CAUSEWAY
A308
Runnymede Park
EGHAM
HUMMER
STRODE ST
MANORVILLE CT
THE AVENUE
RUNNEMEDE RD
PARK RD
KINGS RD
DENHAM
CEDAR CT
RUNNEMEDE CT
HERINDON CL
ORCHID CT
ALBANY PL
CROWN ST
ROAD
HIGH STREET
Police Sta
GREEN LA
INDUSTRIAL ESTATE
LOVETT
HAWTHORN RD
GORDON RD
NEW RD
Eclipse Roundabout
LIT CROFT
RUNNEMEDE RD
HIGH
VICARAGE
MANOR FRM LA
Fire Station
VICARAGE CRES
ST NAZAIRE CL
JUTLAND PL
MONKS WK
CENTURY RD
WENDOVER RD
STRODES COLL
FAIRHAVEN
LANGHAM PL
WETTON PL
Mus
STREET
ARNDALE WY
POOLEY AV
ALEXANDER RD
MULLENS ROAD
FLANDERS
TITE HILL
FALAISE
FALCON DR
ALDER CL
EGHAM HILL
A30
HIGH ST
6th Form Coll
STREET
THE GROVE
TINSEY CL
POOLEY
RHODES CL
MANOR CL
POOLEY GRN CL
ROWAN
FIELD VW
MILTON RD
BLUE BALL LA
CHURCH RD
ST JOHNS CT
SCHOOL LA
DAVIES WY
SWEEPS LA
MT LEE
RISE
LIMES RD
GRANGE RD
STONEY LANDS CT
BAND LA
STATION RD
HARDWELL CL
QUINCEY RD
MANOR LEAZE
CONIFER LA
CHART RD
ROUNDWAY
GLEBE RD
GREENWAYS
MALT HL
THE SPRING
AV
CRESCENT
NORTH ST
QUEENS RD
EGHAM
ELWELL CL
MOWBRAY CRES
GRACE GDNS
LAY DRIVE
ORCHARD CL
VICARAGE AV
MEAD CL
COLLEGE AV
MEAD CT
BROOK
MDW
ARGENT CL
POND
WARDS PL
SPRING
RUSHAM RD
WESLEY DRIVE
FITZROBERT PL
DE ROS PL
Sports Centre
VICARAGE CT
ROAD
EGHAM
HARCOURT CL
CLARENCE STREET
OSBORNE RD
PRINCESS RD
RUSHAM PARK AV
DALEHAM AV
BRAYWOOD AV
MANORCROFT RD
School
TEMPEST RD
LANGTON WAY
B3
RIPLEY AV
IND. EST.
LYNWOOD AV
NOBLES WAY
MOORGROVE CRES
MANOR WY
LANE
STROUDE
M25
VICARAGE
MEDLAKE RD
LEA
SOUTH
DEVILS
STEPHEN CL
THORPE
CONISTON WY
WINDERMERE CL
LA
AYEBRIDGES
PARK
AVENUE
NEW WICKHAM LA
THORPE LEA ROAD
AMBLESIDE WY
GRASSMERE CL
DERWENT RD
BUTTERMERE WY
BARROWDALE CL
HELVELLYN CL
RYDAL WY
KESWICK
THIRLMERE CL
STROUDE RD
WICKHAM LA
CLOCKHOUSE LA WEST
CLOCKHOUSE LA EAST
WAVENDENE AVENUE
ASHLEIGH AV
CLANDON AV
WARWICK AV
THE LEA
B388
ROAD
Level Crossing
PRUNE HILL
WHITEHALL

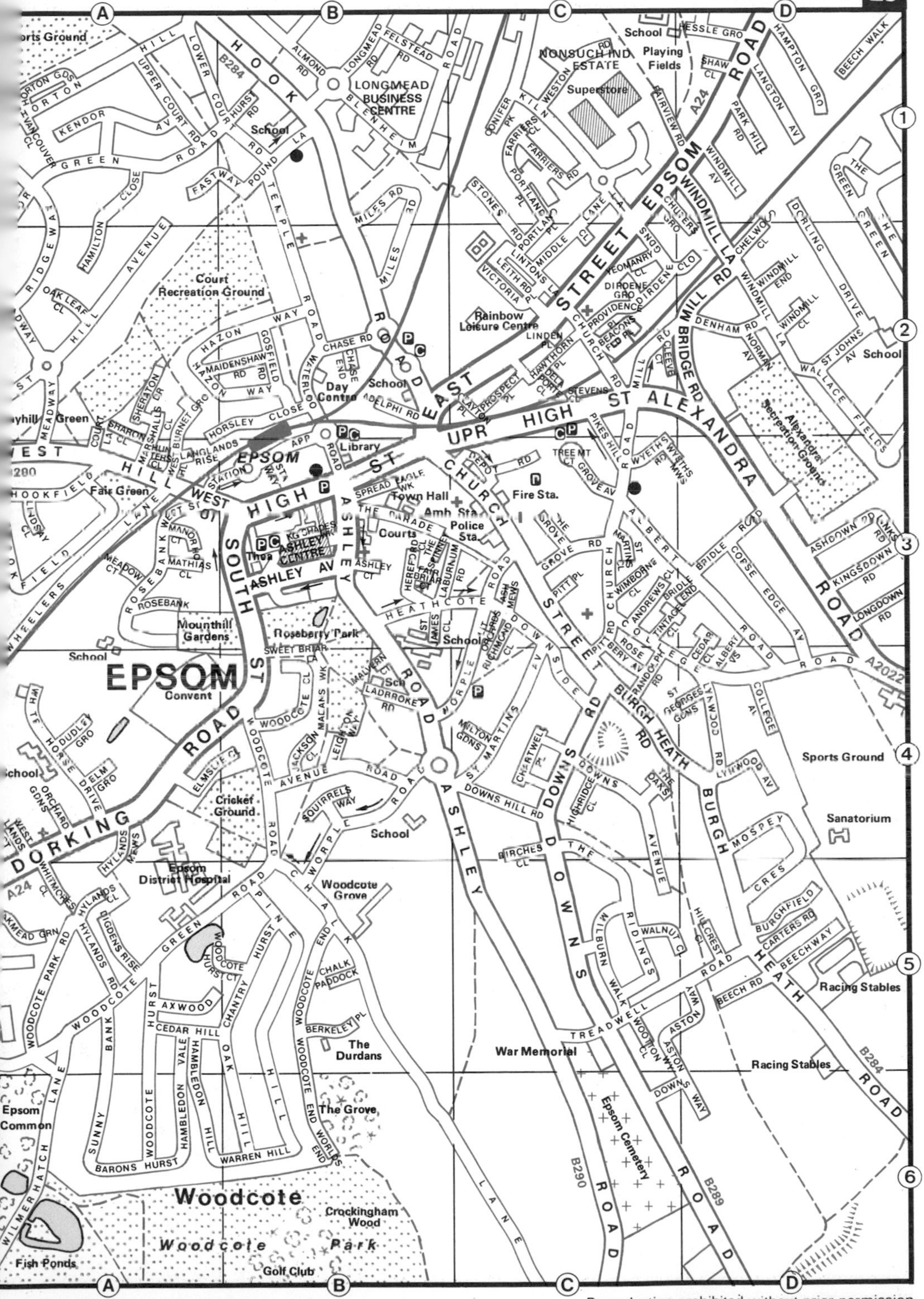
A
B
C
D
1
2
3
4
5
6
Sports Ground
HOOK ROAD
B284
ALMOND RD
LONGMEAD RD
FELSTEAD RD
LONGMEAD BUSINESS CENTRE
BLENHEIM RD
School
NONSUCH IND ESTATE
Playing Fields
Superstore
HESSLE GRO
HAMPTON GRO
BEECH WALK
SHAW CL
LANGTON AV
PARK HILL RD
A24
EAST STREET
EPSOM ROAD
WINDMILL AV
WINDMILL LA
FAIRVIEW RD
KILN WESTON
CONIFER PK
FARRIERS CL
FARRIERS RD
PORTLAND PL
STONES RD
MIDDLE LANE
LINTONS LA
LEITH RD
VICTORIA PL
CHURCH RD
HORTON GDS
HORTON
VANCOUVER CL
KENDOR
UPPER COURT RD
LOWER COURT RD
HURST RD
GREEN
FASTWAY
POUND LA
TEMPLE ROAD
MILES RD
HAMILTON CLOSE
RIDGEWAY
AVENUE
OAK LEAF CL
HILL
Court Recreation Ground
HAZON WAY
MAIDENSHAW RD
GOSFIELD RD
WATERLOO RD
CHASE RD
CHASE END
Day Centre
School
ADELPHI RD
Rainbow Leisure Centre
LINDEN PL
HAWTHORN PL
YEOMANRY CL
DIRDENE GRO
DIRDENE CLO
PROVIDENCE PL
BEACONS FD
CHURCHES GRO
DENHAM RD
NORMAN AV
WINDMILL END
WINDMILL CL
DORLING DRIVE
CHELWOOD CL
THE GREEN
ST JOHNS AV
School
WALLACE FIELDS
Alexandra Recreation Ground
ALEXANDRA ROAD
BRIDGE RD
MILL RD
UPR HIGH ST
PROSPECT PL
STEVENS
PIKES HILL
WYETHS RD
WYETHS MEWS
Meadway
Green
SHARON CL
MARSHALLS CL
SHERATON
BURNET GRO
HORSLEY CLOSE
LANGLANDS RISE
WEST HILL
B280
EPSOM
STATION APP
Library
HOOKFIELD
Fair Green
WEST ST
HIGH ST
SPREAD EAGLE WK
Town Hall
THE PARADE
Amb Sta
Police Sta.
Fire Sta.
DEPOT RD
TREEMT CT
GROVE AV
Courts
ASHLEY CENTRE
Thea
ASHLEY AV
ASHLEY RD
ASHLEY CT
SOUTH ST
MANOR CT
MATHIAS CL
MEADOW CT
ROSEBANK
LINDSAY
WHEELERS LANE
HEATHCOTE RD
HEREFORD CT
LABURNUM RD
The Grove
GROVE RD
PITT PL
CHURCH ST
MARTINS CL
WIMBORNE CL
ANDREWS CL
TINTAGEL
BRIDLE END
BRIDLE RD
COPSE EDGE AV
ASHDOWN RD
KINGSDOWN RD
LONGDOWN RD
ALBERT RD
Mountfield Gardens
Rosebery Park
SWEET BRIAR LA
School
School
EPSOM
Convent
ST JAMES CL
ORCHARD
RICHMOND CL
DOWNSIDE
ROSE BANK
PIT BERRY AV
RANDOLPH RD
CEDAR CL
ALBERT VS
ST GEORGES GDNS
LYNWOOD AV
COLLEGE AV
A2022
Sports Ground
MALVERN
Sch
LADBROKE RD
WORPLE RD
MILTON GDNS
ST MARTINS
CHARTWELL PL
BURGH HEATH RD
DOWNS RD
DOWNS
THE OAKS
HIGHRIDGE CL
DOWNS HILL RD
Sanatorium
WOODCOTE
JACKSON CL
MALANS WK
LEIGHTON WAY
ELMSLIE CL
DUDLEY GRO
HORSE DRIVE
ELM GRO
ORCHARD GDNS
School
Cricket Ground
SQUIRRELS WAY
School
BIRCHES CL
THE DOWNS
AVENUE
BURGH HEATH
MOSPEY CRES
DORKING ROAD
A24
HYLANDS MEWS
WHITMORES CL
Epsom District Hospital
HYLANDS CL
WOODCOTE GREEN ROAD
Woodcote Grove
CHALK LA
BURGHFIELD
CARTERS RD
BEECHWAY
OAKMEAD GRN
WOODCOTE PARK RD
HYLANDS RD
DIGDENS RISE
WOODCOTE HURST CT
PINE HILL
HURST
CHALK PADDOCK
MILBURN WALK
RIDINGS
WALNUT CL
HILLCREST CL
Racing Stables
AXWOOD
CHANTRY
CEDAR HILL
WOODCOTE END
BERKELEY PL
The Durdans
TREADWELL ROAD
ASTON WAY
BEECH RD
HEATH
WOOTTON CL
War Memorial
Racing Stables
B284
ROAD
LANE
BANK
SUNNY
WOODCOTE
VALE
HAMBLEDON
HAMBLEDON HILL
OAK HILL
WOODCOTE END
WORLDS END
The Grove
Epsom Common
WILMERHATCH
BARONS HURST
WARREN HILL
Epsom Cemetery
B290
B289
ROAD
Woodcote
Crockingham Wood
Woodcote Park
Golf Club
Fish Ponds

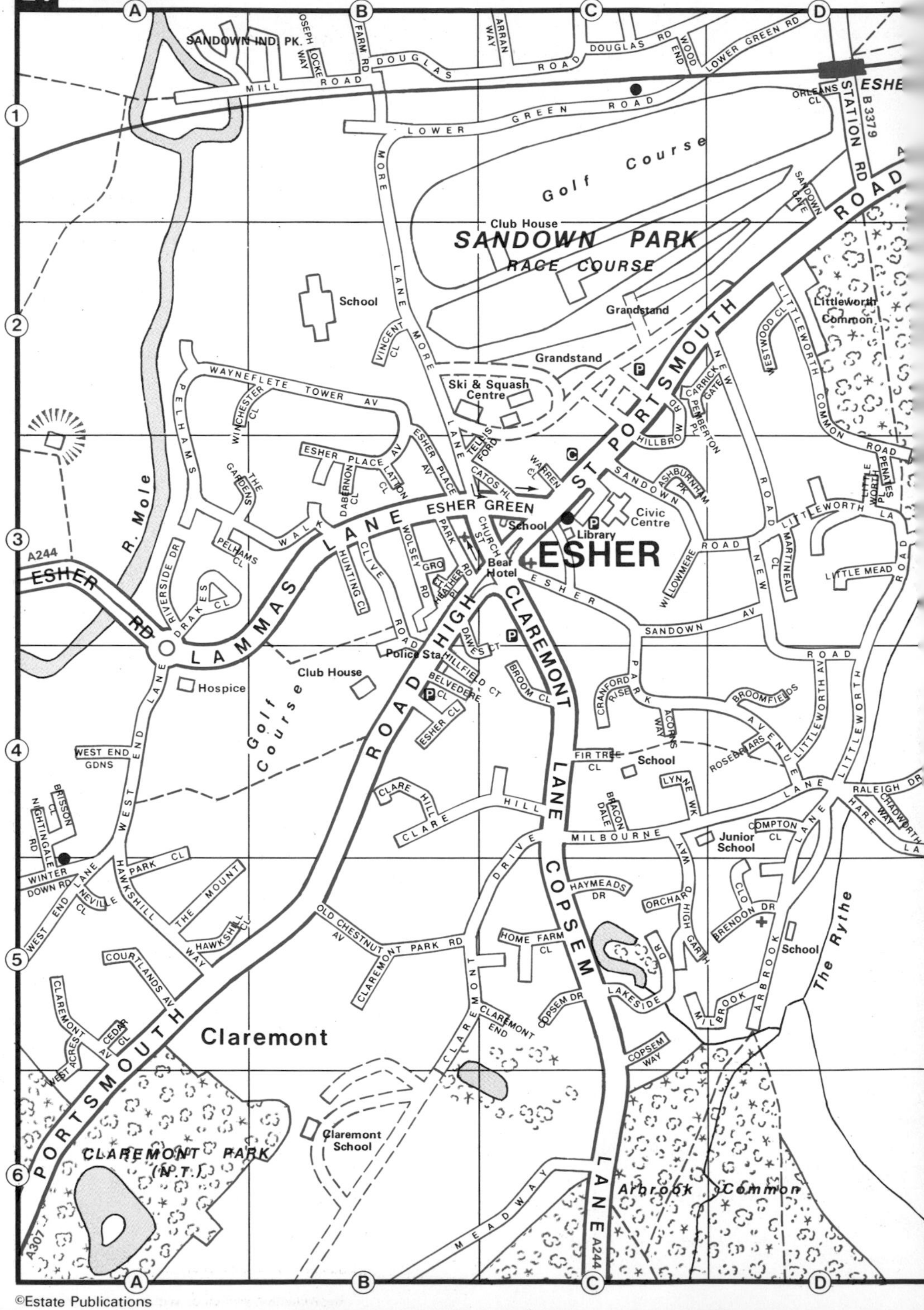
A
B
C
D
1
2
3
4
5
6
SANDOWN IND. PK.
MILL ROAD
FARM RD
DOUGLAS ROAD
ARRAN WAY
DOUGLAS RD
WOOD END
LOWER GREEN RD
LOWER GREEN ROAD
ORLEANS CL
ESHER
STATION RD
B 3379
MORE LANE
Golf Course
Club House
SANDOWN PARK
RACE COURSE
SANDOWN GATE
ROAD
School
Grandstand
Littleworth Common
VINCENT CL
Ski & Squash Centre
WAYNEFLETE TOWER AV
PORTSMOUTH
WESTWOOD CL
LITTLEWORTH
CARRICK GATE
NEW
PEMBERTON PL
HILLBROW RD
COMMON ROAD
PELHAMS
WINCHESTER CL
ESHER PLACE AV
TELLIS FORD
WARREN CL
ST
LITTLEWORTH ROAD
THE GARDENS
DABERNON CL
LATTON CL
CATOS HL
SANDOWN
ASHBURNHAM PK
R. Mole
ESHER GREEN
Civic Centre
LITTLE WORTH PL
PENATES
LITTLEWORTH LA
School
Library
ESHER
A244
WALK
LANE
PELHAMS CL
WOLSEY
CHURCH ST
WILLOWMERE
ROAD
MARTINEAU
LITTLE MEAD
ESHER
RIVERSIDE DR
HUNTING CL
CLIVE
GRO
Bear Hotel
CLAREMONT
DRAKES CL
LAMMAS
HIGH
RD
DAWES CT
SANDOWN AV
ROAD
Police Sta.
HILLFIELD CT
Hospice
Club House
BELVEDERE CL
BROOM CL
CRANFORD RISE
PARK
BROOMFIELDS
Golf Course
ESHER CL
ACORNS WAY
AVENUE
LITTLEWORTH AV
WEST END GDNS
FIR TREE CL
School
ROSEBRIARS
LANE
RALEIGH DR
BRISSON CL
CLARE HILL
HILL
BEACON DALE
LYNNE WK
CHADWORTH WAY
NIGHTINGALE RD
WEST END
CLARE
MILBOURNE
Junior School
COMPTON CL
HARE LA
WINTER DOWN RD
PARK CL
HAWKSHILL
THE MOUNT
DRIVE
COPSEM
HAYMEADS DR
WAY
NEVILLE CL
WEST END LANE
OLD CHESTNUT AV
ORCHARD
HIGH GARTH
BRENDON DR
CLOS
HAWKSHILL CL
HAWKSHILL WAY
HOME FARM CL
School
The Rythe
PARK RD
COURTLANDS AV
CLAREMONT
ARBROOK
CLAREMONT AV
CEDAR CL
COPSEM DR
LAKESIDE
MILBROOK
CLAREMONT END
Claremont
WEST ACRES
COPSEM WAY
PORTSMOUTH
Claremont School
CLAREMONT PARK (N.T.)
Arbrook Common
MEADWAY
A307
LANE
A244

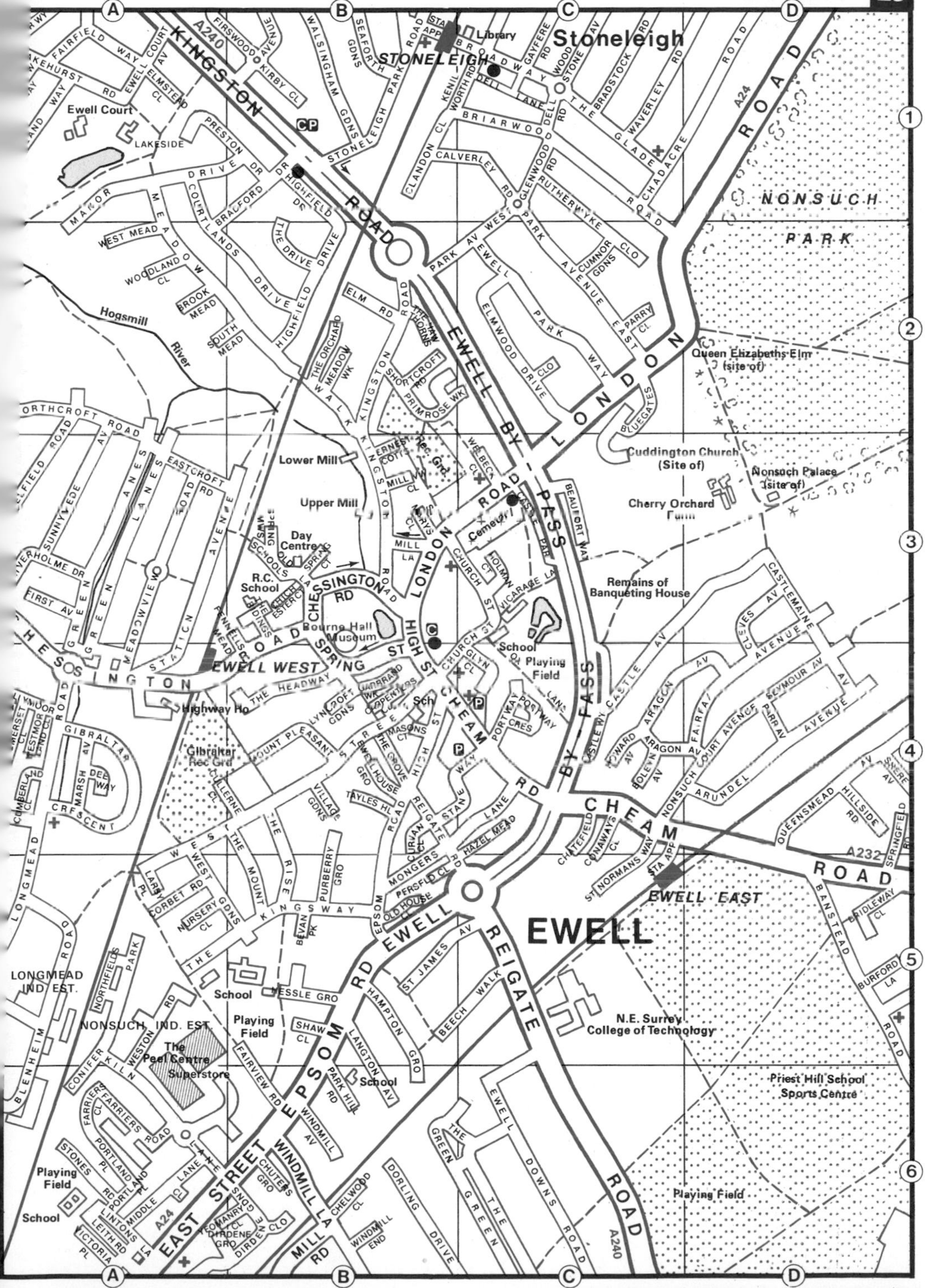

A
B
C
D
1
2
3
4
5
6
Stoneleigh
STONELEIGH
Library
KINGSTON ROAD
A240
FIRSWOOD AVENUE
KIRBY CL
WALSINGHAM GDNS
SEAFORTH GDNS
STONELEIGH PARK ROAD
STONELEIGH BROADWAY
GAYFERE RD
WOODSTONE AV
THE BRADSTOCK RD
WAVERLEY RD
DELL LANE
KENILWORTH RD
BRIARWOOD RD
CALVERLEY RD
CLANDON CL
GLENWOOD RD
RUTHERWYKE CLO
THE GLADE
CHADACRE ROAD
FAIRFIELD WAY
EWELL COURT AV
ELMSTEAD CL
Ewell Court
LAKESIDE
PRESTON DR
MANOR DRIVE
MEADOW
COURTLANDS DRIVE
BRADFORD DR
HIGHFIELD DR
HIGHFIELD DRIVE
THE DRIVE
WEST MEAD
WOODLAND CL
BROOK MEAD
SOUTH MEAD
Hogsmill River
CP
NONSUCH PARK
A24
LONDON ROAD
PARK AV WEST
EWELL PARK WAY
CUMNOR GDNS
PARK AVENUE EAST
PARRY CL
ELMWOOD DRIVE
CLO
BLUEGATES
Queen Elizabeths Elm (site of)
Cuddington Church (Site of)
Nonsuch Palace (site of)
Cherry Orchard Farm
EWELL BY PASS
ELM RD
THE ORCHARD
MEADOW WK
KINGSTON WALK
SHORTCROFT RD
PRIMROSE WK
THE HORNS
ERNEST COTTS
Rec. Grd.
WELBECK CL
MILL VIEW CL
Lower Mill
Upper Mill
KINGSTON ROAD
MILL LA
LONDON ROAD
Cemetery
BEAUFORT WAY
HOLMAN CT
CHURCH ST
VICARAGE LA
Remains of Banqueting House
CASTLEMAINE AV
CLEVES AV
CASTLE AVENUE
NORTHCROFT ROAD
EASTCROFT RD
SUNNYMEDE AV
GREEN LANES
MEADOWVIEW
STATION AVENUE
FIRST AV
Day Centre
R.C. School
SPRING ST
CHESSINGTON RD
Bourne Hall Museum
HIGH ST
CHURCH ST
School
Playing Field
GLYN CL
PORTWAY
PORTWAY CRES
EWELL WEST
CHESSINGTON ROAD
THE HEADWAY
Highway Ho
LYNCROFT GDNS
GARBRAND WK
CARPENTERS CT
Sch
MASONS CT
THE GROVE
EWELL HOUSE GRO
CHEAM RD
STANE WAY
HOWARD AV
ARAGON AV
FAIRFAX AV
BOLEYN AV
NONSUCH COURT AVENUE
SEYMOUR AV
PARR AV
ARUNDEL AV
HILLSIDE RD
QUEENSMEAD
SPRINGFIELD RD
Gibraltar Rec Grd
MOUNT PLEASANT
CULLERNE CL
GIBRALTAR CRESCENT
MARSH AV
DEEWAY
VILLAGE GDNS
TAYLES HL
WEST ST
THE MOUNT
THE RISE
PURBERRY GRO
REIGATE RD
CURJAN CL
HAZEL MEAD
MONGERS LA
PERSFLD CL
OLD HOUSE
CHATFIELD
CONAWAYS CL
NORMANS WAY
STA APP
CHEAM ROAD
A232
EWELL EAST
EWELL
BANSTEAD ROAD
BRIDLEWAY CL
BURFORD LA
LONGMEAD ROAD
LONGMEAD IND. EST.
NONSUCH IND. EST.
CORBET RD
NURSERY GDNS
KINGSWAY
BEVAN PK
EPSOM RD
EWELL RD
ST JAMES AV
REIGATE RD
THE PARK
NORTHFIELDS
School
HESSLE GRO
Playing Field
SHAW CL
HAMPTON GRO
BEECH WALK
N.E. Surrey College of Technology
LANGTON AV
PARK HILL RD
School
The Peel Centre Superstore
KILN WESTON RD
CONIFER
FAIRVIEW RD
EPSOM
WINDMILL AV
FARRIERS CL
FARRIERS ROAD
PORTLAND PL
STONES RD
EWELL DOWNS ROAD
THE GREEN
Priest Hill School Sports Centre
BLENHEIM
Playing Field
School
MIDDLE LANE
LINTONS
LEITH RD
VICTORIA PL
EAST STREET
WINDMILL LA
CHUTERS GRO
YEOMANRY CL
DIRDENE GDNS
DIRDENE GRO
DIRDENE CLO
MILL RD
CHELWOOD CL
WINDMILL END
DORLING DRIVE
THE GREEN
Playing Field
A240

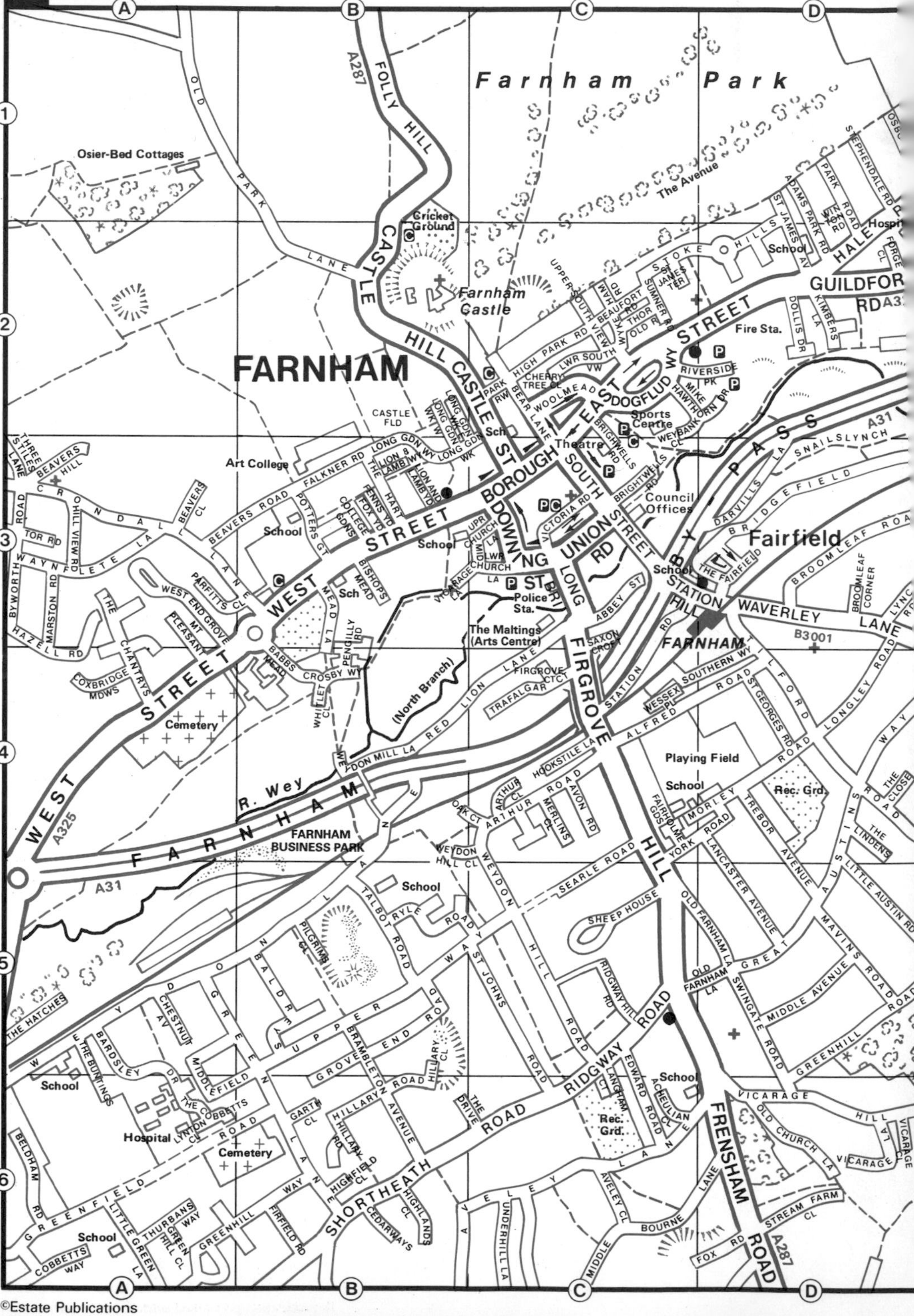
A
B
C
D
1
2
3
4
5
6
Farnham Park
FARNHAM
Osier-Bed Cottages
OLD PARK LANE
FOLLY HILL
A287
CASTLE HILL
Cricket Ground
Farnham Castle
The Avenue
CASTLE FLD
Art College
LONG GDN WY
LONG GDN WK
LION & LAMB WY
LION AND LAMB YD
FALKNER RD
BEAVERS ROAD
BEAVERS HILL
BEAVERS CL
THREE STILES RD
CRONDALL LANE
HILL VIEW RD
TOR RD
WAYNFLETE LA
BYWORTH RD
MARSTON RD
HAZELL RD
THE CHANTRYS
COXBRIDGE MDWS
MT PLEASANT
WEST END GROVE
PARFITTS CL
WEST STREET
A325
Cemetery
School
Sch
POTTERS GT
COLLEGE GDNS
FENNS YD
FOX YD
THE HART
BISHOPS MEAD
MEAD LA
PENGILLY RD
BABBS MEAD
CROSBY WY
WHITLET CL
WEYDON MILL LA
CASTLE ST
BOROUGH
DOWNING ST
UPR CHURCH LA
MID CHURCH LA
LWR CHURCH LA
VICARAGE LA
ST BRI
Police Sta.
The Maltings (Arts Centre)
(North Branch)
R. Wey
RED LION LANE
FIRGROVE CT
TRAFALGAR CT
SAXON CROFT
ABBEY ST
LONG
FIRGROVE HILL
UNION RD
VICTORIA RD
SOUTH STREET
Theatre
Sports Centre
BRIGHTWELLS RD
BRIGHTWELLS
Council Offices
EAST ST
WOOLMEAD
BEAR LANE
PARK RW
CHERRY TREE CL
HIGH PARK RD
LWR SOUTH VW
UPPER SOUTH VIEW
WYKEHAM RD
BEAUFORT RD
THORN
OLD R
SUMNER RD
ST JAMES TER
STOKE HILLS
ST JAMES AV
ADAMS PARK RD
PARK ROAD
WINTON RD
SHEPHERD & FLOCK
SHEPHERDALE RD
HALE
FORGE CL
Hospital
GUILDFORD RD
A31
DOGFLUD WY
STREET
Fire Sta.
RIVERSIDE PK
MIKE HAWTHORN DR
WEYBANK CL
DOLLIS DR
KIMBERS LA
BY-PASS
SNAILSLYNCH
BRIDGEFIELD
DARVILLS LA
Fairfield
THE FAIRFIELD
BROOMLEAF ROAD
BROOMLEAF CORNER
STATION HILL
FARNHAM
WAVERLEY LANE
B3001
SOUTHERN WY
WESSEX PL
STATION
ALFRED ROAD
ST GEORGES RD
FORD
LONGLEY ROAD
HOOKSTILE LA
ARTHUR CL
ARTHUR ROAD
AVON RD
MERLINS CL
OAK CT
Playing Field
Rec. Grd.
FAIRHOLME GDNS
MORLEY ROAD
YORK RD
TREBOR AVENUE
LANCASTER AVENUE
AUSTINS
THE CLOSE
THE LINDENS
LITTLE AUSTIN RD
MAVINS ROAD
FARNHAM
A31
FARNHAM BUSINESS PARK
WEYDON HILL CL
WEYDON HILL ROAD
SEARLE ROAD
SHEEP HOUSE
OLD FARNHAM LA
SWINGATE ROAD
GREAT
MIDDLE AVENUE
GREENHILL ROAD
TALBOT ROAD
RYLE ROAD
PILGRIMS CL
WAY
ST JOHNS ROAD
RIDGWAY HILL RD
RIDGWAY ROAD
BALDREYS
UPPER
GREEN LANE
CHESTNUT AV
MIDDLEFIELD
BARDSLEY DR
THE BUNTINGS
THE COBBETTS
THE HATCHES
WEYDON
GROVE END ROAD
BRAMBLETON AVENUE
HILLARY CL
HILLARY RD
GARTH CL
HIGHFIELD CL
THE DRIVE
LANGHAM CT
EDWARD ROAD
ACHEULIAN CL
FRENSHAM ROAD
VICARAGE HILL
OLD CHURCH LA
VICARAGE CL
VICARAGE LA
STREAM FARM CL
FOX RD
A287
BOURNE
MIDDLE
AVELEY LANE
AVELEY CL
UNDERHILL LA
SHORTHEATH ROAD
HIGHLANDS
CEDARWAYS
FIRFIELD RD
GREENHILL WAY
THURBANS WAY
GREEN HILL CL
LITTLE GREEN LA
COBBETTS WAY
GREENFIELD RD
BELDHAM RD
LINTON CL
Hospital
Cemetery

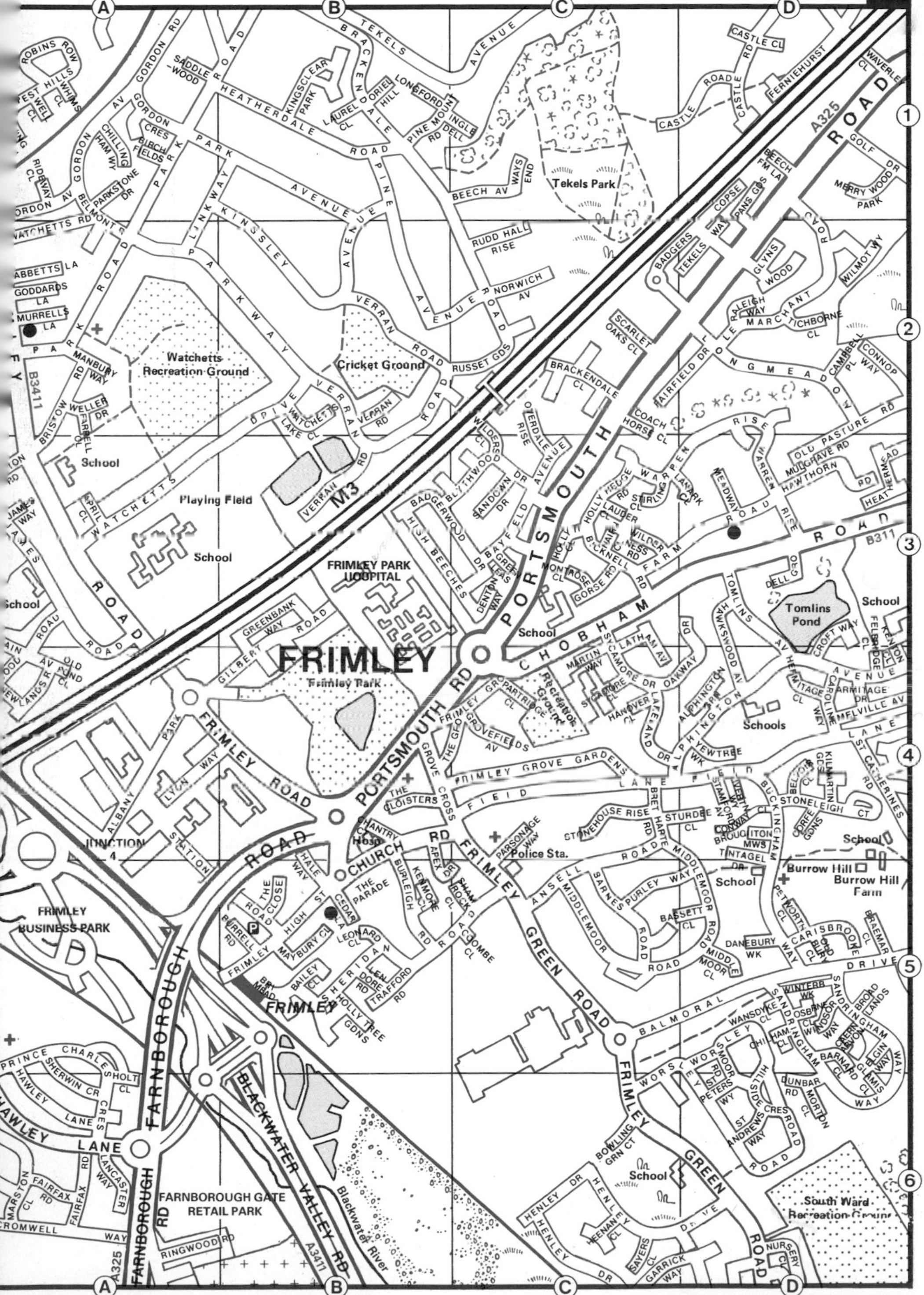
FRIMLEY
Frimley Park
FRIMLEY PARK HOSPITAL
Tekels Park
Watchetts Recreation Ground
Cricket Ground
Playing Field
Tomlins Pond
FRIMLEY BUSINESS PARK
FARNBOROUGH GATE RETAIL PARK
South Ward Recreation Ground
JUNCTION 4
Police Sta.
Burrow Hill
Burrow Hill Farm
Blackwater River
PORTSMOUTH RD
CHOBHAM RD
FRIMLEY RD
FARNBOROUGH RD
BLACKWATER VALLEY RD
FRIMLEY GREEN ROAD
M3
A325
A3411
B3411
B311

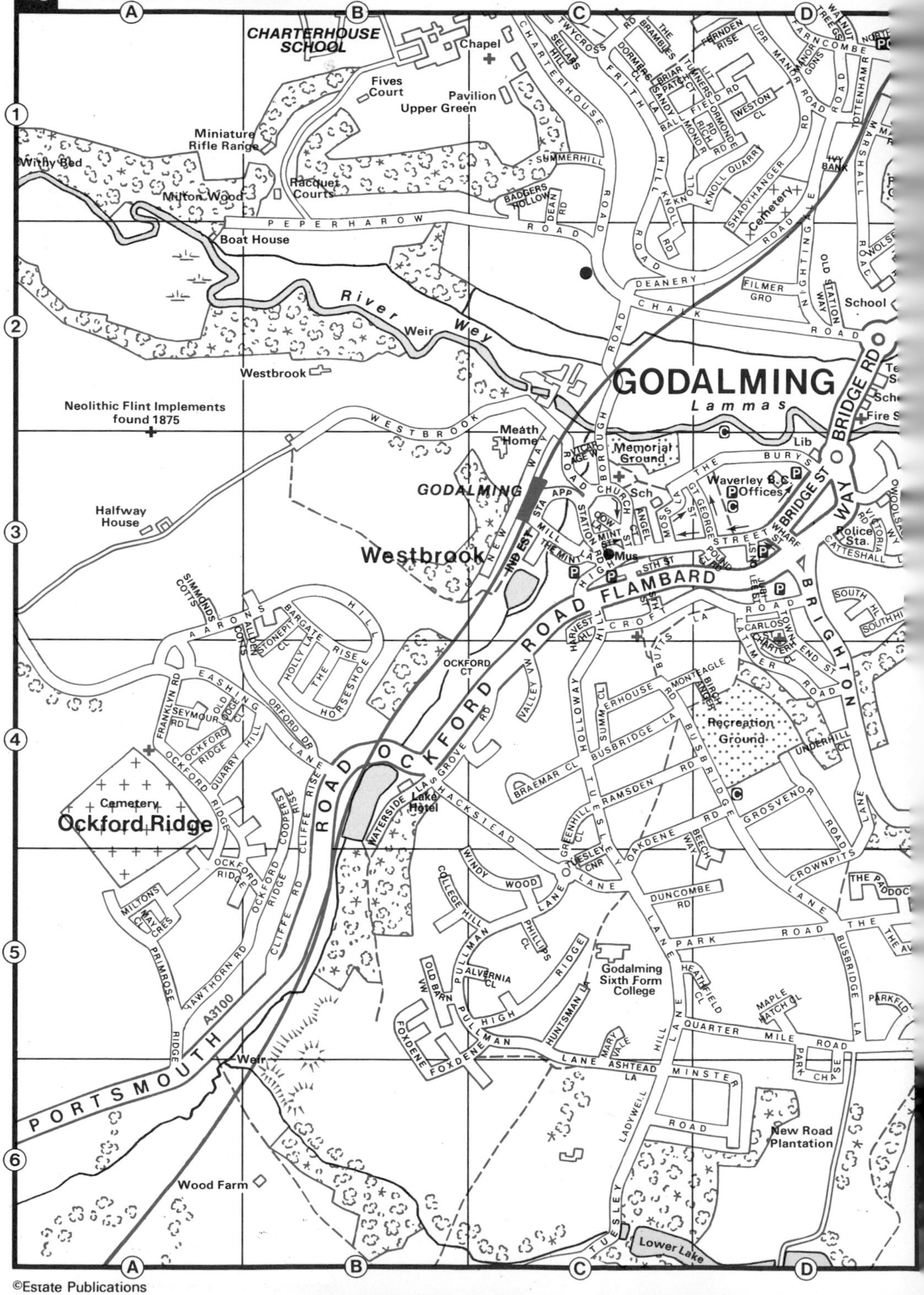
A
B
C
D
1
2
3
4
5
6
CHARTERHOUSE SCHOOL
Chapel
Fives Court
Pavilion
Upper Green
Miniature Rifle Range
Withy Bed
Milton Wood
Racquet Courts
Boat House
PEPERHAROW ROAD
SUMMERHILL
BADGERS HOLLOW
DEAN RD
CHARTERHOUSE ROAD
FRITH HILL ROAD
TWYCROSS RD
SELLARS HILL
THE BRAMBLES
DORMERS CL
BRIAR PATCH
SANDY LA
TUMNERS CT
FERNDEN RISE
FIELD RD
ORMONDE RD
RICHMOND RD
WESTON CL
KNOLL QUARRY
KNOLL RD
SHADYHANGER
Cemetery
UPR MANOR ROAD
MANOR GDNS
FARNCOMBE
TOTTENHAM RD
MARSHALL
IVY BANK
DEANERY
CHALK ROAD
FILMER GRO
NIGHTINGALE ROAD
OLD STATION WAY
School
River Wey
Weir
Westbrook
Neolithic Flint Implements found 1875
WESTBROOK
Meath Home
GODALMING
Lammas
Memorial Ground
BOROUGH ROAD
VICARAGE WK
CHURCH ST
Sch
THE BURYS
Waverley B.C. Offices
Lib
BRIDGE ST
BRIDGE RD
Fire Sta
WAY
Police Sta.
CATTESHALL
VICTORIA
Halfway House
GODALMING
NEW WAY
STA APP
MILL LA
IND EST
THE MINT
STATION RD
MINT ST
Mus
HIGH ST
MOSS LA
ANGEL CT
GT GEORGE ST
STREET
WHARF ST
POUND LA
STH ST
Westbrook
FLAMBARD
JUBILEE
ROAD
BRIGHTON ROAD
SOUTH HL
SOUTHHILL
CARLOS ST
TOWNSEND
CHARTERHOUSE CL
LATIMER
SIMMONDS COTTS
AARONS HILL
ALLDEN COTTS
STONEPIT CL
BARGATE RISE
HOLLY LA
THE HORSESHOE
HILL
OCKFORD CT
ROAD
CROFT RD
HARVEST HL
BUTTS LA
VALLEY VW
OCKFORD
EASHING LANE
FRANKLYN RD
SEYMOUR RD
OLD LODGE CL
OCKFORD RIDGE
QUARRY HILL
ORFORD DR
HOLLOWAY HILL
SUMMERHOUSE RD
MONTEAGLE
BIRCH
BUSBRIDGE LA
Recreation Ground
UNDERHILL CL
GROVE RD
ROAD
WATERSIDE
Lake Hotel
Cemetery
Ockford Ridge
COOPERS RISE
CLIFFE RISE
HACKSTEAD LA
BRAEMAR CL
RAMSDEN RD
TUESLEY
GREENHILL CL
BUSBRIDGE
GROSVENOR ROAD
BEECH WAY
OAKDENE RD
TUESLEY CNR
WINDY WOOD
DUNCOMBE RD
CROWNPITS LANE
THE PADDOCK
OCKFORD RIDGE
MILTONS CRES
WAY CL
COLLEGE HILL
PHILLIPS CL
LANE
PARK ROAD
THE AV
RIDGE
Godalming Sixth Form College
HEATHFIELD CL
PRIMROSE RIDGE
HAWTHORN RD
CLIFFE RD
PULLMAN
ALVERNIA CL
OLD BARN VW
HIGH
HUNTSMAN LA
MAPLE HATCH CL
PARKFLD
A3100
FOXDENE
MARY VALE
QUARTER MILE ROAD
PARK CHASE
BUSBRIDGE LA
PORTSMOUTH ROAD
Weir
ASHTEAD LA
MINSTER ROAD
HILL LANE
LADYWELL
New Road Plantation
Wood Farm
TUESLEY
Lower Lake

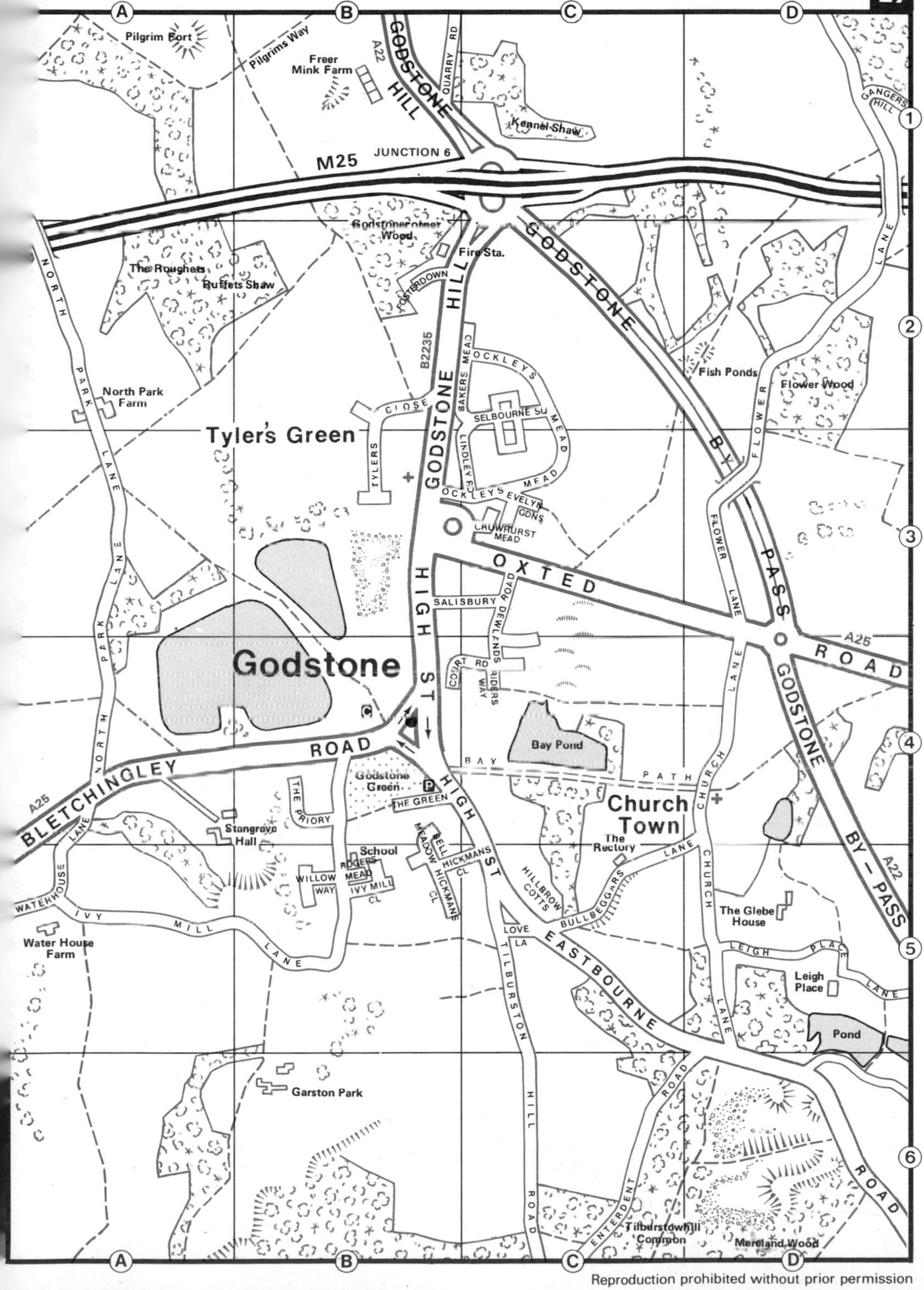
A
B
C
D
1
2
3
4
5
6
Pilgrim Fort
Pilgrims Way
Freer Mink Farm
A22
GODSTONE HILL
QUARRY RD
Kennel Shaw
GANGERS HILL
M25
JUNCTION 6
Godstonecotner Wood
Fire Sta.
GODSTONE
NORTH PARK LANE
The Roughets
Ruffets Shaw
FOSTERDOWN
HILL
LANE
B2235
BAKERS MEAD
OCKLEYS MEAD
SELBOURNE SQ
Fish Ponds
Flower Wood
FLOWER
North Park Farm
CLOSE
Tyler's Green
TYLERS
LINDLEY RD
BY - PASS
EVELYN GDNS
CRUWHURST MEAD
FLOWER LANE
OXTED
SALISBURY
ROAD
DEWLANDS
HIGH ST
A25
ROAD
Godstone
COURT RD
RIDERS WAY
GODSTONE
Bay Pond
BAY PATH
ROAD
BLETCHINGLEY
A25
Godstone Green
P
THE GREEN
THE PRIORY
HIGH ST
Church Town
CHURCH LANE
Stangrove Hall
School
The Rectory
LANE
BELL MEADOW
ROGERS MEAD
HICKMANS CL
WILLOW WAY
IVY MILL CL
HILLBROW COTTS
BULLBEGGARS
CHURCH LANE
BY-PASS
A22
The Glebe House
WATERHOUSE LANE
IVY MILL LANE
LOVE LA
EASTBOURNE
Water House Farm
TILBURSTON HILL ROAD
LEIGH PLACE LANE
Leigh Place
Pond
Garston Park
ROAD
ROAD
ENTERDENT
Tilburstowhill Common
Mereland Wood

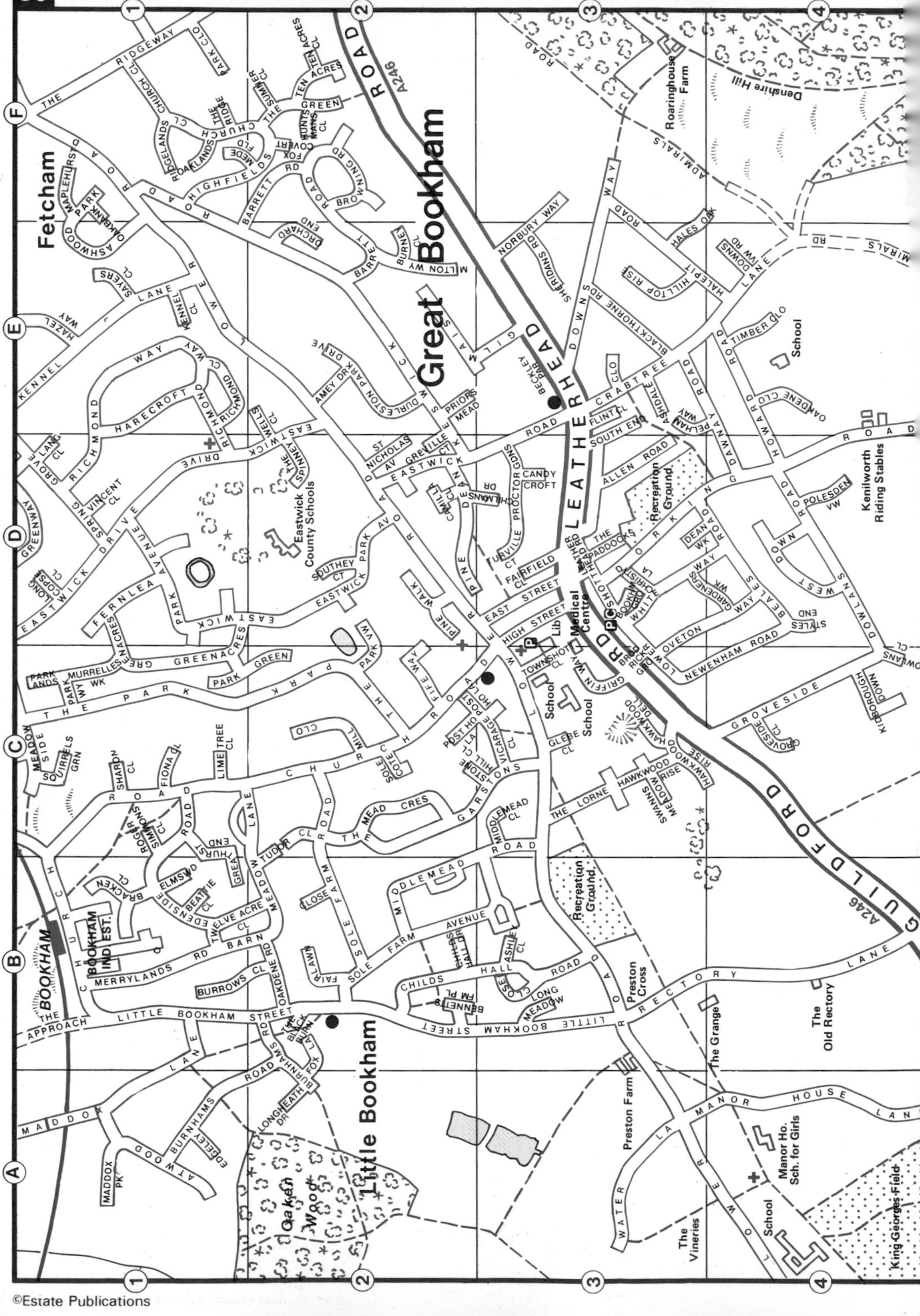

Great Bookham
Little Bookham
Fetcham
BOOKHAM
GUILDFORD ROAD
A246
LEATHERHEAD ROAD
LOWER ROAD
CHURCH ROAD
THE RIDGEWAY
PARK CLO
CHURCH CL
TEN ACRES CL
TEN ACRES
SUMNER CL
THE GREEN
THE RIDGE
CHURCH CL
RIDGELANDS
OAKLANDS
HIGHFIELDS
MEDE FLD
FOX COVERT
HUNTS MANS CL
BROWNING RD
BARRETT RD
ORCHARD END
BURNEY CL
MILTON WY
NORBURY WAY
SHERIDANS RD
ASHWOOD
OAKBANK
PARK
MAPLEHURST
SAYERS CL
KENNEL LANE
KENNEL CL
HAZEL WAY
HARECROFT
RICHMOND WAY
RICHMOND CL
RICHMOND
WELLS CL
EASTWICK
AMEY DR
DURLESTON PARK DRIVE
GILMAIS
PRIORS MEAD
ST NICHOLAS AV
GREVILLE
EASTWICK ROAD
CANDY CROFT
PROCTOR GDNS
CHILMANS DR
DEAN
BECKLEY PAR
DOWNS WAY
HALES OAK
HILLTOP RISE
BLACKTHORNE RD
DOWNS VW RD
HALEPIT ROAD
ADMIRALS RD
Denshire Hill
Roaringhouse Farm
TIMBER CLO
School
OAKDENE CLO
HOWARD ROAD
CRABTREE
FLINT CL
SOUTH END
ASHDALE
PELHAM WAY
ALLEN ROAD
Recreation Ground
DAWNAY ROAD
LOWER SHOT
DORKING ROAD
DEAN WK
POLESDEN VW
Kenilworth Riding Stables
WEST DOWN
LANGLEY GROVE
GREENWAY
SPRING VINCENT CL
EASTWICK DRIVE
THE SPINNEY
Eastwick County Schools
TURVILLE CT
FAIRFIELD CL
PINE WALK
SOUTHEY CT
EASTWICK PARK AV
LONG COPSE CL
FERNLEA AVENUE
PARK
EAST STREET
HIGH STREET
Lib
Medical Centre
THE PADDOCKS
LEATHERHEAD RD
CHRISTIE LA
BOOKHAM GRO
WHITE WAY
GARDENERS WK
BEALES LA
STYLES END
LOWER SHOT
OVETON WAY
NEWENHAM ROAD
DOWLANS CL
DOWLANS
KIDBOROUGH DOWN
GROVESIDE
GROVESIDE CL
GREENACRES
PARK GREEN
PARK VW
THE PARK
PARK LANDS
MURRELLES WK
PARK WY
FIFE WAY
TOWNSHOTT CL
GRIFFIN WAY
ROUNDS CL
HOLLY CT
POST HO LA
VICARAGE CL
GLEBE CL
School
HAWKWOOD DELL
HAWKWOOD RISE
MEADOW SIDE
SQUIRRELS GRN
SHARON CL
FIONA CL
LIME TREE CL
MILL CLO
SOLE COTE
STONE HILL
GARSTONS
MEAD CRES
THE MEAD
MIDDLEMEAD CL
THE LORNE
HAWKWOOD RISE
SWANNS MEADOW
ROGERS CL
SIMMONS CL
HURST END
GREATLANE
TUDOR CL
BRACKEN
ELMSWD
BEATTIE CL
EDENSIDE
TWELVE ACRE CL
BARN
MEADOW RD
SOLE FARM ROAD
MIDDLEMEAD
MIDDLE ROAD
AVENUE
CLOSE
FARM
SOLE FARM
Recreation Ground
BOOKHAM IND EST.
MERRYLANDS RD
BURROWS CL
OAKDENE RD
FAIRLAWN
CHILDS HALL DR
ASHLEY CL
CHILDS HALL ROAD
CLOSE
BENNETTS FM PL
LONG MEADOW
Preston Cross
RECTORY LANE
The Old Rectory
The Grange
THE APPROACH
LITTLE BOOKHAM STREET
THE BLACK BURN
FOX LA
BURNHAMS ROAD
BURNHAMS
LONGHEATH DR
MADDOX LANE
MADDOX PK
ATWOOD
EDGELEY
Oaken Wood
Preston Farm
MANOR HOUSE LANE
WATER LA
LOWER RD
The Vineries
School
Manor Ho. Sch. for Girls
King Georges Field
©Estate Publications

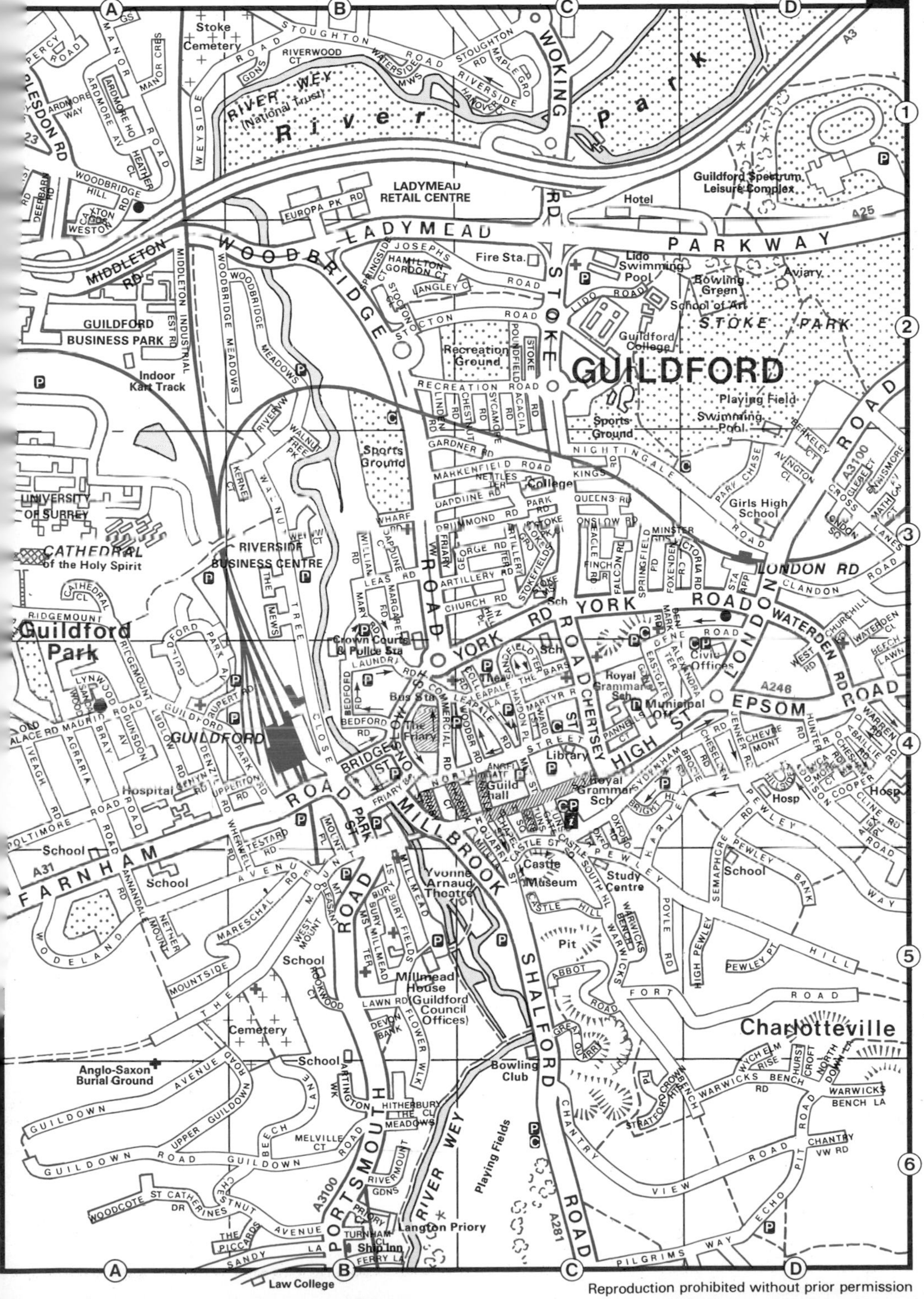
A
B
C
D
1
2
3
4
5
6
Stoke Cemetery
STOUGHTON ROAD
RIVERWOOD CT
WATERSIDE RD
MAPLE GRO
RIVERSIDE
HANOVER CT
WOKING RD
RIVER WEY (National Trust)
River Park
A3
Guildford Spectrum Leisure Complex
Hotel
A25
LADYMEAD RETAIL CENTRE
EUROPA PK RD
LADYMEAD
PARKWAY
MANOR RD
MANOR CRES
ARDMORE WAY
ARDMORE AV
ARDMORE HO
HEATHER CL
WOODBRIDGE HILL
WOODBRIDGE RD
WEYSIDE
DEERBARN RD
WESTON
MIDDLETON RD
MIDDLETON INDUSTRIAL EST RD
GUILDFORD BUSINESS PARK
Indoor Kart Track
WOODBRIDGE MEADOWS
Fire Sta.
ST JOSEPHS
HAMILTON GORDON CT
SPRINGSIDE CT
STOCTON CL
LANGLEY CL
STOCTON ROAD
Lido Swimming Pool
LIDO ROAD
Bowling Green
Aviary
School of Art
STOKE PARK
Guildford College
Recreation Ground
POUNDFIELD
STOKE RD
GUILDFORD
RECREATION ROAD
LINDEN RD
CHESTNUT
SYCAMORE
ACACIA RD
Playing Field
Swimming Pool
Sports Ground
BERKELEY CT
AVINGTON CL
A3100
NIGHTINGALE RD
PARK CHASE
Girls High School
LONDON RD
CLANDON ROAD
GARDNER RD
MARKENFIELD ROAD
NETTLES TER
College
KINGS RD
QUEENS RD
ONSLOW RD
PARK RD
DRUMMOND RD
WHARF RD
DAPDUNE RD
FRIARY
GEORGE RD
ARTILLERY RD
ARTILLERY TER
STOKEFIELDS
STOKE MS
LEAS RD
MARGARET RD
CHURCH RD
HILL PL
WILLIAM RD
MARY RD
UNIVERSITY OF SURREY
CATHEDRAL of the Holy Spirit
RIVERSIDE BUSINESS CENTRE
WALNUT TREE CL
WALNUT TREE PK
KERNEL CT
THE MEWS
RIVERVIEW
CATHEDRAL CL
RIDGEMOUNT
Guildford Park
GUILDFORD PARK AV
YORK RD
YORK ROAD
Crown Courts & Police Sta
LAUNDRY RD
Bus Sta
The Friary
COMMERCIAL RD
LEAPALE RD
SANDFIELD TER
THE BARS
HAYDON PL
MARTYR RD
WARD ST
Royal Grammar Sch
Civic Offices
Municipal Off
DENE ROAD
EASTGATE
ALEXANDRA TER
EPSOM ROAD
WATERDEN RD
CHURCHILL
A246
WARREN RD
HIGH ST
NORTH ST
Guild hall
Library
CHERTSEY ST
BEDFORD RD
BRIDGE ST
FRIARY BR
MILLBROOK
PARK ST
Hospital
FARNHAM ROAD
A31
School
THE MOUNT
MOUNT PL
POLTIMORE RD
ARTILLERY RD
LUDLOW RD
DUNSDON AV
AGRARIA
IVEAGH
MAURICE
OLD PALACE RD
GUILDFORD
DENZIL RD
UPPERTON RD
RUPERT RD
TESTARD RD
WODELAND
MARESCHAL RD
NETHER MOUNT
MOUNTSIDE
WEST MOUNT
MOUNT PLEASANT
Castle
Museum
CASTLE ST
CASTLE HILL
QUARRY ST
Yvonne Arnaud Theatre
MILLMEAD
BURY FIELDS
Study Centre
SOUTH HILL
PEWLEY BANK
PEWLEY HILL
PEWLEY PT
HIGH PEWLEY
POYLE RD
SEMAPHORE RD
Hosp
WARWICKS BENCH
Pit
ABBOT RD
FORT ROAD
Charlotteville
Cemetery
Millmead House (Guildford Council Offices)
LAWN RD
DEVON BANK
FLOWER WLK
ROOKWOOD CT
GREAT QUARRY
Bowling Club
SHALFORD ROAD
Anglo-Saxon Burial Ground
GUILDOWN AVENUE
GUILDOWN ROAD
UPPER GUILDOWN
BEECH LANE
MELVILLE CT
HITHERBURY CL
THE MEADOWS
PORTSMOUTH ROAD
RIVERMOUNT GDNS
A3100
RIVER WEY
Playing Fields
WOODCOTE
ST CATHERINES DR
CHESTNUT AVENUE
THE PICCARDS
SANDY LA
PRIORY
TURNHAM CL
Ship Inn
FERRY LA
Langton Priory
A281
CHANTRY VIEW ROAD
ECHO PIT ROAD
PILGRIMS WAY
STRATFORD CT
CROWN HTS
WYCH ELM RISE
HURST CROFT
NORTH DOWN
WARWICKS BENCH LA
CHANTRY VW RD
Law College

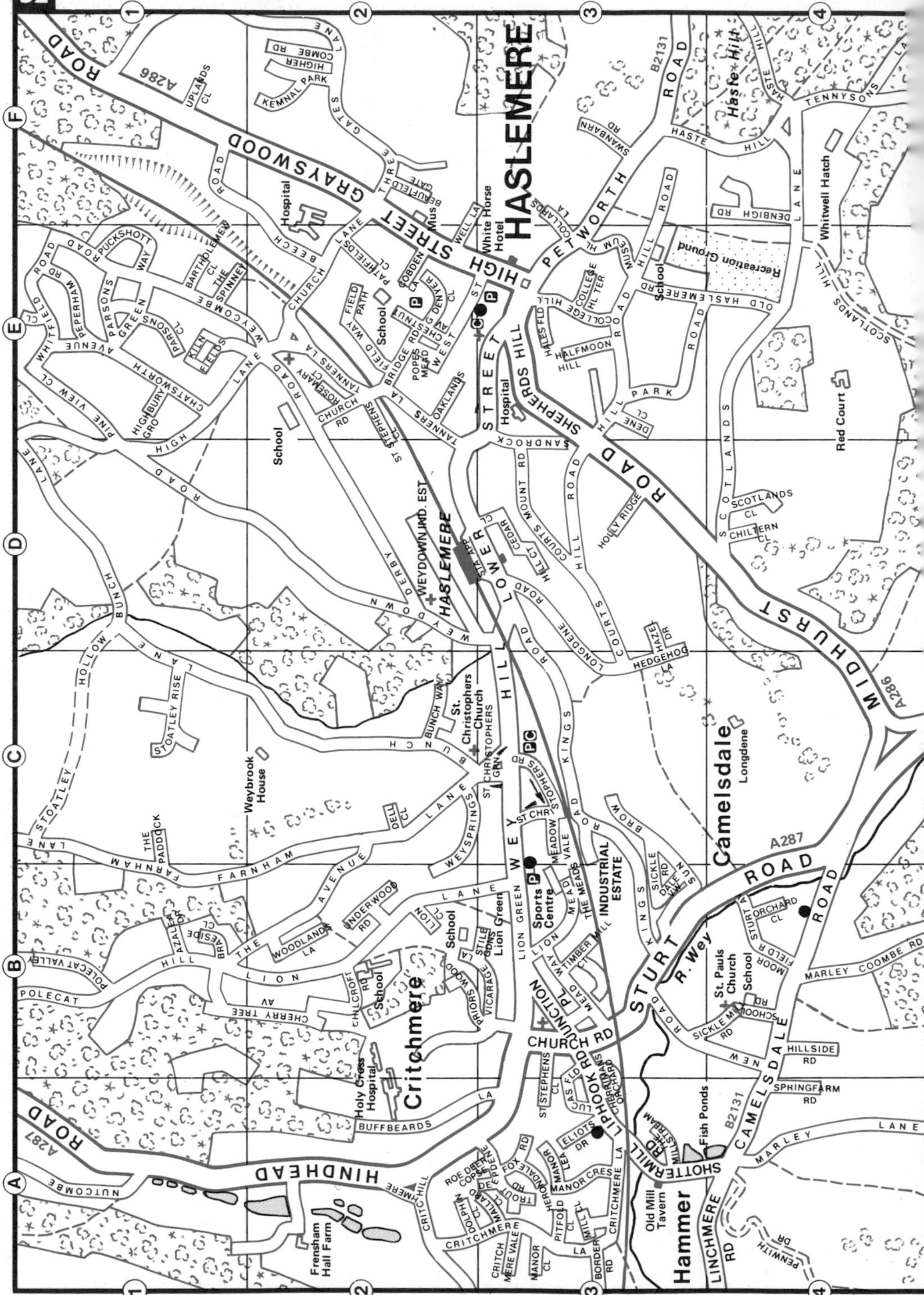
HASLEMERE
GRAYSWOOD ROAD
A286
UPLANDS CL
HIGHER COMBE RD
KEMNAL PARK
GATES LANE
BEAUFIELD GATE
THREE LANE
Hospital
BEECH ROAD
HIGH STREET
WELL LA
Mus
White Horse Hotel
PUCKSHOTT WAY
BARTHOLOMEW CL
THE SPINNEY
WEYCOMBE
CHURCH LANE
PATHFIELDS CL
COBDEN LA
FIELD PATH
FIELD WAY
School
CHESTNUT
DENYER
WEST ST
WHITFIELD CL
PEPERHAM RD
PARSONS GREEN
PARSONS CL
KILN FIELDS
AVENUE
CHATSWORTH
HIGHBURY GRO
PINE VIEW CL
LANE
ROSEMARY CT
TANNERS LA
BRIDGE RD
POPES MEAD
OAKLANDS
CHURCH RD
ST STEPHENS CT
School
HIGH LANE
ROAD
PETWORTH ROAD
B2131
SWANBARN RD
HASTE HILL
Haste Hill
TENNYSONS LA
COLLARDS LA
MUSEUM HL
COLLEGE HL TER
COLLEGE HILL
HALES FLD
HALFMOON HILL
School
Recreation Ground
OLD HASLEMERE RD
DENBIGH RD
Whitwell Hatch
SCOTLANDS HILL
LANE
HILL PARK
DENE CL
SHEPHERDS HILL
Hospital
SANDROCK
STREET
Red Court
SCOTLANDS
SCOTLANDS CL
CHILTERN CL
COURTS MOUNT RD
HOLLY RIDGE
COURTS HILL ROAD
CEDAR CL
LOWER
STA APP
WEYDOWN IND. EST
HASLEMERE
DERBY
WEYDOWN ROAD
LONGDENE ROAD
COURTS
HAZEL DR
HEDGEHOG LA
MIDHURST ROAD
A286
BUNCH LANE
HOLLOW
STATLEY RISE
BUNCH WAY
St. Christophers Church
HILL
PC
ST CHRISTOPHERS GN
ST CHRISTOPHERS RD
Weybrook House
Camelsdale
Longdene
STOATLEY
THE PADDOCK
DELL CL
LANE
WEYSPRINGS
KINGS ROAD
BROW
ST CHR
MEADOW VALE
INDUSTRIAL ESTATE
SICKLE DALE
SUN VALE
A287
ROAD
FARNHAM LANE
AVENUE
LANE
WEY
Sports Centre
P
THE MEADS
AZALEA DR
BRAESIDE CL
UNDERWOOD RD
LION CL
School
STILE GDNS
Lion Green
LION GREEN
LION MEAD
TIMBER MILL
KINGS
STURT
R. Wey
ORCHARD CL
STURT AV
MOOR FIELD RD
MARLEY COOMBE RD
POLECAT VALLEY
HILL
THE WOODLANDS LA
LION
WOOD LA
POLECAT
CHERRY TREE AV
CHILCROFT RD
School
PRIORS
VICARAGE
Critchmere
JUNCTION PL
WAY
MEAD CT
St. Pauls Church
School
SCHOOL RD
SICKLE MILL RD
CAMELSDALE
HILLSIDE RD
NEW
CHURCH RD
Holy Cross Hospital
Critchmere
ST STEPHENS CL
LIPHOOK RD
CHERRIMANS ORCHARD
LUCAS FLD
SPRINGFARM RD
ROAD
A287
BUFFBEARDS LA
HINDHEAD
ELIOTS DR
FOX RD
RILL
THE STREAM
MILLSTREAM
Fish Ponds
B2131
CAMELSDALE
MARLEY LANE
NUTCOMBE
HILL
CRITCH
ROE DEER COPSE
DEEPDENE
TROUT RD
HERON
MANOR LEA
KINDALE
MANOR CRES
SHOTTERMILL
Old Mill Tavern
Hammer
LINCHMERE RD
PENWITH DR
Frensham Hall Farm
DOLPHIN
MALLARD
CRITCHMERE VALE
CRITCH MERE VALE
MANOR CL
PITFOLD CL
MILL LA
CRITCHMERE LA
BORDER RD
1
2
3
4
A
B
C
D
E
F

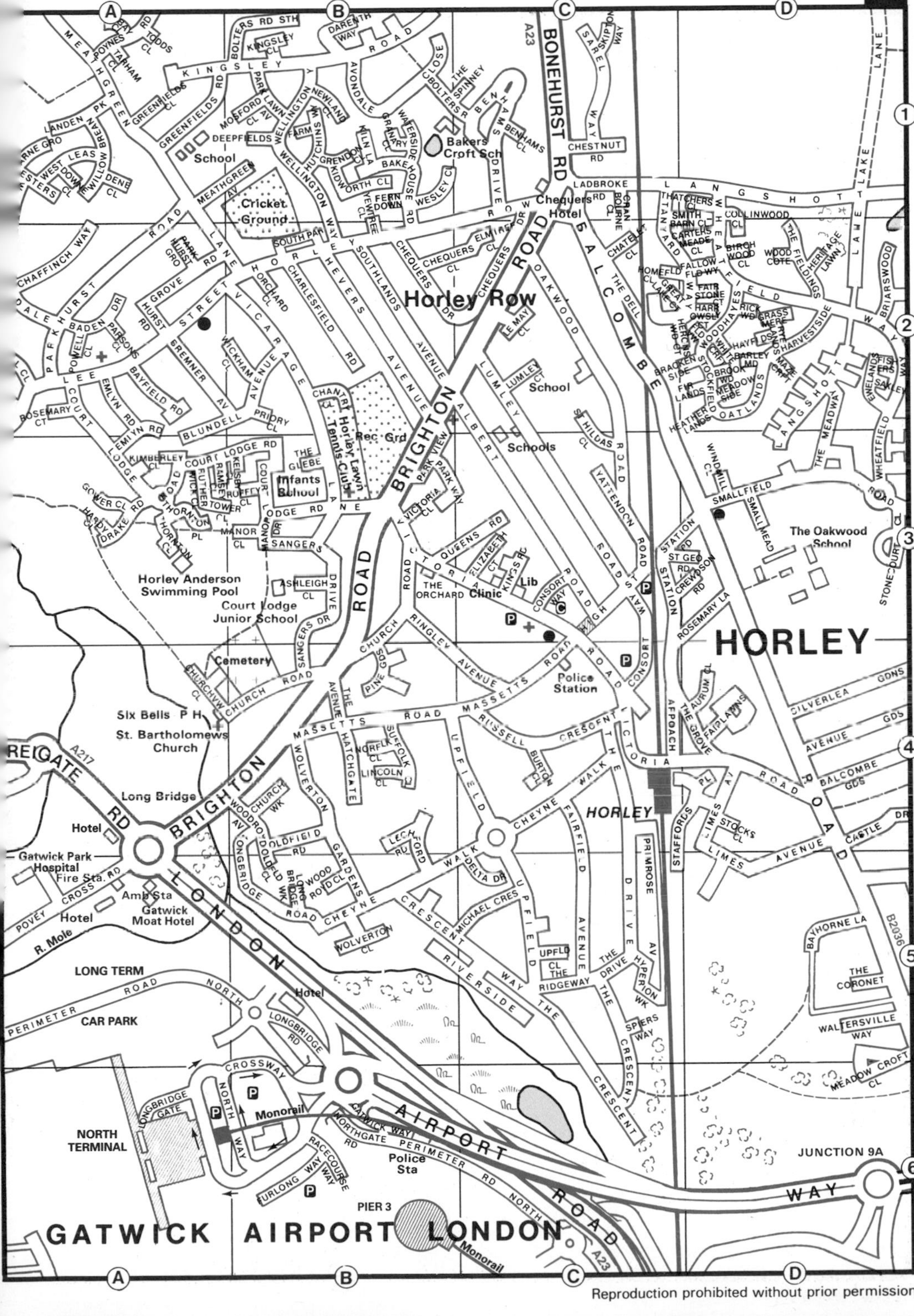

A
B
C
D
1
2
3
4
5
6
BOLTERS RD STH
KINGSLEY RD
DARENTH WAY
ROAD
A23
BONEHURST RD
SARSEL WAY
SKIPTON WAY
MEATH GREEN LANE
POYNES RD
TARHAM CL
TODDS CL
GREENFIELDS RD
PARK LAWN AV
MOSFORD CL
WELLINGTON WAY
NEWLAND CL
AVONDALE
GRANARY CL
WATERSIDE
KILN LA
CLOSE
BOLTERS
THE SPINNEY
BENHAMS DRIVE
BENHAMS CL
Bakers Croft Sch
CHESTNUT RD
LANDEN PK
WEST LEAS
WILLOW BREAN
DENE CL
DEEPFIELDS
School
GRENDON CL
BAKEHOUSE RD
WESLEY CL
FERN DOWN
YEWTREE CL
LADBROKE RD
LANGSHOT
Chequers Hotel
CRANBOURNE CL
THATCHERS CL
SMITH BARN CL
CARTERS MEADE CL
COLLINWOOD CL
Cricket Ground
MEATHGREEN AV
CHAFFINCH WAY
PARKHURST GRO
SOUTH PARK
HORLEY ROW
CHEQUERS CL
ELMTREE CL
CHEQUERS DR
ROAD
CHATELET CL
BIRCH WOOD CL
WOOD COTE
THE FIELDINGS
HERITAGE LAWN
BRIARSWOOD
Horley Row
GROVE RD
PARKHURST RD
STREET
VICARAGE
ORCHARD DR
CHARLESFIELD RD
HEVERS AVENUE
SOUTHLANDS AVENUE
LE MAY CL
OAKWOOD RD
BALCOMBE
THE DELL
HOMEFIELD CL
GREAT LAKE CT
FALLOW FLD WY
FAIR STONE CT
WHEATFIELD WAY
WOODHAYES
GRASSMERE
HARVESTSIDE
BADEN DR
PARSONS CL
POWELL CL
LEE
COURT
BREMNER AV
WICKHAM AVENUE
BAYFIELD RD
EMLYN RD
ROSEMARY CT
LEMLYN RD
BLUNDELL
PRIORY CL
CHANTRY CL
Horley Lawn Tennis Club
Rec. Grd
BRIGHTON
LUMLEY CT
LUMLEY RD
School
ALBERT RD
ST HILDAS CL
BRACKEN SIDE
FIR LANDS
STOCKFIELD
BROOK WD
MEADOWS SIDE
HEATHERLANDS
OATLANDS
LANGSHOTT
THE MEADWAY
EWELANDS
SAKLEY
KIMBERLEY CL
COURT LODGE RD
THE GLEBE
Infants School
PARK VIEW
PARK WAY
Schools
YATTENDON RD
WINDMILL CL
SMALLFIELD ROAD
SMALL MEAD
WHEATFIELD WAY
The Oakwood School
GOWER CL
HARDY CL
DRAKE RD
THORNTON PL
MANOR CL
MANOR DR
LODGE RD
SANGERS
VICTORIA CL
QUEENS RD
ELIZABETH CT
KINGS RD
STATION RD
ST GEO RD
CREWSON RD
STONE COURT
Horley Anderson Swimming Pool
Court Lodge Junior School
ASHLEIGH CL
DRIVE
ROAD
THE ORCHARD
Clinic
Lib
CONSORT WAY
HIGH ROAD
ROSEMARY LA
HORLEY
Cemetery
SANGERS DR
CHURCH RD
RINGLEY AVENUE
PINE GDS
Police Station
CONSORT
APPROACH
AURUM CL
THE GROVE
FAIRLAWNS
SILVERLEA GDNS
AVENUE GDS
CHURCHVW CL
CHURCH ROAD
Six Bells P H
St. Bartholomews Church
REIGATE RD
A217
MASSETTS ROAD
THE AVENUE
HATCHGATE
NORFLK CL
SUFFOLK CL
LINCOLN CL
UPFIELD
RUSSELL CRESCENT
BURTON CL
VICTORIA
BALCOMBE GDS
Long Bridge
BRIGHTON
WOLVERTON
CHURCH WK
WOODROYD AV
OLDFIELD RD
CHEYNE WALK
FAIRFIELD
HORLEY
STAFFORDS PL
LIMES AV
STOCKS CL
CASTLE DR
Hotel
Gatwick Park Hospital
Fire Sta.
CROSS RD
Amb Sta
Gatwick Moat Hotel
POVEY
Hotel
LONGBRIDGE WK
WOOD ROYD CL
GARDENS
LECHFORD RD
DELTA DR
MICHAEL CRES
PRIMROSE DRIVE
LIMES AVENUE
R. Mole
LONDON
CHEYNE ROAD
CRESCENT
AVENUE
HYPERION WK
BAYHORNE LA
B2036
WOLVERTON CL
RIVERSIDE WAY
UPFLD CL
THE RIDGEWAY
THE DRIVE
THE CORONET
LONG TERM
PERIMETER ROAD NORTH
CAR PARK
Hotel
LONGBRIDGE RD
THE CRESCENT
SPIERS WAY
WALTERSVILLE WAY
MEADOW CROFT CL
CROSSWAY
LONGBRIDGE GATE
NORTH WAY
Monorail
GATWICK WAY
WORTHGATE
RACECOURSE WAY
PERIMETER RD NORTH
AIRPORT
Police Sta
NORTH TERMINAL
FURLONG WAY
JUNCTION 9A
WAY
ROAD
PIER 3
GATWICK AIRPORT LONDON
Monorail
A23
P

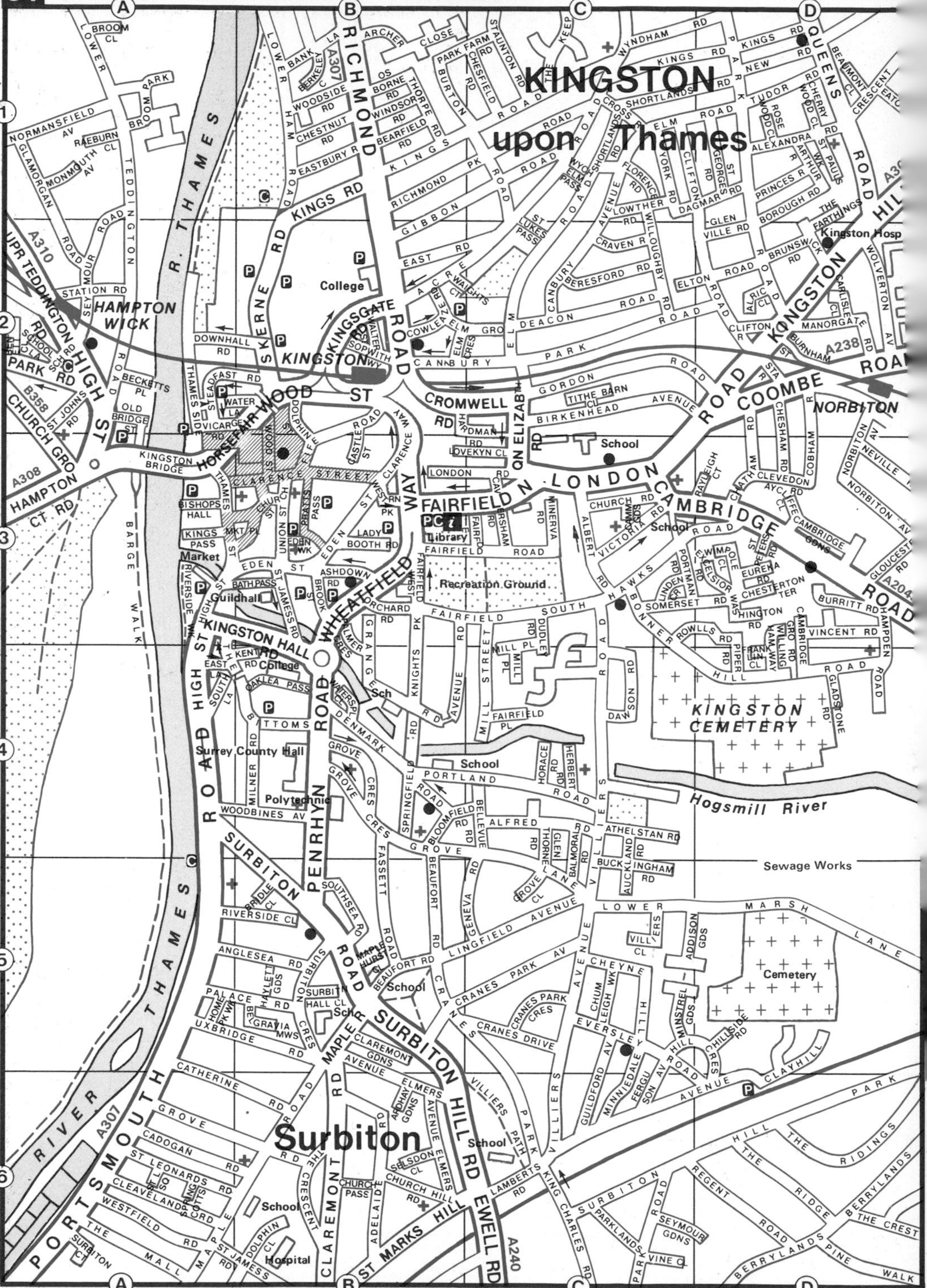
A
B
C
D
1
2
3
4
5
6
KINGSTON
upon Thames
Surbiton
HAMPTON WICK
NORBITON
KINGSTON CEMETERY
Cemetery
Hogsmill River
R. THAMES
RIVER THAMES
Sewage Works
Kingston Hosp
College
Library
Recreation Ground
Guildhall
Market
Surrey County Hall
Polytechnic
School
Sch
Hospital
KINGSTON BRIDGE
KINGSTON HALL RD
HORSEFAIR
WOOD ST
CLARENCE STREET
FAIRFIELD
LONDON RD
CAMBRIDGE ROAD
COOMBE ROAD
KINGSTON HILL
RICHMOND ROAD
KINGS RD
SKERNE RD
KINGSGATE RD
CANBURY PARK RD
CROMWELL RD
WHEATFIELD WAY
PENRHYN ROAD
SURBITON ROAD
SURBITON HILL RD
EWELL RD
PORTSMOUTH ROAD
HIGH ST
HAMPTON CT RD
UPR TEDDINGTON RD
LOWER TEDDINGTON ROAD
BARGE WALK
HAWKS ROAD
VILLIERS ROAD
LOWER MARSH LANE
CRANES PARK AV
LINGFIELD AVENUE
ST MARKS HILL
MAPLE RD
CLAREMONT RD
A307
A310
A308
B358
A238
A240
A204

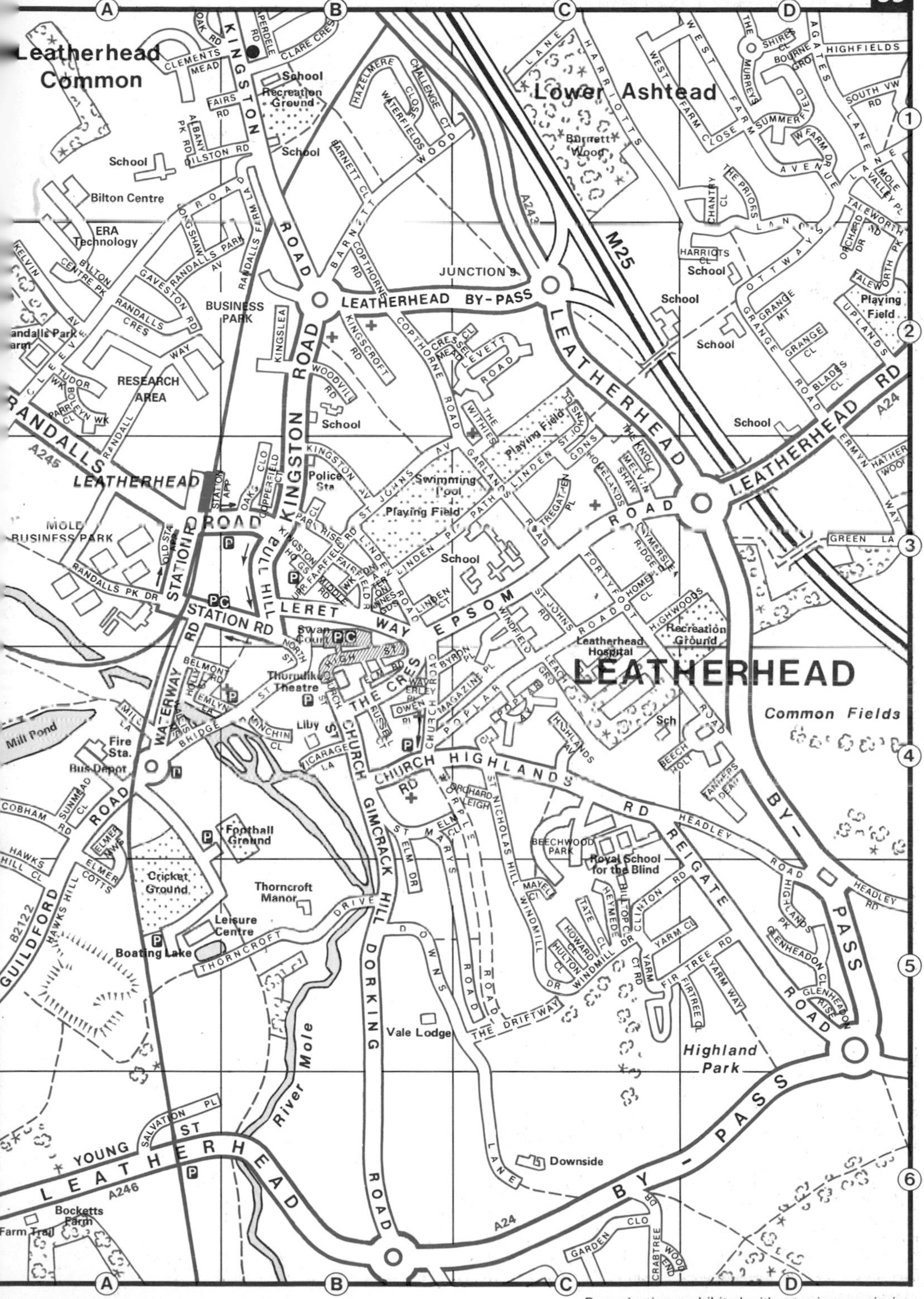
A
B
C
D
1
2
3
4
5
6
Leatherhead Common
Lower Ashtead
Burnett Wood
LEATHERHEAD
Common Fields
Highland Park
KINGSTON ROAD
LEATHERHEAD BY-PASS
JUNCTION 9
M25
A243
A24
A245
A246
B2122
School
Recreation Ground
Bilton Centre
ERA Technology
BUSINESS PARK
RESEARCH AREA
MOLD BUSINESS PARK
Randalls Park Farm
Police Sta.
Swimming Pool
Playing Field
Leatherhead Hospital
Thorndike Theatre
Swan Court
Liby
Fire Sta.
Bus Depot
Mill Pond
Football Ground
Cricket Ground
Thorncroft Manor
Leisure Centre
Boating Lake
River Mole
Vale Lodge
Downside
Bocketts Farm
Farm Trail
BEECHWOOD PARK
Royal School for the Blind
Sch
Playing Field
LEATHERHEAD RD
RANDALLS RD
STATION RD
LERET WAY
EPSOM ROAD
CHURCH ST
HIGH ST
THE CRES
BRIDGE ST
GIMCRACK HILL
DORKING ROAD
GUILDFORD ROAD
COBHAM RD
HAWKS HILL CL
YOUNG ST
SALVATION PL
LEATHERHEAD BY-PASS
REIGATE RD
HEADLEY ROAD
HIGHLANDS RD
CHURCH RD
ST JOHNS AV
COPTHORNE ROAD
LEVETT ROAD
THE WITHIES
DOWNS LANE
ST MARYS ROAD
ST NICHOLAS HILL
WINDMILL DR
THE DRIFTWAY
THORNCROFT DRIVE
FORTYFOOT ROAD
HIGHWOODS
OTTWAYS LANE
GRANGE ROAD
UPLANDS
HARRIOTTS LANE
WEST FARM CLOSE
WEST FARM AVENUE
BARNETT WOOD LANE
HAZELMERE CL
CHALLENGE CT
WATERFIELDS
CLEMENTS MEAD
FAIRS RD
DILSTON RD
ALBANY PK RD
CLARE CRES
RANDALLS PARK AV
GAVESTON RD
RANDALLS CRES
BILTON CENTRE PK
KELVIN AV
CLEEVE WAY
TUDOR WK
BOLEYN WK
PARR CL
RANDALLS PK DR
OLD STA APP
STATION APP
PULL HILL
KINGSLEA
KINGSCROFT RD
WOODVILLE RD
COPPERFIELD CT
OAKS CL
LINDEN PL
LINDEN RD
LINDEN CT
GARLANDS RD
ST JOHNS RD
TREGARTHEN PL
HOMELANDS
MELVINSHAW
THE KNOLL
GREEN LA
BLADES CL
GRANGE CL
GRANGE MT
HIGHFIELDS
SOUTH VW RD
SUMMERFIELD
THE PRIORS
CHANTRY CL
HARRIOTS CL
MOLE VALLEY PL
TALEWORTH RD
ERMYN WAY
HATHERWOOD
BYRON PL
MAGAZINE PL
POPLAR RD
HIGHLANDS AV
BEECH HOLT
TANNERS DEAN
ORCHARD LEIGH
ST MARYS RD
ELM DR
MAYELL CL
HOWARD CL
TATE CL
HULTON CL
HEYMEDE
HILLTOP CL
CLINTON RD
YARM CL
YARM WAY
FIR TREE RD
FIRTREE CL
GLENHEADON CL
GLENHEADON RISE
HIGHLANDS PK
VICARAGE LA
MINCHIN CL
BELMONT RD
WATERWAY RD
SUNMEAD CL
ELMER MWS
ELMER COTTS
HAWKS HILL CL
GARDEN CLO
CRABTREE WOOD

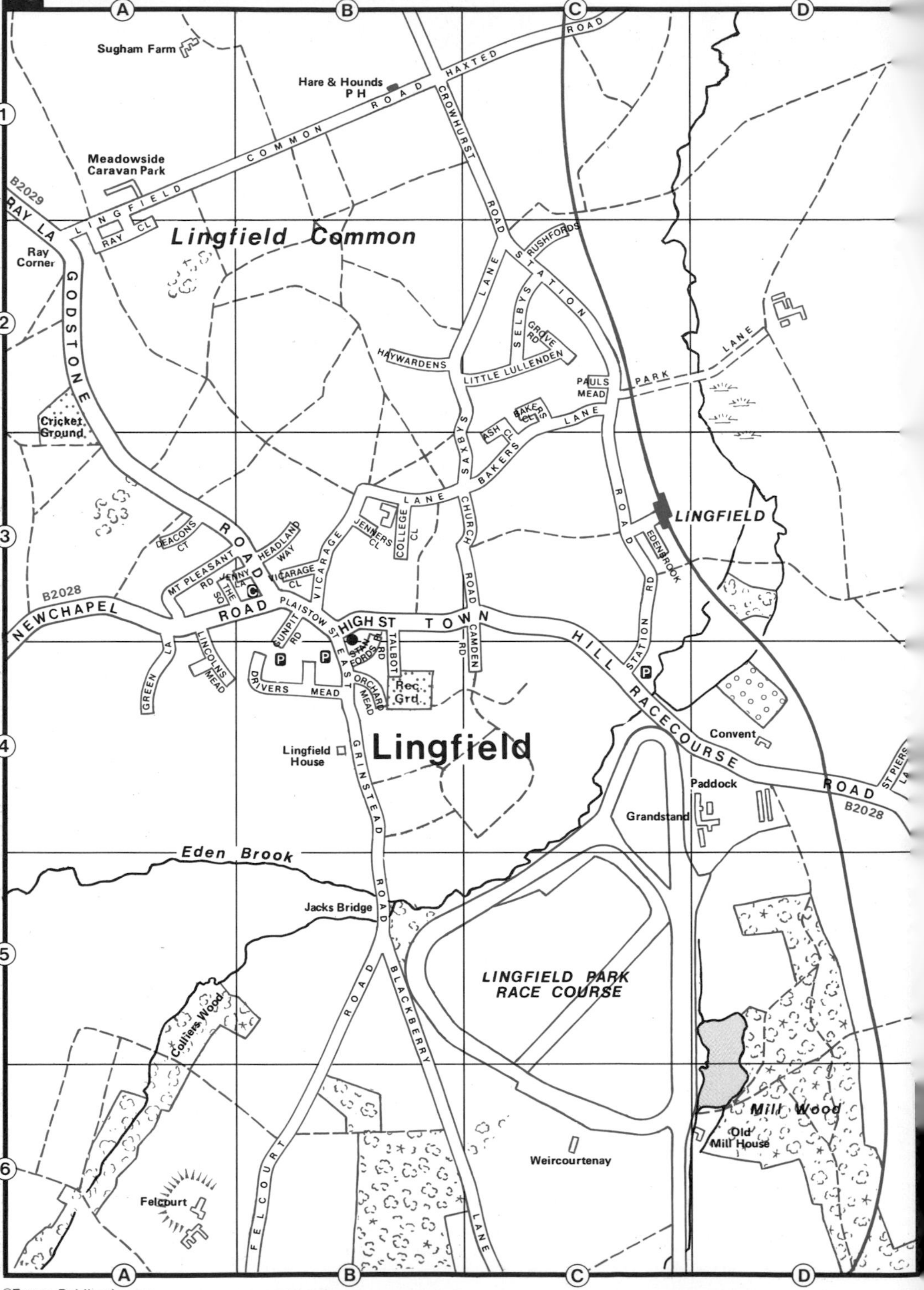

A
B
C
D
1
2
3
4
5
6
Sugham Farm
Hare & Hounds PH
HAXTED ROAD
CROWHURST ROAD
LINGFIELD COMMON ROAD
Meadowside Caravan Park
B2029
RAY LA
RAY CL
Lingfield Common
Ray Corner
GODSTONE ROAD
STATION
LANE
RUSHFORDS
SELBYS
GROVE RD
HAYWARDENS
LITTLE LULLENDEN
PAULS MEAD
PARK LANE
BAKERS CL
ASH CL
BAKERS LANE
SAXBYS
Cricket Ground
LANE
JENNERS CL
COLLEGE CL
CHURCH ROAD
LINGFIELD
DEACONS CT
HEADLAND WAY
MT PLEASANT RD
JENNY LA
THE SQ
VICARAGE
VICARAGE CL
STATION RD
EDEN BROOK
B2028
NEWCHAPEL ROAD
PLAISTOW ST
HIGH ST
TOWN
HILL
GUNPIT RD
STANFORDS PL
TALBOT RD
CAMDEN RD
LA
GREEN
LINCOLNS MEAD
EAST
DRIVERS MEAD
ORCHARD MEAD
Rec Grd
RACECOURSE ROAD
Convent
ST PIERS LA
B2028
Lingfield House
Lingfield
GRINSTEAD ROAD
Paddock
Grandstand
Eden Brook
Jacks Bridge
LINGFIELD PARK RACE COURSE
ROAD
BLACKBERRY LANE
Colliers Wood
Mill Wood
Old Mill House
Weircourtenay
FELCOURT ROAD
Felcourt

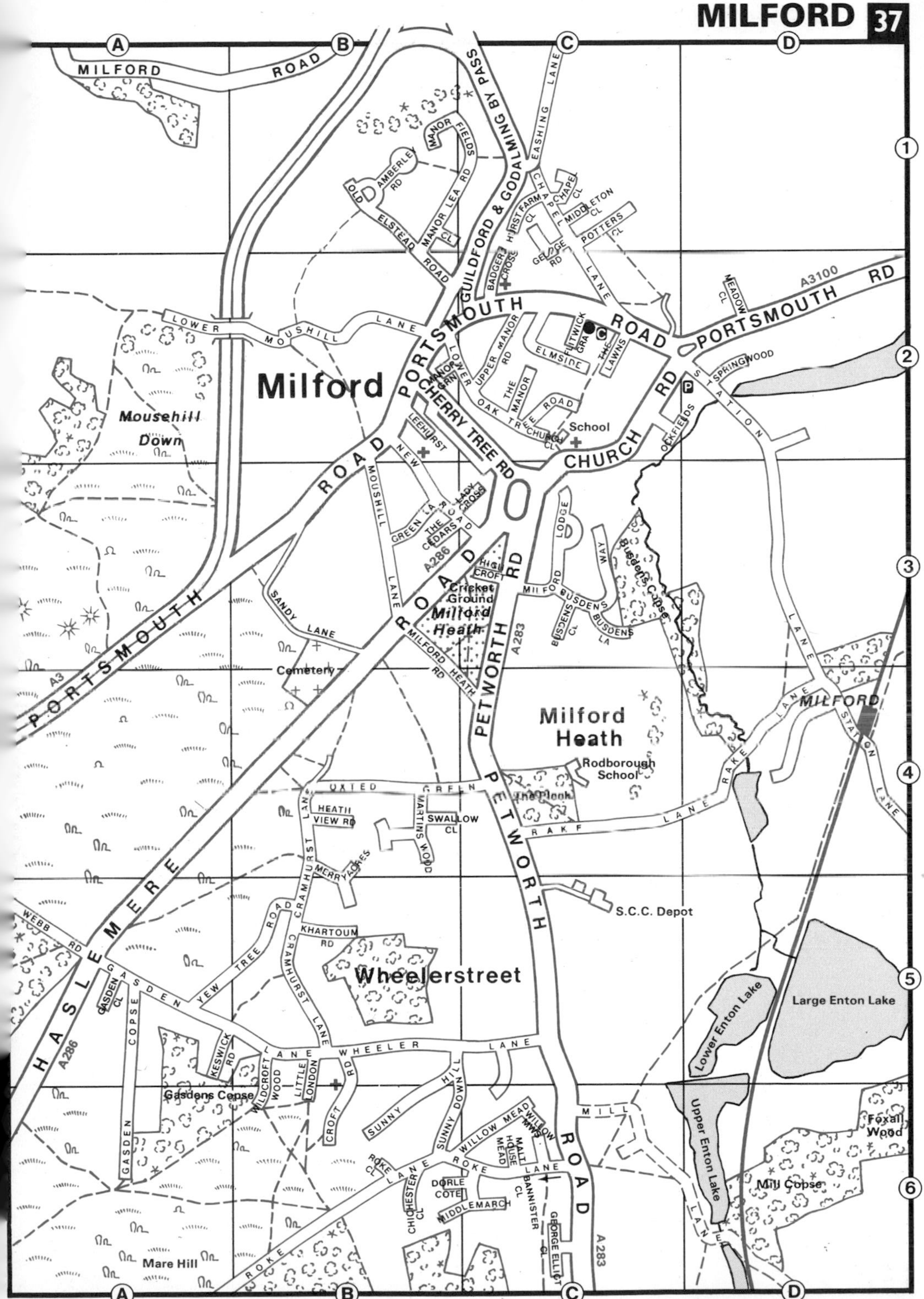
Milford
Mousehill Down
Milford Heath
Wheelerstreet
Gasdens Copse
Mare Hill
Large Enton Lake
Lower Enton Lake
Upper Enton Lake
Foxall Wood
Mill Copse
Cricket Ground
Cemetery
School
Rodborough School
S.C.C. Depot
The Plook
MILFORD ROAD
PORTSMOUTH ROAD
GUILDFORD & GODALMING BY PASS
EASHING LANE
MANOR FIELDS
AMBERLEY RD
OLD ELSTEAD ROAD
MANOR LEA RD
LOWER MOUSHILL LANE
CHAPEL LANE
MIDDLETON CL
POTTERS CL
HIRST FARM CL
GELDGE RD
BADGERS CROSS
MEADOW CL
A3100
PORTSMOUTH RD
FLITWICK GRA
THE LAWNS
ELMSIDE
UPPER MANOR RD
LOWER MANOR GRN
THE MANOR
OAK TREE ROAD
CHURCH CL
CHURCH RD
SPRINGWOOD
STATION LANE
OCKFIELDS
CHERRY TREE RD
LEEHURST
NEW ROAD
MOUSHILL LANE
GREEN LA
THE CEDARS
LADY CROSS
HIGH CROFT
A286
MILFORD HEATH RD
PETWORTH RD
A283
LODGE
WAY
BUSDENS CL
BUSDENS LA
BUSDENS
Busdens Copse
SANDY LANE
A3
MILFORD STATION
RAKE LANE
OXTED GREEN
HEATH VIEW RD
MARTINS WOOD
SWALLOW CL
MERRYACRES
CRAMHURST LANE
KHARTOUM RD
YEW TREE ROAD
WEBB RD
HASLEMERE ROAD
GASDEN CL
GASDEN COPSE
KESWICK RD
WHEELER LANE
WILDCROFT WOOD
LITTLE LONDON
CROFT RD
SUNNY HILL
SUNNY DOWN
WILLOW MEAD
WILLOW MWS
MALT HOUSE MEAD
ROKE CL
ROKE LANE
DORLE COTE
CHICHESTER CL
MIDDLEMARCH
BANNISTER CL
GEORGE ELLIOT CL
MILL LANE
A
B
C
D
1
2
3
4
5
6

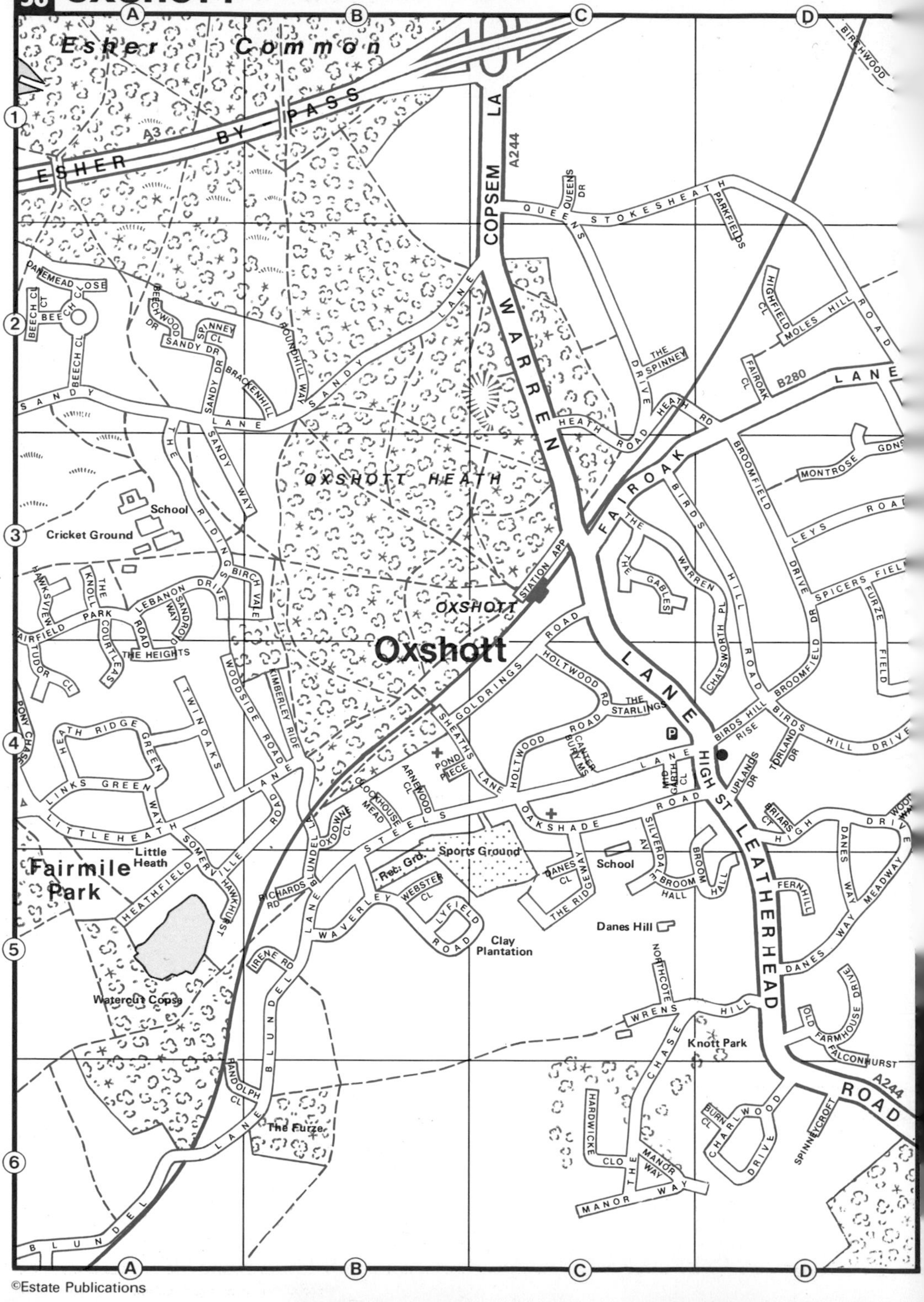

Esher Common

Esher By Pass

A3

Oxshott

OXSHOTT HEATH

Esher Common

Cricket Ground

School

Fairmile Park

Little Heath

Watercut Copse

The Furze

Knott Park

Danes Hill

Sports Ground

Clay Plantation

Oxshott

COPSEM LA
A244

WARREN

FAIROAK LANE

HIGH ST

LEATHERHEAD ROAD
A244

STOKESHEATH
PARKFIELDS
QUEENS DR

MOLES HILL

BIRCHWOOD

B280 LANE

MONTROSE GDNS

LEYS ROAD

SPICERS FIELD

FURZE FIELD

THE DRIVE

HEATH ROAD

THE SPINNEY

HIGHFIELD CL

FAIROAK CL

BROOMFIELD

CHATSWORTH PL

WARREN RD

BIRDS HILL

THE GABLES

STATION APP

GOLDRINGS

HOLTWOOD RD

HOLTWOOD ROAD

SHEATHS LANE

STEELS LANE

ARNEWOOD

CLOCKHOUSE MEAD

STOBANE CL

POND PIECE

OAKSHADE ROAD

THE STARLINGS

BIRDS HILL RISE

UPLANDS

ORLANDO DR

BIRDS HILL DRIVE

CANCER BURMS

DANES CL

SILVERDALE AV

BROOM HALL

BROOM HALL

School

THE RIDGEWAY

FERNHILL

FRIARS

HIGH

DANES WAY

MEADWAY

WOOD DRIVE

OLD FARMHOUSE DRIVE

FALCONHURST

SPINNEYCROFT

BURN CL

CHARLWOOD DRIVE

MANOR WAY

THE MANOR WAY

HARDWICKE CLO

WRENS

NORTHCOTE

CHASE

KNOLL PARK

HAWKSVIEW

AIRFIELD ESTATE

TUDOR CL

PONY CHASE

HEATH RIDGE GREEN

LINKS GREEN WAY

LITTLEHEATH LANE

HEATHFIELD

SOMERVILLE

HAWKHURST

RICHARDS RD

IRENE RD

BLUNDEL LANE

RANDOLPH CL

BLUNDEL LANE

WAVERLEY ROAD

LYFIELD ROAD

WEBSTER CL

Ret. Grd.

COURTLANDS

THE HEIGHTS

LEBANON DRIVE

SANDOWN WAY

RIDING WAY

BIRCH VALE

WOODSIDE ROAD

KIMBERLEY RIDE

TWINOAKS

THE HEIGHTS

PANEMEAD

BEECH CL

BEECH CT

BEECH CL

BEECHWOOD DR

SPINNEY CL

SANDY DR

BRACKENHILL

SANDY LANE

ROUNDHILL WAY

SANDI LANE

THE SANDY WAY

©Estate Publications

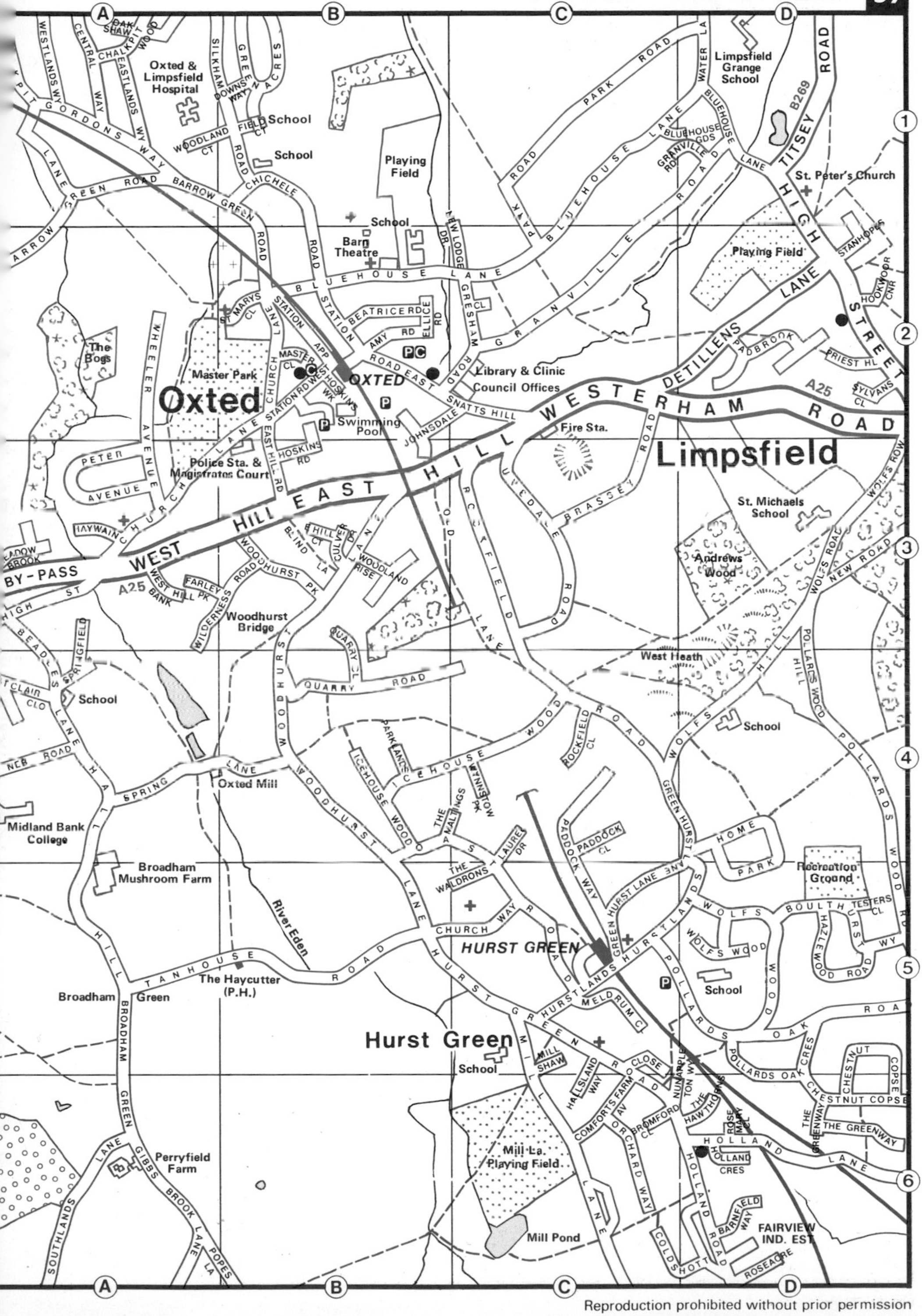
A
B
C
D
1
2
3
4
5
6
Oxted
Limpsfield
Hurst Green
OXTED
HURST GREEN
Oxted & Limpsfield Hospital
School
Playing Field
Barn Theatre
Limpsfield Grange School
St. Peter's Church
Library & Clinic
Council Offices
Master Park
The Bogs
Swimming Pool
Police Sta. & Magistrates Court
Fire Sta.
St. Michaels School
Andrews Wood
West Heath
Woodhurst Bridge
Oxted Mill
Midland Bank College
Broadham Mushroom Farm
River Eden
The Haycutter (P.H.)
Broadham Green
Recreation Ground
Perryfield Farm
Mill La. Playing Field
Mill Pond
FAIRVIEW IND. EST
WESTERHAM ROAD
EAST HILL
WEST HILL
BY-PASS
A25
B269
TITSEY ROAD
HIGH STREET
GORDONS WAY
BARROW GREEN ROAD
BLUEHOUSE LANE
GRANVILLE ROAD
PARK ROAD
DETILLENS LANE
STATION ROAD EAST
STATION ROAD WEST
SNATTS HILL
WHEELER AVENUE
PETER AVENUE
CHURCH LANE
WOODHURST LANE
QUARRY ROAD
ICEHOUSE WOOD
SPRING LANE
TANHOUSE ROAD
HURST GREEN ROAD
HURSTLANDS
POLLARDS WOOD ROAD
POLLARDS OAK ROAD
WOLFS HILL
WOLFS ROW
HOLLAND LANE
HOLLAND ROAD
MILL LANE
ORCHARD WAY
COMFORTS FARM AV
BROADHAM GREEN
GIBBS BROOK LANE
SOUTHLANDS LANE
POPES LA
CHESTNUT COPSE
THE GREENWAY
HOME PARK
BOULTHURST WY
HAZLEWOOD ROAD
UVEDALE ROAD
BRASSEY
ROCKFIELD ROAD
CHURCH WAY
MELDRUM CL
ROSEACRE
BARNFIELD WAY
COLDSHOTT

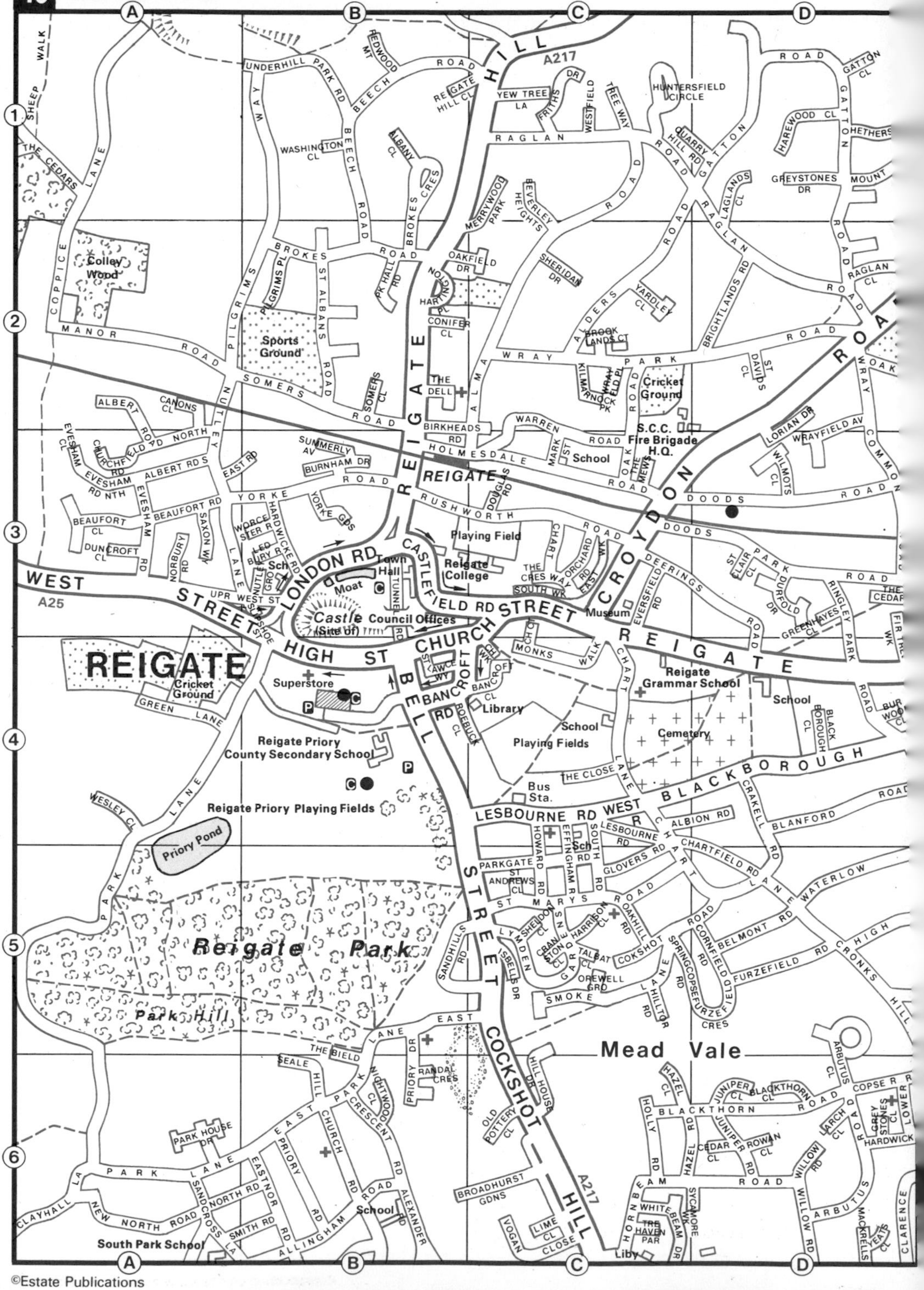

A
B
C
D
1
2
3
4
5
6
SHEEP WALK
THE CEDARS
COPPICE LANE
UNDERHILL PARK RD
REDWOOD MT
BEECH ROAD
REIGATE HILL CL
HILL
A217
YEW TREE LA
FRITHS DR
WESTFIELD
TREE WAY
HUNTERSFIELD CIRCLE
ROAD
GATTON CL
GATTON
RAGLAN
QUARRY HILL RD
HAREWOOD CL
HETHERS
WASHINGTON CL
ALBANY CL
BROKES CRES
GREYSTONES DR
MOUNT
MERRYWOOD PARK
BEVERLEY HEIGHTS
LAGLANDS CL
Colley Wood
BROKES ROAD
PK HALL RD
OAKFIELD DR
HARTINGTON PL
SHERIDAN DR
BRIGHTLANDS RD
RAGLAN CL
PILGRIMS PL
PILGRIMS WAY
ST ALBANS ROAD
Sports Ground
CONIFER CL
ALDERS ROAD
YARDLEY CL
BROOK LANDS CT
MANOR ROAD
REIGATE
ALMA
WRAY PARK ROAD
ST DAVIDS CL
WRAY
OAK
SOMERS ROAD
SOMERS CL
THE DELL
KILMARNOCK PK
WRAY FIELD PL
Cricket Ground
ALBERT RD
CANONS
NUTLEY LANE
BIRKHEADS RD
WARREN ROAD
S.C.C. Fire Brigade H.Q.
LORIAN DR
WRAYFIELD AV
EVESHAM CL
CHURCHFIELD RD
NORTH
SUMMERLY AV
HOLMESDALE ROAD
MARK ST
School
OAK RD
THE MEWS
WILMOTS CL
COMMON
ALBERT RDS
EAST RD
BURNHAM DR
REIGATE
EVESHAM RD NTH
YORKE ROAD
DOUGLAS RD
CROYDON
DOODS ROAD
BEAUFORT RD
BEAUFORT CL
SAXON WAY
HARDWICKE RD
YORKE GDS
RUSHWORTH ROAD
DOODS
DUNCROFT CL
NORBURY RD
WORCESTER RD
LEDBURY RD
Playing Field
CHART
ORCHARD
ST CLAIR CL
PARK
DEERINGS ROAD
WEST
A25
LONDON RD
Town Hall
CASTLEFIELD RD
Reigate College
THE CRES
WAY
EAST WK
EVERSFIELD RD
DURFOLD DR
RINGLEY PARK
THE CEDARS
Sch
NUTLEY GRO
UPR WEST ST
Moat
TUNNEL RD
SOUTH WK
Museum
GREENHAYES CL
FIR TREE WK
STREET
SLIPSHOE ST
Castle (Site of)
Council Offices
STREET
CHURCH
REIGATE
HIGH ST
LAWCE WY
MONKS WALK
REIGATE
Cricket Ground
Superstore
BANCROFT
BANCROFT RD
Reigate Grammar School
School
BLACKBOROUGH CL
BURY WOOD
GREEN LANE
BELL
ROEBUCK CL
Library
School
Playing Fields
Cemetery
Reigate Priory County Secondary School
BLACKBOROUGH
CHART LANE
THE CLOSE
CRAKELL RD
ROAD
WESLEY CL
LANE
Reigate Priory Playing Fields
Bus Sta.
LESBOURNE RD WEST
ALBION RD
BLANFORD
Priory Pond
HOWARD RD
EFFINGHAM RD
SOUTH RD
Sch
LESBOURNE RD
CHARTFIELD RD
PARKGATE
ST ANDREWS CL
GLOVERS RD
RYS
WATERLOO
PARK
ST MARYS ROAD
ROAD
LANE
Reigate Park
SANDHILLS RD
LYMDEN GDNS
SHELDON CL
CRANSTON CL
HARRISON CL
OAKHILL RD
BELMONT RD
CORNFIELD RD
HIGH
CRONKS
TALBOT CL
COKSHOT
SPRINGCOPSE RD
FURZEFIELD RD
FURZEFIELD CRES
Park Hill
ISBELLS DR
OREWELL GRD
SMOKE LANE
HILLTOP RD
HILL
EAST
COCKSHOT
THE BIELD
LANE
SEALE HILL
PRIORY DR
RANDAL CRES
HILL HOUSE DR
Mead Vale
ARBUTUS CL
HAZEL CL
JUNIPER CL
BLACKTHORN CL
COPSE R
LOWER
HOLLY RD
BLACKTHORN ROAD
LARCH CL
GREY STONES CL
HARDWICK
NIGHTWOOD CL
CHURCH
CRESCENT
PARK HOUSE DR
OLD POTTERY CL
HAZEL RD
CEDAR CL
JUNIPER RD
ROWAN CL
WILLOW RD
EAST PARK
PRIORY RD
ALEXANDER RD
CLAYHALL LA
PARK LANE
EASTNOR RD
NORTH RD
ROAD
BROADHURST GDNS
HORNBEAM ROAD
SYCAMORE WK
WHITEBEAM DR
ARBUTUS
WILLOW RD
NEW NORTH ROAD
SANDCROSS LA
SMITH RD
ALLINGHAM
School
VOGAN CL
LIME CL
CLOSE
THE HAVEN PAR
Liby
MACKRELLS
YEATS CL
CLARENCE
South Park School

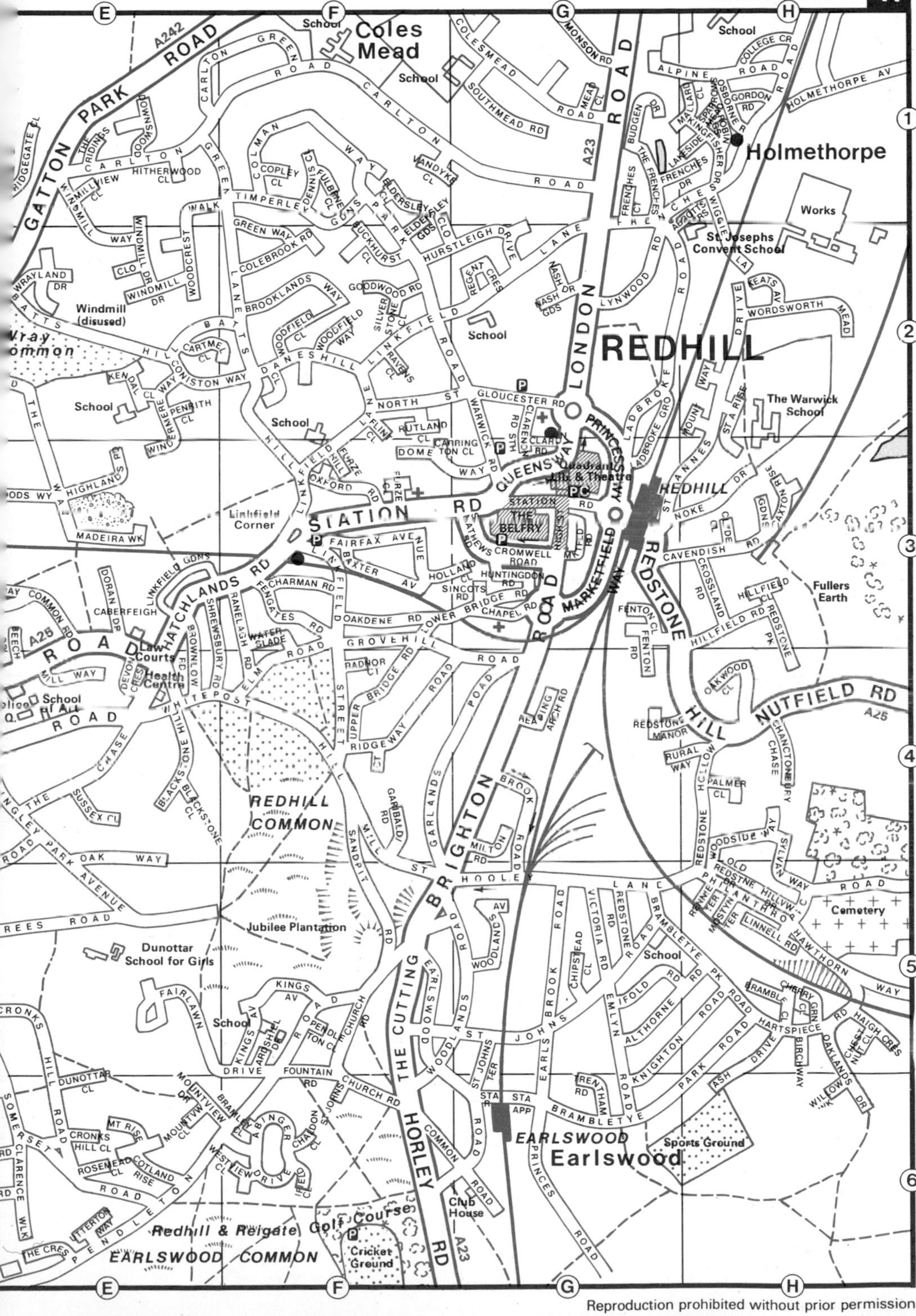
E
F
G
H
1
2
3
4
5
6
Coles Mead
School
Holmethorpe
Works
St Josephs Convent School
REDHILL
The Warwick School
Windmill (disused)
Wray Common
School
Quadrant Lib & Theatre
THE BELFRY
REDHILL
Linkfield Corner
Fullers Earth
Law Courts
Health Centre
REDHILL COMMON
Jubilee Plantation
Dunottar School for Girls
Cemetery
Sports Ground
EARLSWOOD
Earlswood
Club House
Redhill & Reigate Golf Course
Cricket Ground
EARLSWOOD COMMON
GATTON PARK ROAD
A242
CARLTON GREEN
CARLTON ROAD
COLESMEAD ROAD
SOUTHMEAD RD
MONSON RD
LONDON ROAD
A23
HOLMETHORPE AV
ALPINE ROAD
COLLEGE CR
FRENCHES ROAD
THE FRENCHES
LINKFIELD LANE
HURSTLEIGH DRIVE
LYNWOOD RD
KEATS AV
WORDSWORTH MEAD
BATTS HILL
CONISTON WAY
DANESHILL
NORTH ST
GLOUCESTER RD
WARWICK ROAD
PRINCESS WAY
QUEENSWAY
LADBROKE GRO
STATION RD
CROMWELL ROAD
MARKETFIELD WAY
REDSTONE HILL
CAVENDISH RD
HILLFIELD RD
NUTFIELD RD
A25
HATCHLANDS RD
CHARMAN RD
OAKDENE RD
LOWER BRIDGE RD
CHAPEL RD
GROVEHILL ROAD
WHITEPOST HILL
MADEIRA WK
BRIGHTON ROAD
GARLANDS RD
HOOLEY LANE
RIDGEWAY
MILL ST
ST JOHNS
EARLSBROOK ROAD
VICTORIA RD
REDSTONE RD
BRAMBLETYE PK ROAD
KNIGHTON PARK ROAD
HAWTHORN WAY
WOODLANDS RD
THE CUTTING
HORLEY RD
KINGS AV
FOUNTAIN DRIVE
CHURCH RD
PENDLETON ROAD
CRONKS HILL ROAD
SOMERSET RD
CLARENCE WLK
PRINCES ROAD
BRAMBLETYE
ASH DRIVE
OAKLANDS
HAIGH CRES
STA APP

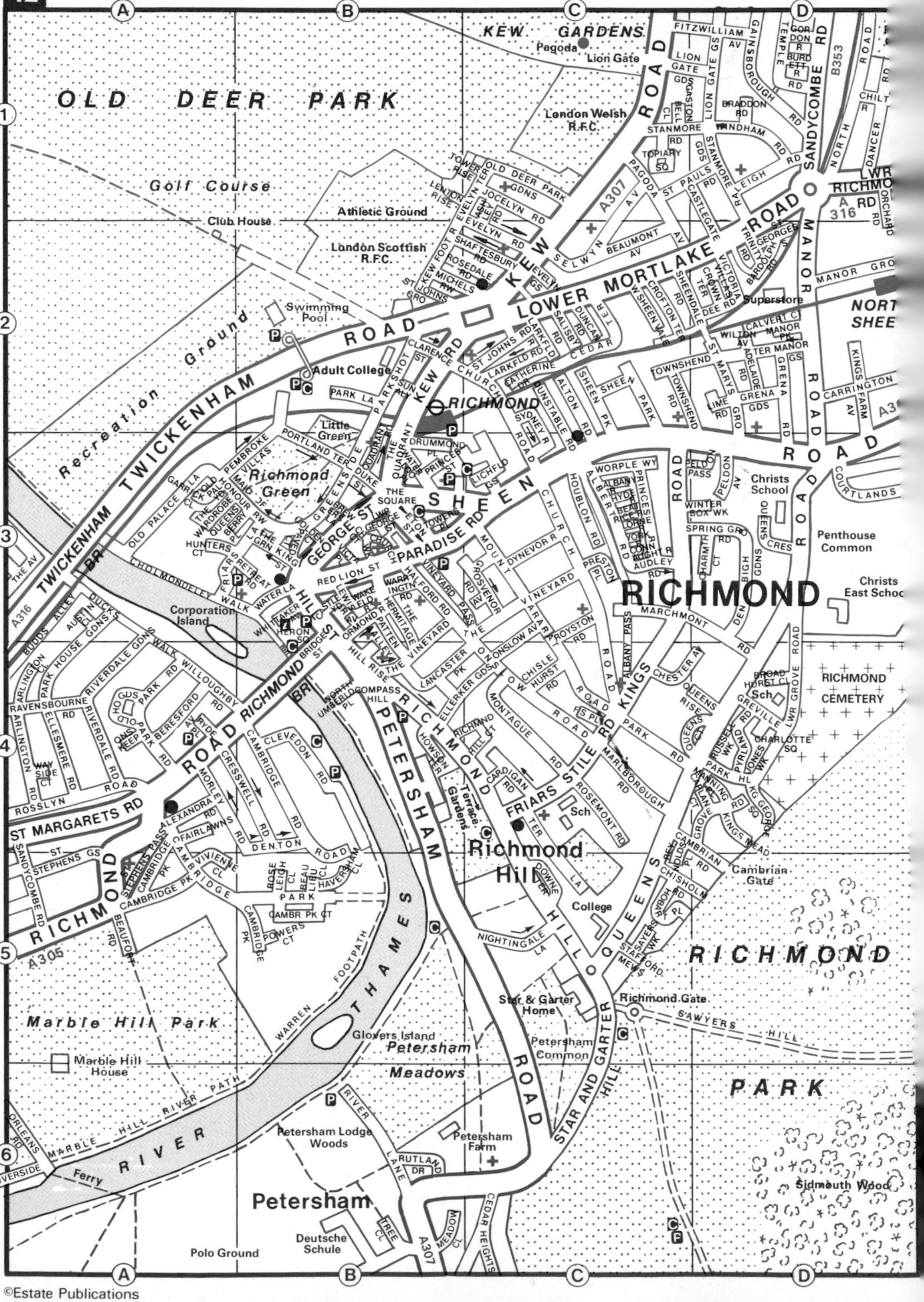

KEW GARDENS

OLD DEER PARK

Golf Course

Club House

Athletic Ground

London Scottish R.F.C.

London Welsh R.F.C.

Swimming Pool

Adult College

Park La

RICHMOND

Little Green

Richmond Green

SHEEN

PARADISE RD

RICHMOND

LOWER MORTLAKE ROAD

Superstore

Christs School

Penthouse Common

Christs East School

RICHMOND CEMETERY

TWICKENHAM BR

Recreation Ground

Corporation Island

ROAD RICHMOND BRI

St Margarets Rd

Marble Hill Park

Marble Hill House

Glovers Island

Petersham Meadows

Petersham Lodge Woods

Petersham Farm

Richmond Hill

College

Star & Garter Home

Richmond Gate

Petersham Common

RICHMOND

PARK

THAMES

RIVER

Ferry

RIVERSIDE

Petersham

Deutsche Schule

Polo Ground

Sidmouth Wood

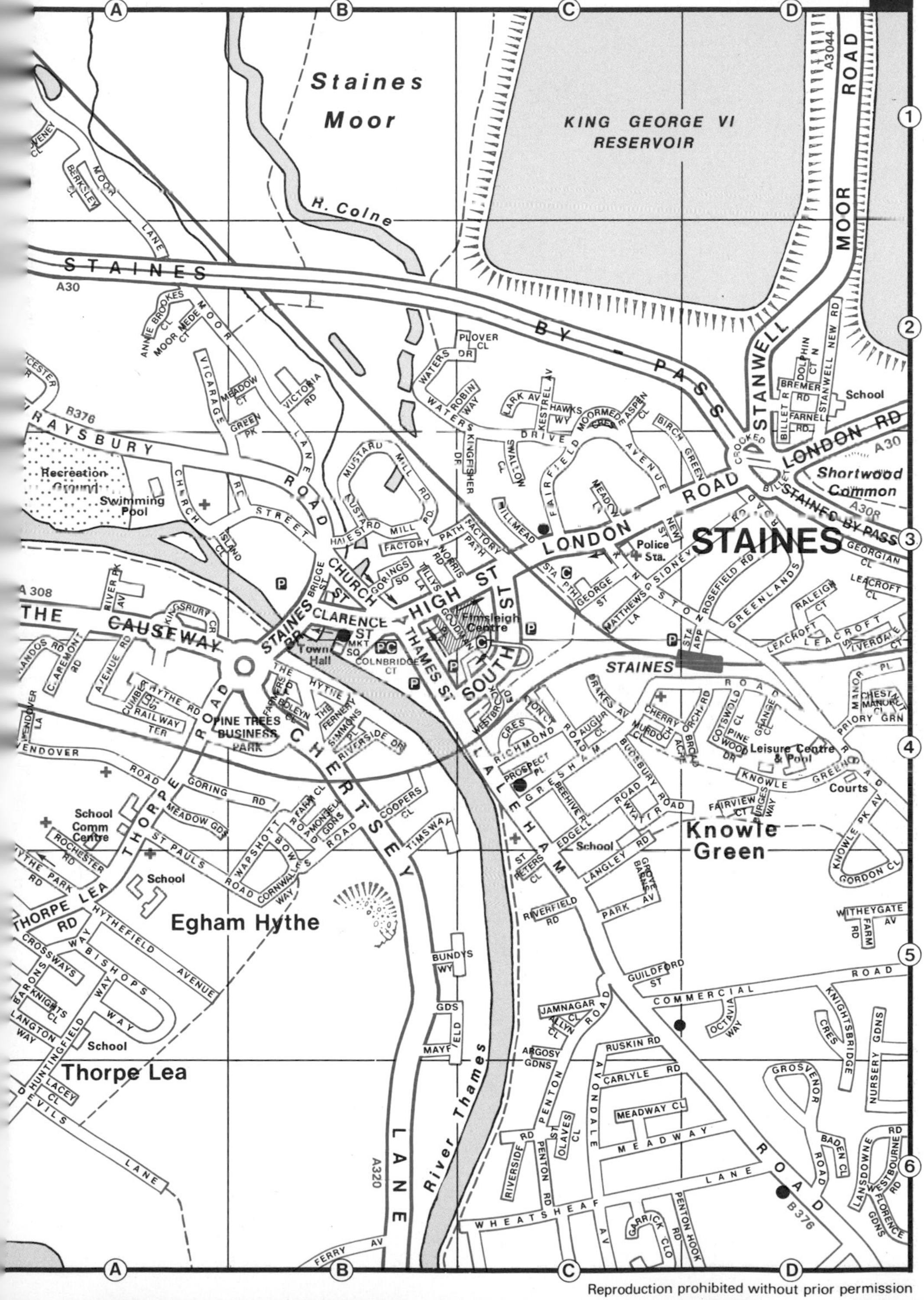
A
B
C
D
1
2
3
4
5
6
Staines Moor
KING GEORGE VI RESERVOIR
R. Colne
STAINES BY - PASS
A30
A3044
MOOR ROAD
STANWELL MOOR ROAD
STANWELL NEW RD
DOLPHIN CT
BREMER RD
FARNELL RD
BILLET RD
School
CROOKED BILLET
LONDON RD
Shortwood Common
A308
STAINES BY PASS
GEORGIAN CL
LEACROFT CL
LEACROFT
RALEIGH CT
RIVERDALE
STAINES
Police Sta.
LONDON ROAD
KINGSTON RD
SIDNEY RD
ROSEFIELD RD
GREENLANDS
MOOR LANE
BERKSLEY CL
ANNIE BROOKES CL
MOOR MEDE CT
VICARAGE
MEADOW CT
GREEN PK
VICTORIA RD
CHURCH LANE
WRAYSBURY ROAD
B376
Recreation Ground
Swimming Pool
CHURCH ST
ISLAND CL
STREET
PLOVER CL
WATERS DR
ROBIN WAY
WATERSIDE
KINGFISHER DR
LARK AV
KESTREL AV
HAWKS WY
MOORMEDE CRES
ASPEN CL
BIRCH GREEN
DRIVE
SWALLOW CL
FAIRFIELD AVENUE
MEADOW
HILLMEAD
NEW RD
MUSTARD MILL RD
FACTORY PATH
NORRIS RD
TILLYS LA
GORINGS SQ
HIGH ST
SOUTH ST
BRIDGE ST
CLARENCE ST
MKT SQ
Town Hall
COLNBRIDGE CT
Elmsleigh Centre
THAMES ST
STA PTH
GEORGE ST
MATTHEWS LA
STA APP
A 308
RIVER PK AV
THE CAUSEWAY
STAINES BR
CHANDOS RD
CLAREMONT RD
AVENUE RD
HYTHE RD
CUMBERLAND
RAILWAY TER
THE HYTHE
FARMERS RD
BOLEYN CT
THE FERNERY
SIMMONS PL
RIVERSIDE DR
PINE TREES BUSINESS PARK
WENDOVER RD
CHERTSEY LANE
WESTBROOK RD
CRES
RICHMOND
PROSPECT PL
AUGUR CL
DRAKES AV
CHERRY ORCHARD RD
BROAD ACRE
MURDOCH
COTSWOLD CL
PINE WOOD DR
GRANGE CL
Leisure Centre & Pool
MANOR PL
CHESTNUT MANOR CL
PRIORY GRN
KNOWLE GREEN ROAD
Courts
GRESHAM ROAD
BEEHIVE RD
BUCKSBURY ROAD
WYATT RD
FAIRVIEW CT
BURGES WAY
Knowle Green
KNOWLE PK AV
GORDON CL
LALEHAM
EDGELL RD
School
LANGLEY RD
GROVE BARNS AV
ST PETERS CL
GORING RD
MEADOW GDS
ST PAULS ROAD
WAPSHOTT ROAD
FARM CL
MONTROSE GDNS
BOWES
CORNWALL WAY
COOPERS CL
TIMSWAY
School Comm Centre
ROCHESTER RD
THORPE LEA RD
HYTHE PARK RD
School
Egham Hythe
HYTHEFIELD AVENUE
CROSSWAYS
BISHOPS WAY
BARONS
KNIGHTS CL
LANGTON WAY
HUNTINGFIELD
School
Thorpe Lea
LACEY CL
DEVILS LANE
RIVERFIELD RD
PARK AV
WITHEYGATE AV
FARM RD
BUNDYS WY
GDS
MAYFIELD
River Thames
A320
FERRY AV
GUILDFORD ST
COMMERCIAL ROAD
JAMNAGAR CL
ALLYN CL
ROAD
OCTAVIA WAY
KNIGHTSBRIDGE CRES
NURSERY GDNS
ARGOSY GDNS
RUSKIN RD
CARLYLE RD
AVONDALE AV
PENTON
MEADWAY CL
MEADWAY
LANE
ST OLAVES CL
RIVERSIDE RD
PENTON RD
GROSVENOR
BADEN CL
LANSDOWNE RD
WESTBOURNE RD
FLORENCE GDNS
WHEATSHEAF
GARRICK CLO
PENTON HOOK RD
B376

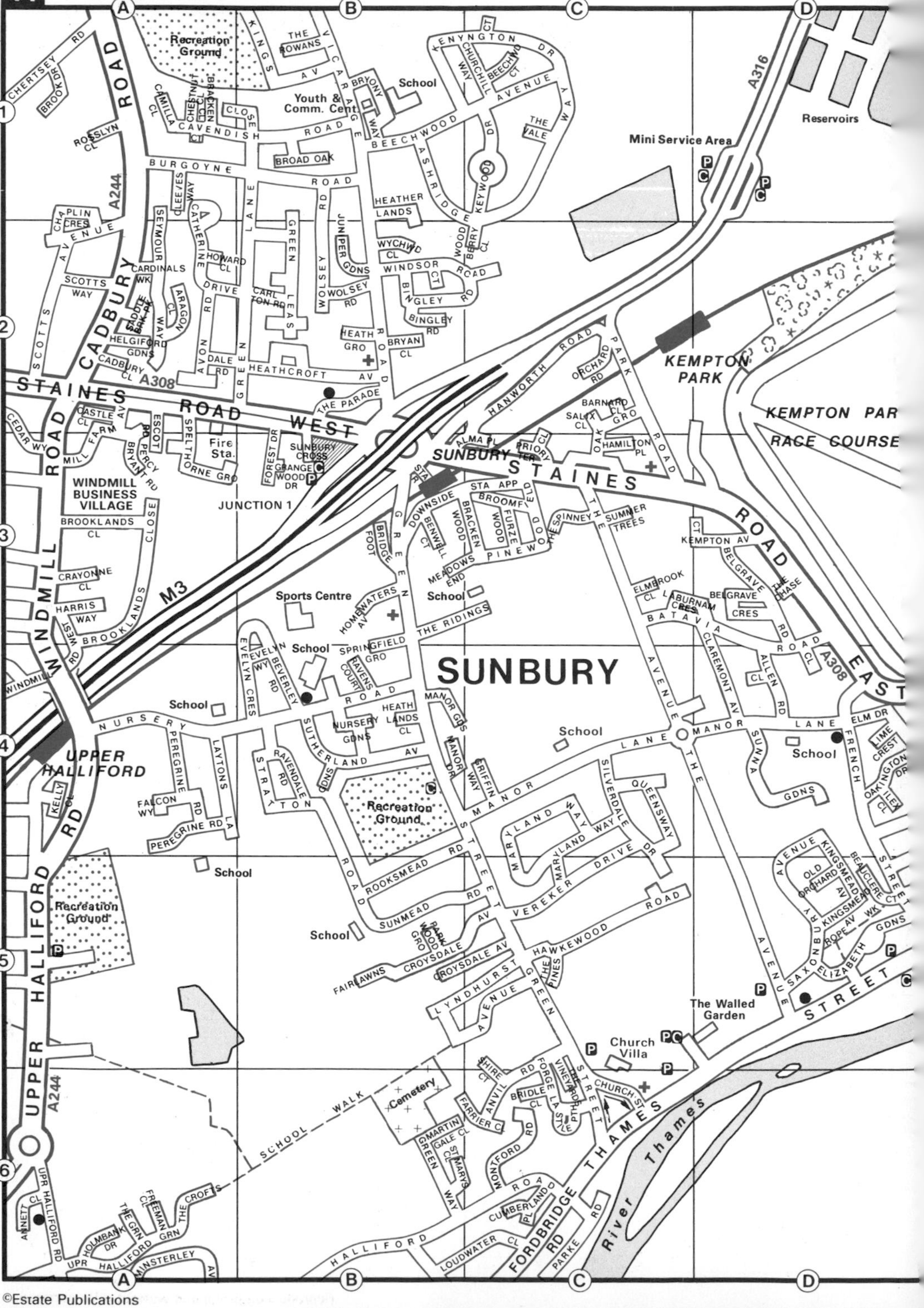

SUNBURY

KEMPTON PARK

KEMPTON PARK RACE COURSE

Reservoirs

Mini Service Area

Recreation Ground

Youth & Comm. Cent.

School

WINDMILL BUSINESS VILLAGE

UPPER HALLIFORD

Sports Centre

School

Recreation Ground

Recreation Ground

The Walled Garden

Church Villa

Cemetery

River Thames

STAINES ROAD WEST

STAINES ROAD

CADBURY ROAD

WINDMILL ROAD

UPPER HALLIFORD

DOLPHIN IND. EST.

Fire Sta.

SUNBURY CROSS

JUNCTION 1

M3

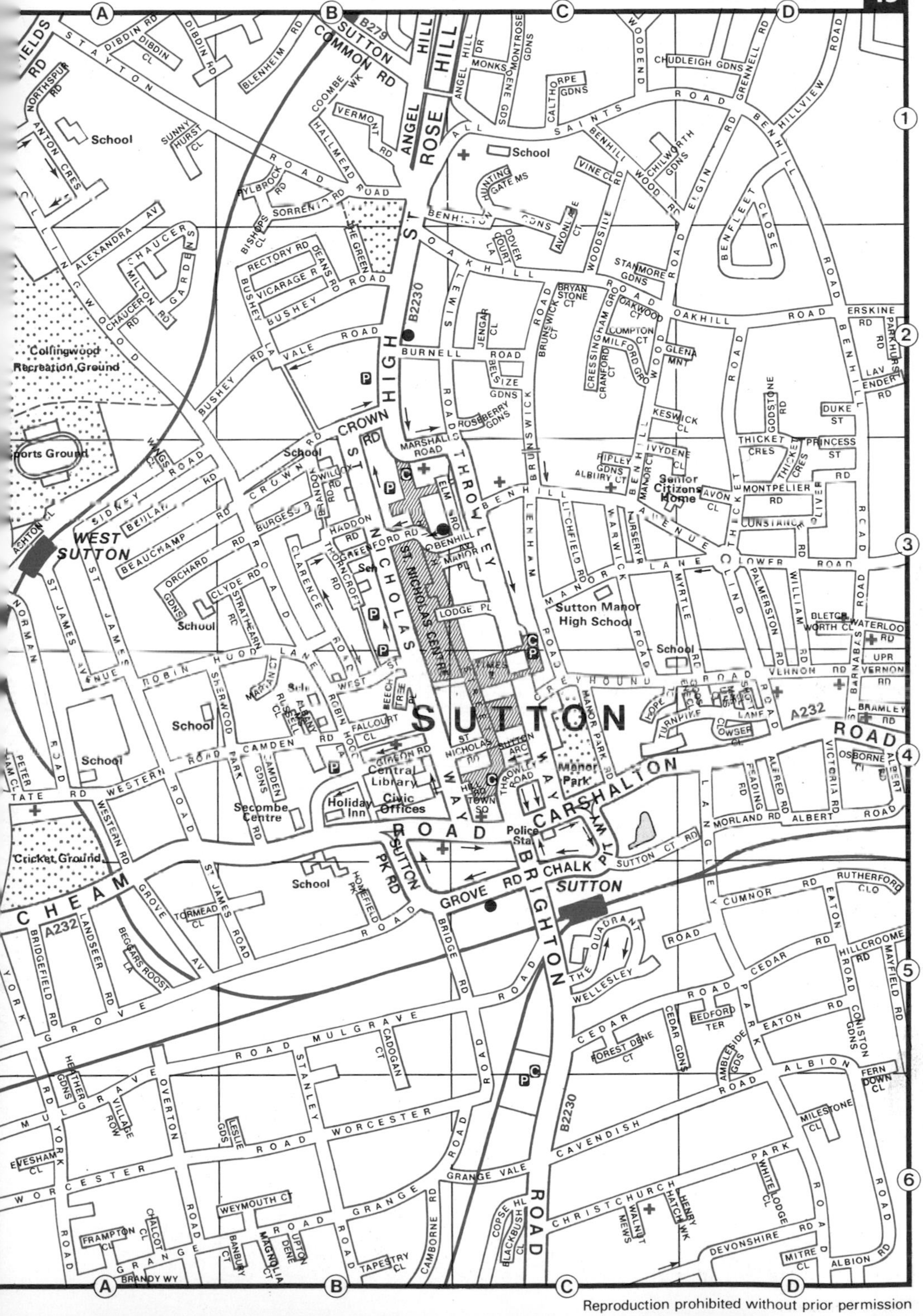
SUTTON
West Sutton
Sutton
A
B
C
D
1
2
3
4
5
6
B279
B2230
A232
Sutton Common Rd
Angel Hill
Rose Hill
High St
All Saints Road
Benhill Wood Rd
Elgin Rd
Benhill Rd
Hillview Rd
Benfleet Close
Chudleigh Gdns
Grennell Rd
Woodend
Calthorpe Gdns
Monks Dr
Montrose Gdns
Dibdin Rd
Dibdin Cl
Blenheim Rd
Stayton Rd
Northspur Rd
Anton Cres
Collingwood Rd
Sunnyhurst Cl
Vermont Rd
Hallmead Rd
Coombe Wk
Rylbrock Rd
Sorrento Rd
Bishops Cl
The Green
Rectory Rd
Vicarage Rd
Deans Rd
Bushey Road
Vale Road
Alexandra Av
Chaucer Gardens
Milton Rd
Chaucer Rd
Benhilton Gdns
Hunting Gate Ms
Avonmore Ct
Dover Court La
Oakhill Road
Woodside
Vine Cl
Chilworth Gdns
Stanmore Gdns
Bryanstone Ct
Brunswick Ct
Oakwood Ct
Compton Ct
Milford Gro
Cressingham Gro
Cranford Ct
Glena Mnt
Lewis Road
Jengar Cl
Burnell Road
Belsize Gdns
Rosebery Gdns
Erskine Rd
Parkhurst Rd
Lavender Rd
Godstone Rd
Duke St
Princess St
Thicket Cres
Thicket Gro
Montpelier Rd
Constance Rd
Keswick Cl
Ivydene Cl
Ripley Gdns
Albury Ct
Manor Ct
Senior Citizens Home
Avon Cl
Collingwood Recreation Ground
Sports Ground
Crown Road
Marshalls Road
Throwley Road
Benhill Av
Lenham Road
Litchfield Rd
Warwick Road
Nursery Rd
Myrtle Rd
Palmerston Rd
William Rd
Manor Lane
Lower Road
Sutton Manor High School
School
Greyhound Road
Vernon Rd
Upr Vernon Rd
Waterloo Rd
Bletchworth Cl
St Barnabas Rd
Bramley Rd
Turnpike Lane
Cowser Cl
Carshalton Road
Manor Park Rd
Manor Park
Sidney Rd
Beulah Rd
Burgess Rd
Beauchamp Rd
Orchard Gdns
Clyde Rd
Strathearn Rd
Clarence Rd
Thorncroft Rd
Greenford Rd
Haddon Rd
St Nicholas Rd
St Nicholas Centre
Lodge Pl
Elm Rd
Manor Pl
Robin Hood Lane
West St
Beech Tree Pl
Albany Ms
Russell Cl
Sherwood Park Rd
Camden Road
Camden Gdns
Falcourt Cl
Gibson Rd
Central Library
Civic Offices
Holiday Inn
Secombe Centre
Western Rd
Norman Av
St James Rd
Peterham Cl
Cricket Ground
Sutton Court Rd
Chalk Pit Way
Sutton Park Rd
Homefield Pk
Grove Rd
Bridge Rd
Brighton Road
Police Sta
Hill Rd
Town Sq
Sutton Arc
Throwley Way
Cheam Road
Tormead Cl
Landseer Rd
Beggars Roost La
Bridgefield Rd
York Rd
The Quadrant
Wellesley Road
Cedar Road
Cedar Gdns
Bedford Ter
Forest Dene Ct
Ambleside Gdns
Cumnor Road
Rutherford Clo
Eaton Rd
Hillcroome Rd
Mayfield Rd
Coniston Gdns
Albion Road
Fern Down Cl
Milestone Cl
Park Road
White Lodge Cl
Christchurch Park
Henry Hatch Wk
Walnut Mews
Devonshire Rd
Mitre Cl
Cavendish Road
Grange Vale
Grange Road
Mulgrave Road
Cadogan Ct
Stanley Road
Worcester Road
Overton Rd
Heather Gdns
Village Row
Leslie Gdns
Evesham Cl
Weymouth Ct
Chalcot Cl
Frampton Cl
Banbury Ct
Magnolia Ct
Upton Dene
Tapestry Cl
Camborne Rd
Copse Hl
Blackbush Cl
Brandy Wy
Morland Rd
Albert Road
Osborne Cl
Victoria Rd
Alfred Rd
Reading Rd
Langley Park Road
Lind Road
Benhill Avenue

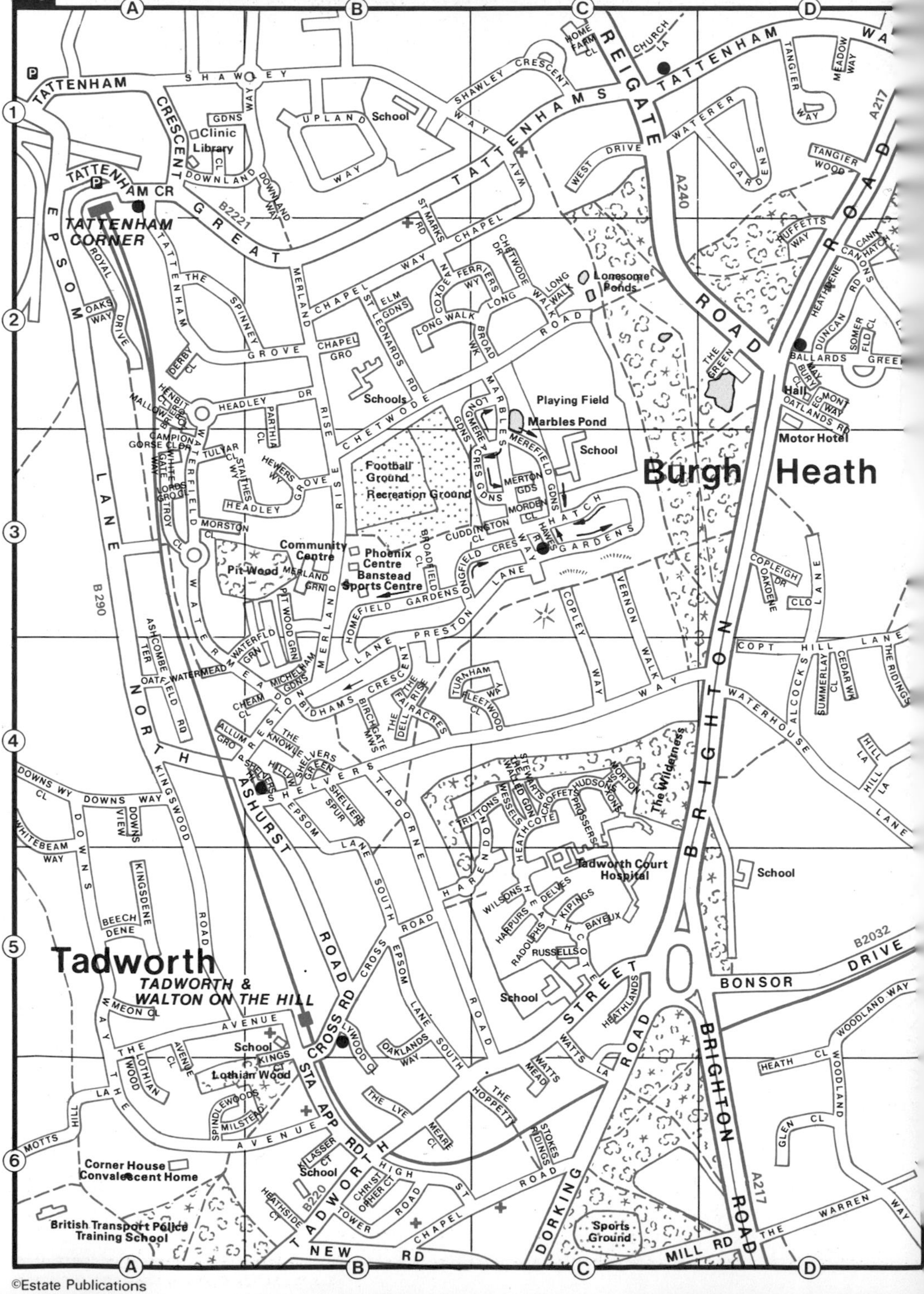

Burgh Heath

Tadworth

TADWORTH &
WALTON ON THE HILL

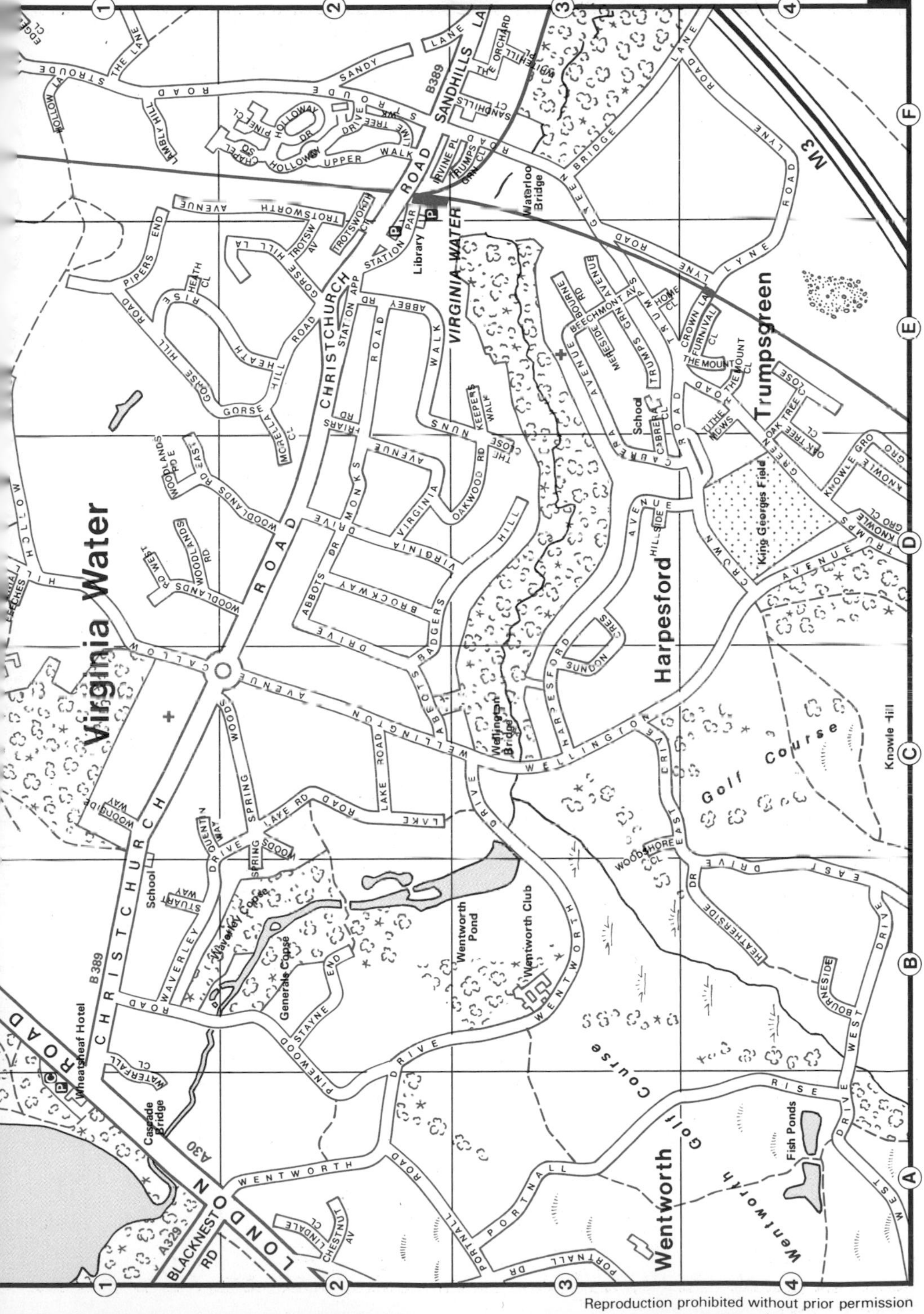
Virginia Water
Harpesford
Trumpsgreen
Wentworth
VIRGINIA WATER
Library
Christchurch Road
B389
A30
A329
London Road
Blacknest Rd
Wellington Avenue
Callow Hill
Stroude Road
Sandy Lane
Sandhills La
Sandhills Ct
The Orchard
Holloway Dr
Holloway Hill
Upper Walk
Lime Tree Walk
Pine Cl
Chapel Sq
Lambly Hill
The Lane
Edgel Cl
Trotsworth Avenue
Trotsworth Ct
Trotsw Av
Pipers End
Gorse Hill Road
Gorse Hill La
Heath Rise
Heath Cl
Morella Cl
Woodlands Rd East
Woodlands Rd West
Woodlands Rd
Woodlands Ride
Station App
Station Pde
Abbey Rd
Friars Rd
Monks Road
Monks Drive
Virginia Avenue
Virginia Drive
The Nuns Walk
Keepers Walk
The Close
Oakwood Rd
Virginia Hill
Abbots Dr
Abbots Drive
Brockway
Badgers Hill
Lake Road
Laye Rd
Spring Woods
Spring Drive
Quentin Way
Woodside Way
Stuart Way
Waverley Drive
Waverley Copse
Generals Copse
Stayne End
Pinewood Drive
Wentworth Drive
Wentworth Road
Wentworth Pond
Wentworth Club
Wentworth Golf Course
Portnall Rise
Portnall Road
Portnall Dr
Chestnut Av
Lindale Cl
Waterfall Cl
Wheatsheaf Hotel
Cascade Bridge
Wellington Bridge
Waterloo Bridge
Green Bridge Road
Trumps Grn Cl
Trumps Grn Av
Trumps Green Road
Irvine Pl
Beechmont Av
Bourne Avenue
Bourne Rd
Merlesie Av
Home Cl
Crown La
Furnival Cl
The Mount
The Mount Cl
Tithe Mews
Oak Tree Cl
Oak Tree Close
Knowle Gro
Knowle Gro Cl
Knowle Hill
Cabrera Cl
Cabrera Avenue
Hillside Avenue
Harpesford Avenue
Sundon Cres
Crown Avenue
King Georges Field
East Drive
Woodshore Cl
Heatherside Dr
Bourneside
West Drive
Fish Ponds
Golf Course
Lyne Road
Lyne Lane
M3
School
1
2
3
4
A
B
C
D
E
F

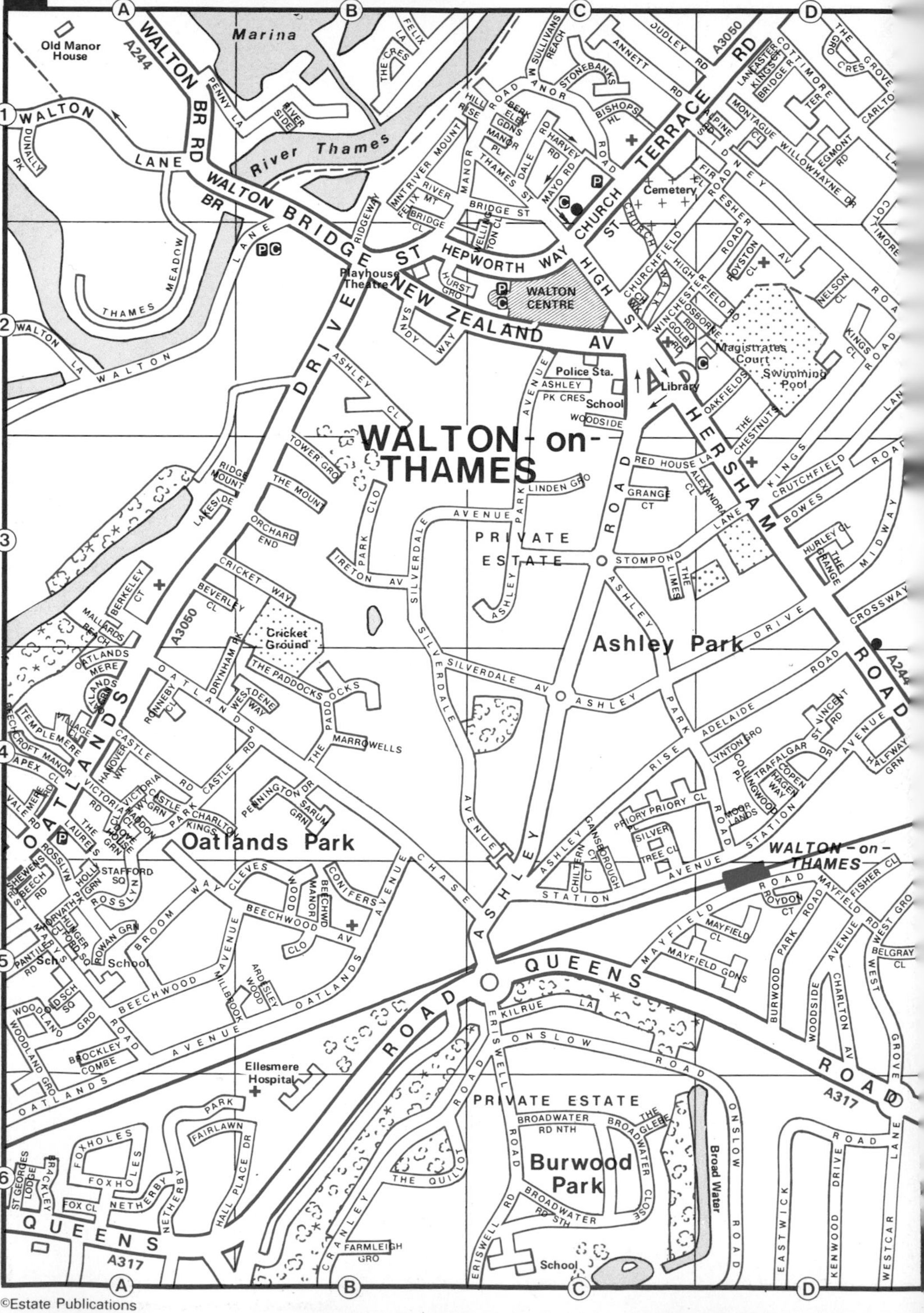
A
B
C
D
1
2
3
4
5
6
Old Manor House
Marina
River Thames
WALTON LANE
WALTON BR RD
A244
WALTON BRIDGE
WALTON BR LANE
DUNALLY PK
PENNY LA
RIVER SIDE
FELIX LA
THE CRES
THAMES MEADOW
WALTON LA
WALTON
BRIDGE ST
HEPWORTH WAY
NEW ZEALAND AV
Playhouse Theatre
WALTON CENTRE
HURST GRO
SANDY WAY
RIDGEWAY
DRIVE
MANOR RD
SULLIVANS REACH
STONEBANKS
ANNETT RD
DUDLEY RD
A3050
BISHOPS HL
HILL RISE
BERKELEY GDNS
MANOR PL
HARVEY RD
DALE RD
MAYO RD
THAMES ST
MOUNT
RIVER MT
BRIDGE CL
WELLINGTON CL
CHURCH ST
CHURCH TERRACE RD
HIGH ST
Cemetery
ALPINE CL
FIR CL
SIDNEY RD
MONTAGUE CL
COTTIMORE TER
COTTIMORE CRES
LANCASTER
KINGSCL
BRIDGER CL
THE GROVE
CRES
WILLOWHAYNE DR
EGMONT RD
CARLTON
ESHER AV
ROYSTON CL
CHURCHFIELD RD
CHURCHFIELD WALK
HIGHFIELD RD
WINCHESTER CL
OSBORNE CL
GOLDBI RD
NELSON CL
KINGS RD
Magistrates Court
Swimming Pool
Library
Police Sta.
ASHLEY PK CRES
School
WOODSIDE
OAKFIELDS
THE CHESTNUTS
HERSHAM ROAD
WALTON-on-THAMES
ASHLEY CL
TOWER GRO
THE MOUNT
RIDGE MOUNT
LAKESIDE
ORCHARD END
PARK CLO
IRETON AV
SILVERDALE AVENUE
PARK AVENUE
PRIVATE ESTATE
LINDEN GRO
RED HOUSE LA
ALEXANDRA LANE
GRANGE CT
STOMPOND LANE
THE LIMES
KINGS CL
CRUTCHFIELD LA
BOWES RD
HURLEY CL
THE GRANGE
MIDWAY
CROSSWAY
ASHLEY RD
BERKELEY CT
BEVERLEY CL
CRICKET WAY
Cricket Ground
MALLARDS REACH
OATLANDS MERE
OATLANDS DRIVE
OATLANDS CHASE
DRYNHAM PK
THE PADDOCKS
WESTDENE WAY
RONNEBY CL
MARROWELLS
Ashley Park
ASHLEY DRIVE
SILVERDALE AV
ASHLEY PARK RD
ASHLEY RISE
ADELAIDE RD
LYNTON GRO
ST VINCENT RD
TRAFALGAR DR
COLLINGWOOD PL
COPENHAGEN WAY
HALFWAY GRN
A244
PRIORY CL
SILVER TREE CL
MOORLANDS
GAINSBOROUGH CT
CHILTERN CT
STATION AVENUE
STATION RD
WALTON-on-THAMES
TEMPLEMERE
BEECHCROFT MANOR
APEX CL
VALE RD
CASTLE RD
HANOVER WK
VICTORIA RD
KINGS CL
CASTLE GRN
CHARLTON
PARK
PENNINGTON DR
SARUM GRN
Oatlands Park
THE LAURELS
ROSSLYN
STAFFORD SQ
CLEVES WAY
WOOD MANOR
BEECHWD
CONIFERS
BEECHWOOD AV
CLO
BROOM WAY
BEECHWOOD AVENUE
MILLBROOK
ARDESLEY WOOD
ROWAN GRN
School
PANTILE RD
WOODLAND GRO
BROCKLEY COMBE
OATLANDS AVENUE
Ellesmere Hospital
QUEENS ROAD
ROYDON CT
MAYFIELD CL
MAYFIELD GDNS
MAYFIELD RD
FISHER CL
WEST GRO
BELGRAY CL
BURWOOD PARK RD
WOODSIDE AVENUE
CHARLTON AV
GROVE
A317
KILRUE LA
ONSLOW ROAD
ERISWELL ROAD
PRIVATE ESTATE
BROADWATER RD NTH
THE GLEBE
BROADWATER CLOSE
Burwood Park
BROADWATER RD STH
Broad Water
School
FAIRLAWN
PARK
HALL PLACE DR
FOXHOLES
NETHERBY
FOX CL
ST GEORGES LODGE
BRACKLEY
QUEENS
A317
THE QUILLOT
CRANLEY RD
FARMLEIGH GRO
EASTWICK RD
KENWOOD DRIVE
WESTCAR LANE

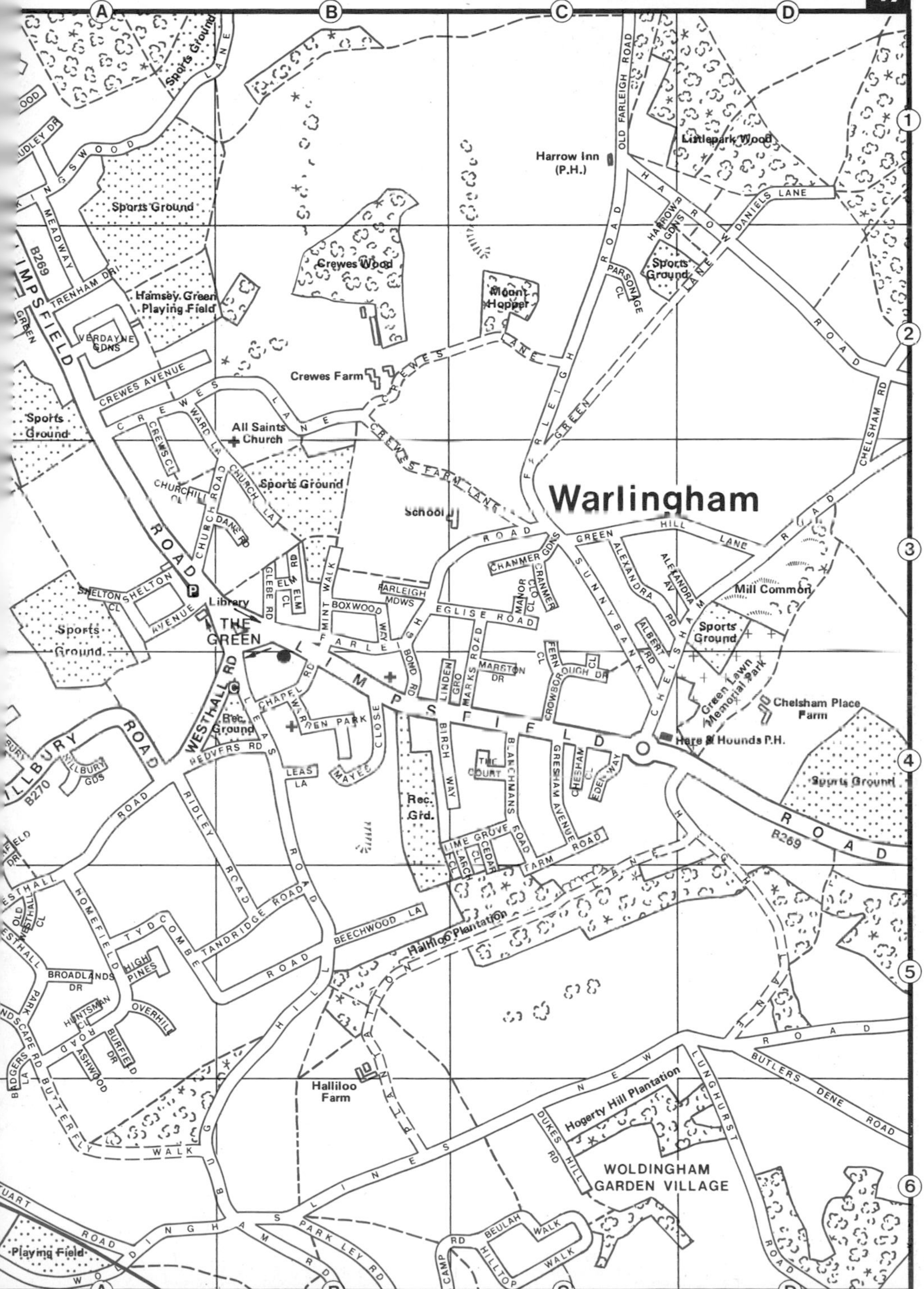
A
B
C
D
1
2
3
4
5
6
Sports Ground
LANE
KINGSWOOD
MEADWAY
B269
LIMPSFIELD
TRENHAM DR
Hamsey Green Playing Field
VERDAYNE GDNS
CREWES AVENUE
Sports Ground
Crewes Wood
Mount Hopper
Crewes Farm
CREWES LANE
All Saints Church
CREWES CL
WARD LA
CHURCHILL CL
CHURCH ROAD
CHURCH LA
DANE RD
Sports Ground
CREWES FARM LANE
School
Harrow Inn (P.H.)
OLD FARLEIGH ROAD
Littlepark Wood
HARROW GDNS
DANIELS LANE
Sports Ground
PARSONAGE CL
FARLEIGH ROAD
GREEN
CHELSHAM RD
Warlingham
GREEN HILL LANE
CHANMER GDNS
CRANMER
ALEXANDRA RD
ALEXANDRA AV
SUNNYBANK
Mill Common
SHELTON CL
SHELTON AVENUE
Library
THE GREEN
Sports Ground
GLEBE RD
ELM CL
ELM RD
MINT WALK
FARLEIGH MDWS
BOXWOOD WAY
EGLISE ROAD
MANOR CL
FARLEIGH
BOND RD
LINDEN GRO
MARKS ROAD
MARSTON DR
FERN CL
CROWBOROUGH DR
ALBERT RD
Sports Ground
Green Lawn Memorial Park
Chelsham Place Farm
Hare & Hounds P.H.
CHELSHAM ROAD
LIMPSFIELD ROAD
WESTHALL RD
CHAPEL RD
WARREN PARK
CLOSE
Rec. Ground
LEAS
HILLBURY ROAD
HILLBURY GDS
B270
REDVERS RD
MAYES
LEAS LA
BIRCH WAY
THE COURT
BLANCHMANS ROAD
GRESHAM AVENUE
CHESHAM CL
EDEN WAY
Sports Ground
B269
Rec. Grd.
LIME GROVE
LARCH CL
CEDAR
FARM ROAD
RIDLEY ROAD
ROAD
TANDRIDGE ROAD
BEECHWOOD LA
Halliloo Plantation
TYDCOMBE ROAD
HOMEFIELD
HIGH PINES
BROADLANDS DR
HUNTSMAN CL
OVERHILL
LANDSCAPE RD
ASHWOOD
BURFIELD DR
BADGERS LA
BUTTERFLY WALK
WESTHALL
OLD WESTHALL CL
PARK
HILL
Halliloo Farm
NEW LINES
Hogerty Hill Plantation
DUKES HILL RD
LUNGHURST ROAD
BUTLERS DENE ROAD
WOLDINGHAM GARDEN VILLAGE
STUART ROAD
Playing Field
WOLDINGHAM
ROAD
PARK LEY RD
BEULAH WALK
CAMP RD
HILLTOP WALK

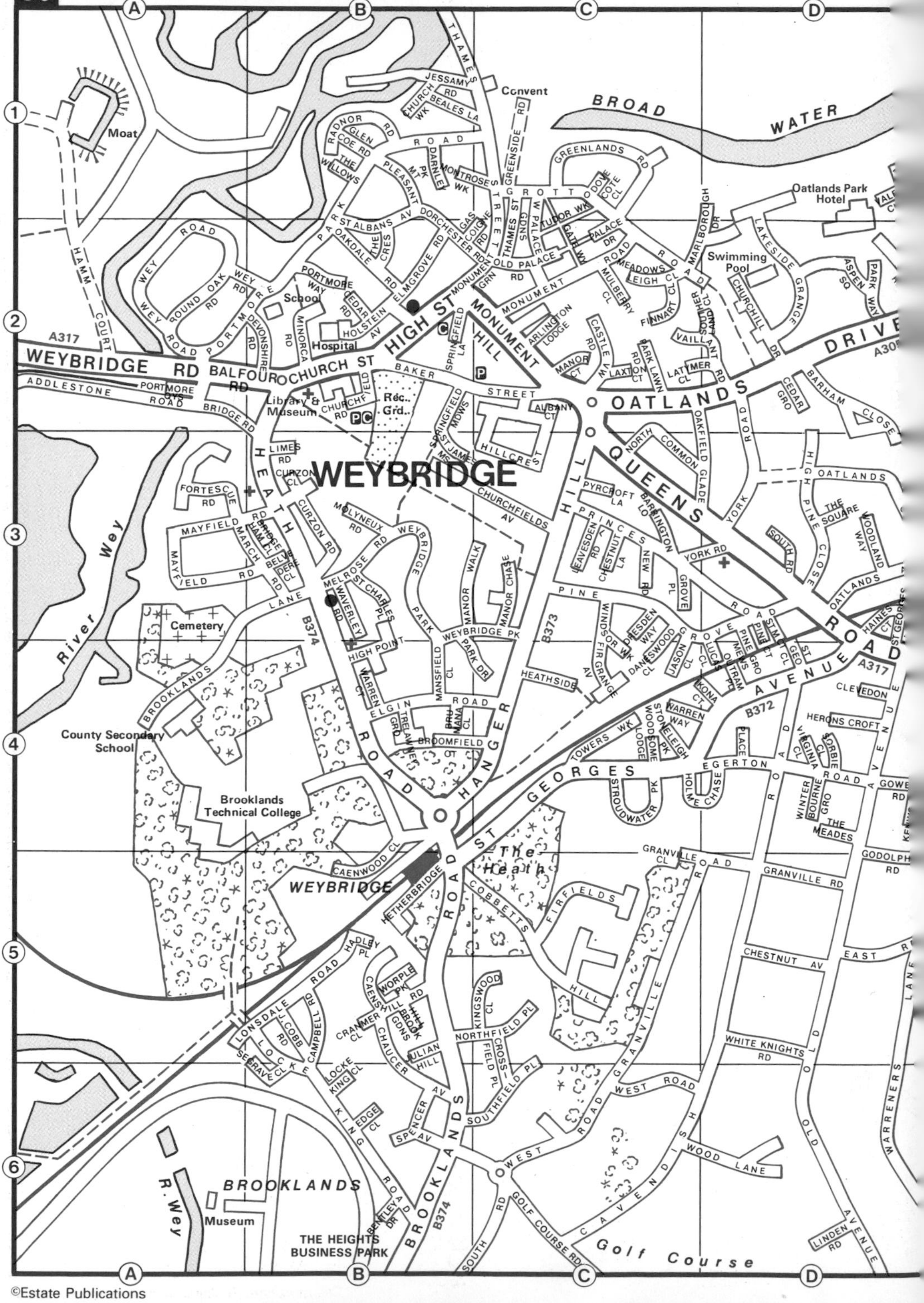
A
B
C
D
1
2
3
4
5
6
Moat
Convent
BROAD WATER
JESSAMY RD
CHURCH WK
BEALES LA
RADNOR RD
GLEN
COE RD
THE WILLOWS
ROAD
DARNLEY PK
MONTROSE WK
PLEASANT PK
GREENSIDE RD
THAMES ST
GREENLANDS RD
DOVE COTE CL
GROTTO
THAMES STREET
W GDNS
TUDOR WK
GATE WY
PALACE DR
MARLBOROUGH DR
Oatlands Park Hotel
LAKESIDE
GRANGE
ASPEN SQ
PARK WAY
Swimming Pool
CHURCHILL DR
ST ALBANS AV
DORCHESTER RD
OAKDALE
THE CRES
ELMGROVE RD
GAS
COLONE
WEY ROAD
ROUND OAK RD
WEY RD
PORTMORE WAY
PORTMORE
DEVONSHIRE
School
MINORCA RD
CEDAR RD
HOLSTEIN AV
Hospital
MONUMENT GRN
OLD PALACE RD
MONUMENT
MEADOWS
LEIGH CL
MULBERRY CL
FINNART CL
SOUTHERLAND CL
VAILLANT RD
ARLINGTON LODGE
CASTLE RD
MANOR CT
WALTON
LAXTON CT
PARK LAWN RD
LATYMER CL
DRIVE
A3050
HAMM COURT
A317
WEYBRIDGE RD
ADDLESTONE ROAD
PORTMORE GDS
BALFOUR RD
CHURCH ST
HIGH ST
SPRINGFIELD LA
HILL
MONUMENT
BAKER STREET
Library & Museum
CHURCH ST
CHURCHFIELD RD
Rec. Grd.
BRIDGE RD
HEATH
LIMES RD
CURZON CL
SPRINGFIELD MDWS
ST JAMES MS
HILLCREST
AUBANY CT
OATLANDS
QUEENS
NORTH
COMMON
OAKFIELD GLADE
ROAD
CEDAR GRO
BARHAM CLOSE
WEYBRIDGE
FORTESCUE RD
CURZON RD
MOLYNEUX RD
WEYBRIDGE
CHURCHFIELDS AV
PYRCROFT LA
BARRINGTON LO
YORK
HIGH PINE CLOSE
OATLANDS
THE SQUARE
WOODLAND WAY
SOUTH RD
River Wey
MAYFIELD RD
HAMILTON
BRIDGE
MARCH
BELVEDERE CL
MAYFIELD RD
MELROSE RD
ST CHARLES PL
WAVERLEY RD
PARK
MANOR WALK
MANOR CHASE
PRINCES RD
LEAVESDEN RD
CHESTNUT LA
NEW RD
GROVE PL
YORK RD
OATLANDS
PINE ROAD
LANE
Cemetery
B374
WEYBRIDGE PK
PARK DR
B373
WINDSOR WK
FIR GRANGE AV
DRESDEN WAY
DANESWOOD
JASON CL
LUCAS
PINE MEWS
PINE GRO
ST GEORGES
GROVE
OUTRAM PL
KONA CT
HAINES CT
ST GEORGES
A317
HIGH POINT
WARREN CT
MANSFIELD CL
BROOKLANDS
ELGIN ROAD
TRELAWNEY GRO
BRUMANA CL
BROOMFIELD
HEATHSIDE
AVENUE
WARREN WAY
B372
CLEVEDON
HERONS CROFT
County Secondary School
ROAD
HANGER
TOWERS WK
WOODSTONE LODGE
STONELEIGH PK
PLACE
VIRGINIA CL
SORBIE CL
ST GEORGES
EGERTON ROAD
STROUDWATER PK
HOLME CHASE
WINTERBOURNE GRO
GOWER RD
Brooklands Technical College
ROAD
THE MEADES
AVENUE
The Heath
CAENWOOD CL
GRANVILLE CL
ROAD
GRANVILLE RD
GODOLPHIN RD
WEYBRIDGE
HETHERBRIDGE
ROAD
COBBETTS
FIRFIELDS
HADLEY PL
ROAD
WORPLE PK
CAENSHILL RD
BROOK GDNS
KINGSWOOD CL
CHESTNUT AV
EAST RD
HILL
GRANVILLE
LANE
LONSDALE RD
CAMPBELL RD
J. COBB RD
CRANMER CL
JULIAN HILL
NORTHFIELD PL
CROSSFIELD PL
SEGRAVE CL
LOCKE
LOCKE KING CL
CHAUCER
SOUTHFIELD PL
WHITE KNIGHTS RD
OLD
WARRENERS
KING EDGE CL
SPENCER AV
SPENCER AV
WEST ROAD
WEST
CAVENDISH
WOOD LANE
BROOKLANDS
R. Wey
ROAD
BENTLEY DR
B374
BROOKLANDS
Museum
SOUTH RD
GOLF COURSE RD
Golf Course
THE HEIGHTS BUSINESS PARK
LINDEN RD
AVENUE

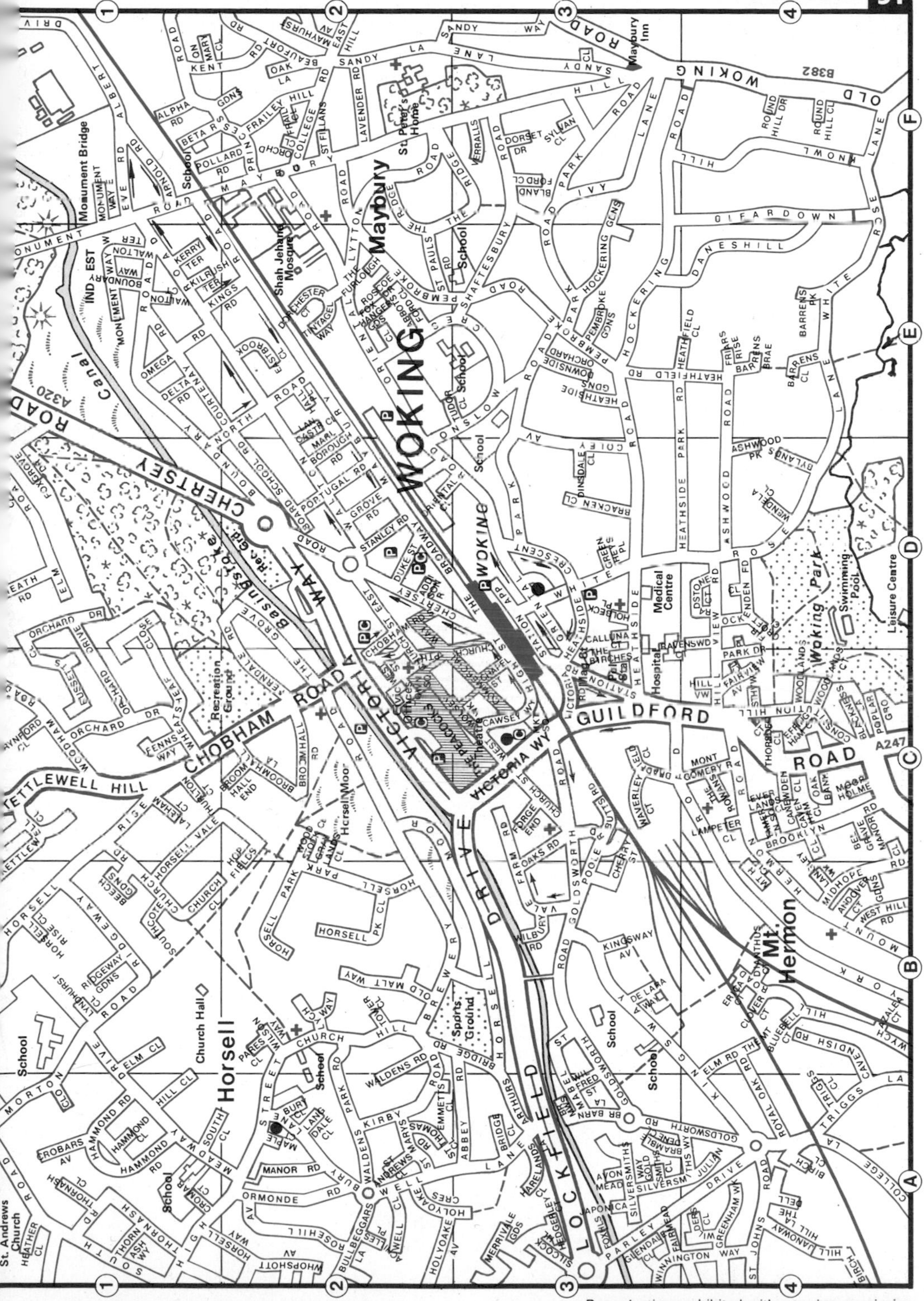
WOKING
Maybury
Horsell
Mt. Hermon
CHERTSEY ROAD
A320
Canal
Basingstoke
CHOBHAM ROAD
GUILDFORD ROAD
A247
VICTORIA WAY
HORSELL MOOR
KETTLEWELL HILL
WOKING OLD ROAD
B382
MAYBURY ROAD
MAYBURY HILL
SANDY LANE
ORIENTAL ROAD
HEATHSIDE ROAD
HEATHSIDE PARK ROAD
HEATHSIDE CRESCENT
HOCKERING ROAD
WHITE ROSE LANE
YORK ROAD
MOUNT HERMON ROAD
CONSTITUTION HILL
BROADWAY
DUKE ST
COMMERCIAL WAY
CHURCH ST
HIGH ST
CHOBHAM RD
VICTORIA
THE GROVE
NORTH ROAD
MONUMENT ROAD
Monument Bridge
IND. EST
Shah Jehan Mosque
St. Peter's Home
Maybury Inn
School
Church Hall
Recreation Ground
Rec. Grd
Sports Ground
Woking Park
Swimming Pool
Leisure Centre
Medical Centre
Hospital
Theatre
The Peacocks
Police Station
Civic Offices
St. Andrews Church
HORSELL MOOR
BREWERY ROAD
HORSELL RISE
CHURCH HILL
HIGH STREET
KIRBY ROAD
GOLDSWORTH ROAD
LOCKFIELD DRIVE
ST JOHNS ROAD
ROYAL OAK ROAD
TRIGGS LANE
COLLEGE LANE
PARLEY DRIVE
KINGSWAY AV
WALDENS PARK RD
MEADWAY DRIVE
SOUTH ROAD
HORSELL PARK
BULLBEGGARS LA
WHOPSHOTT AV
ROSEHILL AV
HOLYOAKE CRES
HAMMOND RD
MORTON ROAD
BIRCH CL
A
B
C
D
E
F
1
2
3
4

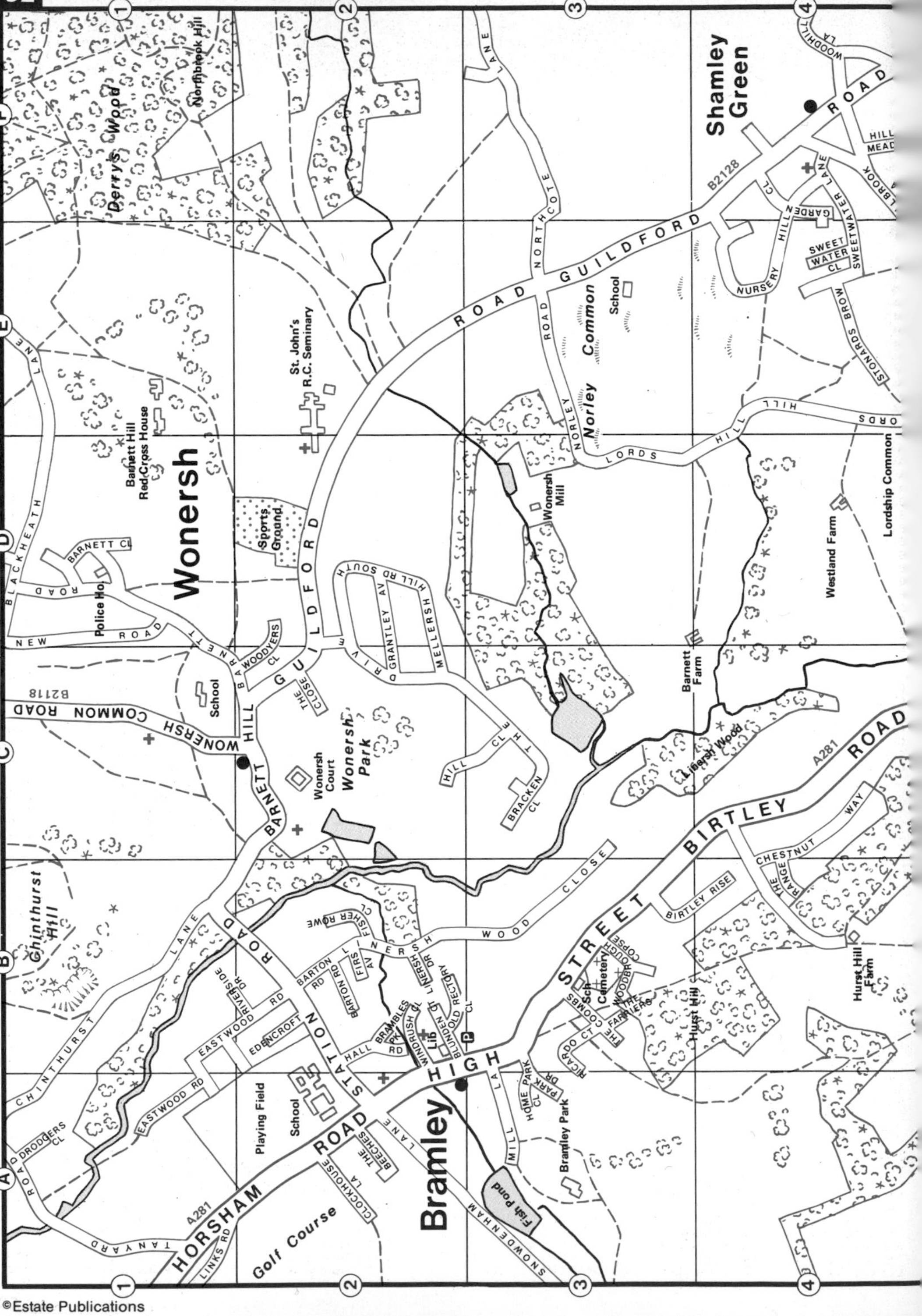
Derry's Wood
Northbrook Hill
Shamley Green
WOODHILL LA
GUILDFORD ROAD
B2128
HILL MEAD
NORTHCOTE ROAD
HILL CL
GARDENS
NURSERY HILL
SWEETWATER LANE
SWEET WATER CL
SCHOOL
Norley Common
STONARDS BROW
St. John's R.C. Seminary
LORDS HILL
NORLEY LANE
Lordship Common
Westland Farm
BLACKHEATH LANE
Barnett Hill Red Cross House
Wonersh
Wonersh Mill
Sports Ground
BARNETT CL
BLACKHEATH ROAD
Police Ho.
NEW ROAD
HILL RD SOUTH
GRANTLEY AV
MELLERSH HILL
DRIVE
BARNETT HILL
WOODYERS CL
THE CLOSE
Barnett Farm
B2118
COMMON ROAD
WONERSH COMMON
School
Wonersh Park
Wonersh Court
HILL CL
THE
BRACKEN CL
Linersh Wood
A281
BIRTLEY ROAD
WAY
CHESTNUT
THE RANGE
Chinthurst Hill
BIRTLEY RISE
STREET
WOOD CLOSE
FISHER ROWE CL
LINERSH
COPSE
COUGH
Cemetery
Sch
Hurst Hill
Hurst Hill Farm
RIVERSIDE DR
ROAD
BARTON RD
FIRS AV
LINERSH DR
RECTORY
OLD
BLUNDEN CL
WINDRUSH CL
BRAMBLES PK
Lib
COOMBS
WOODBRIDGE
THE FARRIERS
EASTWOOD RD
EDENCROFT
HALL RD
STATION
HIGH
RICARDO CT
PARK DR
HOME PARK CL
CHINTHURST LANE
EASTWOOD RD
Playing Field
School
MILL LA
Bramley Park
DRODGERS CL
ROAD
BEECHES
THE
HORSHAM ROAD
CLOCKHOUSE LA
LANE
Bramley
Fish Pond
SNOWDENHAM
TANYARD
A281
LINKS RD
Golf Course
A
B
C
D
E
F
1
2
3
4

BANSTEAD

Ashley Dri	11 C2	Palmersfield Rd	11 C2
Avenue Rd	11 D3	Park Downs	11 D5
Banstead Rd	11 A1	Park Rd	11 D3
Barnfield	11 D2	Pembroke Clo	11 D5
Basing Rd	11 B2	Picquets Way	11 A5
Beacon Way	11 A4	Poplar Dri	11 A2
Beechfield	11 D1	Pound Rd	11 B5
Blue Cedars	11 A2	Rosehill Farm Meadow	11 D3
Bolters La	11 B2	Roundwood Way	11 A3
Briarwood	11 C3	Ruffetts Way	11 A6
Brighton Rd	11 A6	Salisbury Rd	11 D2
Buckles Way	11 A4	Sandersfield Gdns	11 C3
Buff Av	11 D2	Sandersfield Rd	11 C2
Burgh Mt	11 B3	Shelley Clo	11 A3
Burgh Wood	11 A3	Shrubland Rd	11 B4
Burns Dri	11 A4	Stirling Clo	11 B5
Cann Hatch	11 A6	Sutton La	11 D2
Canons La	11 A6	Sycamore Dri	11 A2
Castelton Clo	11 C2	Tangier Way	11 A5
Castleton Dri	11 C2	Tangier Wood	11 A6
Chalk Pit Rd	11 C5	Tattenham Way	11 A5
Chaucer Clo	11 A2	The Beeches	11 C4
Cheviot Clo	11 D3	The Brindles	11 B5
Cheyne Ct	11 D3	The Drive	11 A4
Chiltons Clo	11 D3	The Gables	11 B4
Chipstead Rd	11 B5	The Horseshoe	11 B3
Clifton Pl	11 C3	The Laurels	11 B5
Colcokes Rd	11 C4	The Maples	11 D1
Commonfield Rd	11 C1	The Orchard	11 B3
Court Rd	11 C3	The Oval	11 C2
Courtlands Cres	11 C3	The Tracery	11 D3
Croydon La	11 D2	Thornfield Rd	11 C5
Croydon Lane Sth	11 D2	Tudor Clo	11 A3
Cypress Way	11 A2	Tumble Beacon	11 A4
Daniel Way	11 C2	Tumblewood Rd	11 A4
De Burgh Pk	11 D3	*Upper Dunnymans	
Diceland Rd	11 B4	Mews, Basing Rd	11 B2
Dunnymans Rd	11 B2	*Upper Sawley Wood,	
East Gate	11 A2	Basing Rd	11 B2
Ferndale Rd	11 D1	Warren Rd	11 A2
Fiddicroft Av	11 D2	Waterer Gdns	11 A6
Fir Tree Rd	11 A1	Wellesford Clo	11 B5
Follyfield Rd	11 C2	Whiteoaks	11 D1
Free Down La	11 D1	Wilmot Way	11 C2
Gale Cres	11 C5	Winkworth Pl	11 B2
Garden Clo	11 C3	Winkworth Rd	11 C2
Garrard Rd	11 C4	Wood La	11 B5
Garratts La	11 B4	Woodgavil	11 B4
Gerrards Mead	11 B4	Woodmansterne La	11 D3
Glenfield Rd	11 C3	Yewlands Clo	11 D3
Grange Gdns	11 D1		
Grange Meadow	11 D1		
Great Ellshams	11 C4		
Green Curve	11 B2		
Greenhayes Av	11 C2		
Greenhayes Gdns	11 C3		
Harbourfield Rd	11 D2		
Hawthorn Clo	11 A2		
Heath Clo	11 D2		
Heights Clo	11 A4		
High Beeches	11 A2		
High St	11 C3		
Higher Dri	11 A1		
Hillside	11 A3		
Hillside Clo	11 A4		
Holly Hill Dri	11 C4		
Holly La	11 C4		
Holly La East	11 C4		
Holly La West	11 D5		
Home Meadow	11 C4		
Horse Croft	11 B4		
Kenilworth Clo	11 D4		
Kingsley Av	11 C3		
Lambert Rd	11 C2		
Lancaster Ct	11 B2		
Larchwood Clo	11 A3		
*Lower Dunnymans			
Mews, Basing Rd	11 B2		
*Lower Northfield Rd,			
Basing Rd	11 B2		
*Lower Sawley Wood,			
Basing Rd	11 B2		
Lyme Regis Rd	11 B4		
Meadow Way	11 A5		
Mellow Clo	11 D1		
Monks Rd	11 C4		
Neville Clo	11 C2		
Nork Gdns	11 A2		
Nork Way	11 A3		
North Acre	11 B4		
Oakley Gdns	11 D2		
Orchard Clo	11 A3		
Osier Way	11 A2		

BYFLEET

Abbotts Clo	12 E1	Dartnell Av	12 C3
Acacia Clo	12 A1	Dartnell Clo	12 C3
Acacia Dri	12 A1	Dartnell Ct	12 D2
Amberley Dri	12 A1	Dartnell Cres	12 C2
Amis Av	12 B1	Dartnells Keep	12 C3
Aprilwood Clo	12 A2	Dartnell Park Rd	12 C2
Avro Way	12 F1	Dartnell Pl	12 C3
Barnato Clo	12 F3	Dashwood Clo	12 D2
Barnes Wallis Dri	12 F2	Dawson Rd	12 E2
Basset Clo	12 D1	De Havilland Dri	12 F1
Beech Clo	12 B3	Dodds Cres	12 C4
Berrys La	12 E2	Dorset Way	12 E1
Birch Walk	12 B3	Dunfee Way	12 F2
Birchdale Clo	12 D2	Eden Clo	12 C1
Birchwood Dri	12 B3	Eden Grove Rd	12 F4
Birchwood Rd	12 B3	Elmstead Rd	12 B4
Blackwood Clo	12 D3	Fairford Clo	12 A4
Blenheim Clo	12 A4	Fairlawn	12 A2
Bourne Cres	12 C4	Fairleigh Rd	12 B2
Braeside	12 C2	Faris Barn Dri	12 A2
Brantwood Dri	12 A4	Faris La	12 A2
Brantwood Gdns	12 B4	Ferney Rd	12 E2
Brewery La	12 F3	Fleetwood Ct	12 B3
Briar Clo	12 D2	Florence Av	12 B2
Briar Walk	12 B3	Fosse Way	12 A4
Broadoaks Cres	12 C4	Fulbrook Av	12 B2
Broomfield Rd	12 C2	Fulmer Way	12 A1
Bruce Clo	12 F4	Gorselands Clo	12 D2
Bucks Clo	12 C4	Grafton Clo	12 A3
Byfleet Rd	12 E1	Grange Rd	12 C1
Caillard Rd	12 F2	Greenway Clo	12 B4
Camphill Ct	12 B3	Greenwood Clo	12 A2
Camphill Rd	12 B3	Hart Rd	12 F4
Canada Rd	12 E2	Haydon Ct	12 C1
Cheniston Clo	12 B3	Heather Clo	12 C1
Chertsey Rd	12 E2	Heathervale Rd	12 C1
Church Rd	12 B4	High Rd	12 F3
Clare Clo	12 B4	Highfield Clo	12 B3
Claremont Rd	12 B3	Highfield Rd	12 B4
Cobs Way	12 D1	Hobbs Clo	12 C3
Copthall Way	12 B1	Hollies Av	12 A3
Cresta Dri	12 A1	Holly Av	12 B1
		Hopfield Av	12 F3

INDUSTRIAL ESTATES:

Camphill Ind Est	12 C2	Pyrford Rd	12 B4
Inglehurst	12 C1	Queen Marys Dri	12 A1
Junewood Clo	12 A2	Queen's Av	12 E3
Keston Av	12 B2	Rectory Clo	12 F4
King Georges Dri	12 B1	Rectory La	12 F3
Kings Av	12 E2	Regency Dri	12 A4
Kings Rd	12 C1	Rosemount Av	12 B4
Kingshead La	12 E2	Royston Av	12 F3
Kingston Rise	12 B1	Royston Rd	12 F3
Knowle Gdns	12 A3	Salisbury Pl	12 D2
Lake Clo	12 E3	Sanway Rd	12 F4
Langshott Clo	12 A2	Scotland Bridge Rd	12 B1
Lavender Park Rd	12 B3	Selbourne Av	12 C1
Leisure La	12 C3	Selsdon Rd	12 B2
Linden Clo	12 B2	Sheerwater Av	12 A2
Lindsay Rd	12 C1	Sheerwater Rd	12 A3
Little Orchard	12 B2	Shires House	12 F4
Lyndale Ct	12 B3	Squirrel Keep	12 C3
Madeira Clo	12 B3	Squirrel Wood	12 C3
Madeira Cres	12 B4	Starwood Clo	12 D2
Madeira Rd	12 A4	Station App	12 B3
Maitland Clo	12 B4	Station Rd	12 B3
Manor Dri	12 B1	Stoop Ct	12 C2
Maxwell Dri	12 D2	Stream Clo	12 F3
Mayfield Av	12 D1	Tewkesbury Clo	12 E2
Mayfield Clo	12 D1	The Avenue	12 B1
Melbury Clo	12 B4	The Broadway	12 B1
Millen Clo	12 C1	The Close	12 B4
Mowbray Av	12 F3	The Moat	12 D4
Murrays La	12 E4	The Oaks	12 C4
Nursery Clo	12 A1	The Paddocks	12 C1
Oak End Way	12 A3	The Willows	12 F3
Oakcroft Clo	12 A4	Thistle Dene	12 A3
Oakcroft Rd	12 A4	Trevose Av	12 A4
Oakfields	12 C4	Vickers Dri Nth	12 F1
Old Parvis Rd	12 D3	Vickers Dri Sth	12 F2
Old Woking Rd	12 A4	Viscount Gdns	12 F2
Old Wood	12 D3	Wakefield Clo	12 F2
Old Wood Pond	12 D3	Walnut Tree La	12 E3
Orchard Av	12 A2	Warren Rd	12 B1
Orchards Clo	12 B4	Wendley Dri	12 A1
Oyster La	12 F2	Westwood Av	12 A2
Park Clo	12 D1	Wey Clo	12 C4
Park Side	12 C1	Wild Acres	12 D2
Parvis Bridge	12 E3	Willow Clo	12 A2
Parvis Rd	12 C3	Willow Way	12 D2
Pendennis Clo	12 B4	Winern Glebe	12 E4
Petersham Av	12 F2	Wingfield Clo	12 C1
Petersham Clo	12 F3	Wintersells Rd	12 F1
Petersham Ct	12 F3	Woodham La	12 A2
Pine Clo	12 C2	Woodham Park Rd	12 A1
Pinewood Av	12 D1	Woodham Park Way	12 A1
Pinewood Gro	12 C2	Woodlands Av	12 A3
Pinewood Pk	12 C2	Woodmancote Gdns	12 B4
		York Clo	12 F3
		York Rd	12 F2

CAMBERLEY

Academy Clo	13 C1	Clewborough Dri	13
Albert Rd	13 B4	College Clo	13
Alison Dri	13 D4	College Ride	13
Amberwood Dri	13 D2	Collingwood Grange	
Appley Ct	13 A4	Clo	13
Appley Dri	13 A4	Collingwood Rise	13
Ashwell Av	13 D3	Conifer Dri	13
Ballard Rd	13 E1	Connaught Rd	13
Barn Clo	13 C3	Coolarne Rise	13
Barrossa Rd	13 B2	Copse Clo	13
Bath Rd	13 B3	Copse End	13
Beaufront Clo	13 F2	Cornwall Clo	13
Beaufront Rd	13 F2	Cornwalles Rd	13
Bellever Hill	13 C4	Court Gdns	13
Belton Rd	13 C4	Crawley Dri	13
Berkshire Rd	13 D1	Crawley Hill	13
Bietigheim Way	13 B3	Crawley Ridge	13
Birch Clo	13 C1	Crawley Wood Clo	13
Bracknell Clo	13 E1	Cromwell Rd	13 B
Bracknell Rd	13 E1	Crosby Hill Dri	13 D
Branksome Clo	13 C4	Dawnay Rd	13 A
Branksome Park Rd	13 C3	Deep Well Dri	13 C
Burgoyne Rd	13 F3	Deer Rock Rd	13 D
Caesars Camp Rd	13 E1	Dennistoun Clo	13 B
Caesars Clo	13 E2	Devonshire Dri	13 E
Cambrian Clo	13 A4	Diamond Hill	13 C
Cambridge Walk	13 B4	Diamond Ridge	13 C
Carlinwark Dri	13 D2	Duke of Cornwall Av	13 F
Carshalton Rd	13 E1	Dundaff Clo	13 F
Castle Rd	13 D4	Earls Gro	13 C
Chatsworth Heights	13 F3	Eliot Clo	13 F
Chaucer Gro	13 B4	Elsenwood Cres	13 E
Chesters Rd	13 F4	Elsenwood Dri	13 E
Chestnut Av	13 F3	Epsom Clo	13 A
Church Hill	13 C4	Esher Rd	13 F
Claremont Av	13 E4	Everest Rd	13 B
Clarewood Clo	13 C3	Fairway Heights	13 F4
		Firlands Av	13 B4
		Firwood Dri	13 A4
		Fossewood	13 B2
		Foxdown Clo	13 A4
		France Hill Dri	13 A4
		Frimley Hall Dri	13 D3
		Gainsborough Clo	13 D3
		Georgian Clo	13 C3
		Gibbet La	13 E2
		Goodwood Clo	13 A1
		Grace Reynolds Walk	13 B3
		Grand Av	13 A3
		Grange Rd	13 D4
		Green La Clo	13 A2
		Grove Rd	13 D4
		Hall Clo	13 D3
		Hampshire Rd	13 D1
		Hartford Rise	13 B3
		Heath Rise	13 C4
		Heathcote Rd	13 B4
		Heathway	13 C4
		Heathway Clo	13 C4
		High St	13 C3
		Highbury Cres	13 F2
		Highclere Dri	13 E2
		Highland Rd	13 D2
		Hillcrest Rd	13 F2
		Horseshoe Clo	13 D1
		Horseshoe Cres	13 D1
		Iberian Way	13 F3
		Kestrel Clo	13 E4
		Kings Cres	13 B1
		Kings Ride	13 B3
		Kingston Rd	13 E1
		Knightsbridge Gro	13 D3
		Knightsbridge Rd	13 D3
		Knoll Rd	13 B3
		Knoll Walk	13 B3
		Langley Dri	13 C3
		Larch Clo	13 D1
		Larchwood Glade	13 E2
		Lime Av	13 E3
		Linden Ct	13 D2
		Little Paddock	13 F1
		Loddon Clo	13 F3
		London Rd	13 A3
		Lorraine Rd	13 D2
		Lower Charles St	13 A3
		Lower Gordon Rd	13 A3
		Marlborough Rise	13 D3
		Matthews Rd	13 B1
		Maultway Clo	13 F1
		Maultway Cres	13 F1
		Maultway North	13 F1
		Maywood Dri	13 F2
		Middle Gordon Rd	13 B4
		Middleton Rd	13 D3
		Mitcham Rd	13 F1
		Mulroy Dri	13 F3
		Napier Dri	13 E2
		North Gate Dri	13 E2

elisk Way 13 B3
Dean Rd 13 B2
Green La 13 A2
ddock Clo 13 E3
rk La 13 B4
rk Rd 13 B4
rk St 13 A3
schal Rd 13 E1
mbroke Bdwy 13 B4
ppyhills Rd 13 D2
rtesbery Hill Dri 13 C3
rtesbery Rd 13 B4
rtsmouth Rd 13 E3
ncess Way 13 B4
or End 13 C4
ior Rd 13 E4
een Elizabeth Rd 13 B1
venswood Dri 13 E4
wdon Rise 13 F4
dcrest Gdns 13 D4
pley Clo 13 D2
wan Clo 13 D1
ddleback Rd 13 C1
Georges Rd 13 B3
ndy La 13 C3
eymour Dri 13 F2
halbourne Rise 13 C4
lverwood Dri 13 E2
im Rd 13 A3
outhcote Dri 13 E4
outhern Rd 13 A4
outhwell Park Rd 13 A4
parvell Way 13 B3
pring Gdns 13 F4
pringfield Rd 13 F4
taff College Rd 13 A3
tar Post Rd 13 D1
tockwood Rise 13 E4
utton Rd 13 F1
ekels Av 13 B4
he Avenue 13 A4
he Buchan 13 E2
he Pines 13 D2
own Square 13 B3
reetops Av 13 F2
urf Hill Rd 13 D2
Jpland Rd 13 B2
Jpper Charles St 13 A3
Jpper College Ride 13 C1
Jpper Gordon Rd 13 B4
Jpper Park Rd 13 C4
Valroy Clo 13 B3
Walkers Ridge 13 D4
Waverley Dri 13 D4
West Rd 13 C4
Whitehill Clo 13 B2
Wickham Rd 13 D2
Willington Clo 13 A4
Wimbledon Clo 13 D1
Wimbledon Rd 13 E1
Wishmoor Clo 13 D1
Wishmoor Rd 13 D1
Woodbridge Dri 13 C3
Wychwood Pl 13 F1
Yeomans Way 13 C4
York Pl 13 B3
York Rd 13 B3
Youlden Clo 13 F4
Youlden Dri 13 F4

CATERHAM

Abbots Walk 14 D3
Addison Clo 14 A2
Addison Rd 14 A1
Alderwood Clo 14 A6
Alexanders Walk 14 C6
Annes Walk 14 B1
Auckland Rd 14 A3
Avenue Rd 14 A3
Banstead Rd 14 A2
Beech Gro 14 A6
Beechwood Gdns 14 D3
Beechwood Rd 14 C3
Berkshire Clo 14 A2
Birch Av 14 A4
Bourne La 14 A2
Bradenhurst Clo 14 B6
Brambles Clo 14 B2
Broad Walk 14 B2
Burntwood Clo 14 D1
Burntwood La 14 B2
Buxton Av 14 A1
Buxton La 14 A1
Caterham By-Pass 14 D1
Chaldon Rd 14 A4
Church Hill 14 B5
Church Rd 14 B4
Church Walk 14 C4
Clareville Rd 14 C5
Clifton Clo 14 A3
Colburn Av 14 C5
Colin Rd 14 C4
Colliers 14 D5
Commonwealth Rd 14 C3
Coulsdon Rd 14 A3
Court Rd 14 A4
Crescent Rd 14 C4
Croydon Rd 14 C3
Deansfield 14 B6
Deerswood Clo 14 D5
Dunedin Dri 14 B6
Elgin Cres 14 D3
Elm Gro 14 A2
Essendene Clo 14 B3
Essendene Rd 14 B3
Everard La 14 D2
Farningham Cres 14 C3
Farningham Rd 14 C3
Foxacre 14 B3
Foxon Clo 14 A2
Foxon La 14 A1
Foxon La Gdns 14 A2
Francis Rd 14 A3
Fulford Rd 14 A2
Furrows Pl 14 B3
Gaist Av 14 D3
Garland Way 14 A2
Godstone Rd 14 D5
Gordon Rd 14 A2
Grange Rd 14 C6
Greenhill Av 14 D1
Greenwood Gdns 14 D5
Harestone Dri 14 D5
Harestone Hill 14 C6
Harestone La 14 D5
Harestone Valley Rd 14 B6
Hayes La 14 A1
Heath Rd 14 A4
High St 14 B3
High Trees Clo 14 C3
Highfield Rd 14 D2
Highview 14 B5
Highwoods 14 B5
Hillhurst Gdns 14 A1
Holly Tree Rd 14 A2
Homesdale Rd 14 A4
Homestead Rd 14 A4
Kenley Clo 14 A1
Knowle Lodge 14 C4
Kynaston Ct 14 B6
Le Personne Rd 14 A2
Livingstone Rd 14 A3
London Rd 14 A4
Longmead Clo 14 A2
Loxford Rd 14 B6
Loxford Way 14 B6
Macaulay Rd 14 A2
Manor Av 14 B5
Markfield Rd 14 D6
Markville Gdns 14 D6
Matlock Rd 14 B2
Maurice Av 14 A3
Mead Rd 14 B4
Milner App 14 C2
Milner Rd 14 C2
Money Av 14 A3
Money Rd 14 A3
Monks Pl 14 D2
Mount Pleasant Rd 14 C4
Nelson Rd 14 A4
Newstead Rise 14 D6
Ninehams Clo 14 A1
Ninehams Gdns 14 A1
Ninehams Rd 14 A1
Oak Rd 14 A3
Orchard End 14 B3
Park Av 14 B5
Park Rd 14 A4
Pepper Clo 14 B5
Pine Walk 14 B3
Poplar Walk 14 B4
Portley La 14 B2
Portley Wood Rd 14 C1
Queens Park Rd 14 B4
Reid Av 14 A1
Rochester Gdns 14 B3
Rogers Clo 14 D3
Rosebriars 14 A1
Rosedale 14 A4
Russett Ct 14 C5
Ryelands Clo 14 A2
St Katherines Rd 14 C6
Salmons La 14 B1
Salmons La West 14 A1
Spencer Rd 14 A2
Stafford Clo 14 C4
Stafford Rd 14 C3
Stanstead Rd 14 A6
Station Av 14 C4
Stonehouse Gdns 14 A6
Strathmore Clo 14 B2
Succombs Hill 14 D1
Taunton Av 14 B4
The Copse 14 C6
The Hill 14 C4
The Ridings 14 C6
Tillingdown Hill 14 D2
Tillingdown La 14 D5
Timber Hill Rd 14 C4
Timber La 14 C4
Townend 14 B3
Townend Clo 14 B3
Trenholm Ct 14 C3
Tupwood Ct 14 C5
Tupwood La 14 C6
Underwood Ct 14 B6
Underwood Rd 14 B6
Waller La 14 B4
Waltham Rd 14 D2
Westway 14 A3
White Knobs Way 14 D6
Whyteleafe Rd 14 B1
Willey La 14 A6
William Rd 14 A3
Woldingham Rd 14 D1
Wood La 14 A4
Woodside Clo 14 B5
Yew Tree Dri 14 B6

CHERTSEY

Abbey Gdns 15 C2
Abbey Grn 15 C2
Abbey Rd 15 D3
Alwyns Clo 15 C2
Alwyns La 15 C2
Barker Rd 15 B3
Bedmonds 15 C3
Bedmonds Row 15 C3
Bell Bridge Rd 15 B4
Bittams La 15 B6
Blacksmiths La 15 C3
Bramley Clo 15 D4
Bretlands Rd 15 A5
Bridge Rd 15 D3
Brook Side 15 A3
Burley Orchard 15 C2
Canford Dri 15 D5
Corotus Pl 15 B3
Charles St 15 C4
Chaseside Gdns 15 D3
Chertsey Rd 15 D5
Chilsey Green Rd 15 A2
Clifton Clo 15 D5
Cogmore Farm Clo 15 B3
Colonels La 15 C2
Corderoy Pl 15 B2
Courland Rd 15 D6
Cowley Av 15 B3
Cowley La 15 B3
Cowper Clo 15 B2
Crown Rise 15 B4
Curfew Bell Rd 15 C3
Dianthus Clo 15 A3
Douglas Rd 15 D6
Drill Hall Rd 15 C3
Eastworth Rd 15 C4
Elm Tree Clo 15 A5
Erkenwald Clo 15 B3
Fairway 15 D4
Ferndale Av 15 A6
Fernlands Clo 15 A6
Ferry La 15 D1
Flemish Fields 15 C3
Ford Rd 15 D4
Fordbridge Clo 15 D4
Fordwater Rd 15 D4
Foundry Ct 15 C3
Fox La N 15 B4
Fox La S 15 B4
Free Prae Rd 15 C4
Friars Way 15 C2
Frithwald Rd 15 B3
Galsworthy Rd 15 C3
Gogmore La 15 C3
Gordon Clo 15 B6
Gordon Dri 15 A6
Green La 15 A5
Green Lane Clo 15 A5
Greenmore Clo 15 D6
Grove Rd 15 B2
Guildford Rd 15 A6
Guildford St 15 B4
Hamilton Clo 15 B4
Hanworth La 15 B4
Hardwick La 15 A5
Harrow Clo 15 D5
Hatch Clo 15 D6
Heriot Rd 15 C3
Herrings La 15 C2
Highfield Rd 15 C4
Hillcrest Av 15 A6
Holloway Hill 15 A5
INDUSTRIAL ESTATES:
Fordwater Trading Estate 15 D4
Hanworth Trading Est 15 B4
Inglewood 15 B6
Jersey Clo 15 B6
King St 15 C4
Knoll Pk Rd 15 B4
Laburnum Rd 15 C4
Langton Clo 15 D6
Lasswade Rd 15 B3
Little Green La 15 A6
London St 15 C3
Longbourne Way 15 B2
Lyndhurst Way 15 A5
Masonic Hall Rd 15 B2
Meadhurst Rd 15 D4
Melbury Clo 15 C3
Merrylands 15 B6
North Gro 15 B2
Oaklands Ct 15 D6
Oldbury Rd 15 A3
Onslow Mews 15 C2
Paddocks Way 15 D4
Pannells Clo 15 B4
Pound Rd 15 D3
Prairie Clo 15 D6
Prairie Rd 15 D6
Pretoria Rd 15 B4
Pycroft Rd 15 B3
Queen St 15 C4
Rickman Cres 15 D6
Riversdell Clo 15 C3
Roakes Av 15 D5
Rosemead 15 D3
Rutherwyk Rd 15 A3
Ruxbury Rd 15 A2
St Anns Clo 15 B2
St Anns Hill Rd 15 A2
St Anns Rd 15 A2
St Peters Way 15 C6
Sandalwood Av 15 A6
School La 15 C6
South Gro 15 B2
Springfields Clo 15 D4
Squires Ct 15 D4
Staines La 15 C2
Staines Lane Clo 15 B1
Staines Rd 15 B1
Station Rd 15 C4
Stepgates Mead La 15 D3
Styventon Pl 15 B3
The Barracks 15 D6
The Knoll 15 B4
Thorpe Rd 15 A1
Victory Rd 15 C4
Vincent Clo 15 B3
Vincent Rd 15 A3
Waverley Dri 15 A6
Weir Rd 15 D3
Wheatash Rd 15 D5
White Hart Row 15 C3
Willow Walk 15 D3
Windsor St 15 C2

CHOBHAM

Alpha Rd 16 B3
Bagshot Rd 16 A4
Barnmead 16 C4
Beta Rd 16 C3
Borough Grn 16 A2
Bowling Grn Rd 16 B3
Bracken Way 16 C3
Brimshot La 16 B2
Broadford La 16 B5
Brook Grn 16 C3
Brook La 16 A4
Brookleys 16 C3
Broom La 16 B2
Burrhill La 16 B3
Cannon Cres 16 B4
Castle Gro Rd 16 B5
Chertsey Rd 16 C3
Chobham Park La 16 D3
Clappers La 16 A4
Delta Clo 16 C3
Delta Rd 16 C3
Elm Dri 16 C3
Fowlers Mead 16 B3
Gorse La 16 B2
Gracious Pond Rd 16 C1
Green La 16 C3
Grosvenor Rd 16 A6
Guildford Rd 16 A6
Heather Way 16 A1
High St 16 B4
Killy Hill 16 B2
Leslie Rd 16 A3
Little Heath Rd 16 B2
Medhurst Clo 16 C3
Mincing La 16 C2
Mount Rd 16 D5
Oakdene 16 C3
Oakhurst 16 B2
Red Lion Rd 16 B2
Sandpit Hall Rd 16 D5
Sandy La 16 B2
Scotts Gro Clo 16 A6
Scotts Gro Rd 16 A6
Station Rd 16 C5
Steep Hill 16 A1
The Avenue 16 C2
The Grange 16 B3
Thompsons La 16 A2
Turfhouse La 16 B2
Vicarage Rd 16 B4
Waterperry La 16 C3
Watery La 16 A4
Windlesham Rd 16 A2
Windsor Court La 16 B2
Windsor Rd 16 A1

COBHAM/STOKE D'ABERNON

Anvil La 17 A2
Anyards Rd 17 B2
Ashcroft Park 17 E1
Ashford Gdns 17 D4
Ashlyns Pk 17 E1
Aspen Clo 17 E4
Avenue Rd 17 D4
Beechmeads 17 D1
Bennett Clo 17 A1
Between Streets 17 A2
Birchgrove 17 C2
Blundel La 17 F4
Bramble Rise 17 C2
Bray Rd 17 E4
Bridge Way 17 A1
Broad Highway 17 D3
Brook Farm Rd 17 D3
Brooklands Clo 17 E3
Brunswick Gro 17 C1
Burleigh Park 17 E1
Burstead Clo 17 D1
Canada Rd 17 C1
Cedar Av 17 C3
Cedar Rd 17 B2
Church St 17 B3
Cleeves Clo 17 B2
Cobham Gate 17 B2
Copse Rd 17 B2
Coveham Cres 17 A1
D'Abernon Dri 17 E4
Denby Rd 17 C1
Downside Bridge Rd 17 B3
Downside Rd 17 B4
Drift La 17 F4
Eaton Pk 17 E2
Eaton Park Rd 17 E2
Elm Grove Rd 17 D3
Evelyn Way 17 F4
Fairbourne 17 D1
Fairfield Pk 17 D3
Fairmeads 17 F1
Fairmile Av 17 E2
Fairmile La 17 E1
Fairmile Park Copse 17 F1
Fairmile Park Rd 17 F1
Farm Vw 17 D4
Ferndown Gdns 17 C2
Four Acres 17 E1
Four Wents 17 C2
Freelands Rd 17 B2
French Gdns 17 C2
Gavell Rd 17 A1

Grenville Clo 17 D1
Haleswood 17 C2
Hamilton Av 17 A1
Harebell Hill 17 D2
Hawksview 17 F1
High St 17 B3
Hogshill La 17 B2
Hollyhedge Rd 17 B3
Icklingham Rd 17 C1
Knipp Hill 17 F1
Knowle Pk 17 E3
Lambourne Dri 17 D3
Larkfield 17 A1
Leigh Corner 17 C3
Leigh Court Clo 17 C2
Leigh Hill Rd 17 C2
Leigh Pl 17 C3
Leigh Rd 17 B2
Lockhart Rd 17 C1
Lodge Clo 17 F4
Longboyds 17 B3
Lushington Dri 17 B2
Matthew Arnold Clo 17 A2
Meadowlands 17 A1
Miles La 17 E1
Mill Rd 17 C3
Millhedge Clo 17 E4
Mizen Clo 17 D2
Mizen Way 17 D3
Molesworth Rd 17 A1
Mossfield 17 A1
Northfield Rd 17 B1
Oak Rd 17 D3
Oakdene Par 17 B2
Oakdene Rd 17 B2
Oakfield Rd 17 B2
Old Common Rd 17 B1
Oxshott Rise 17 E2
Oxshott Way 17 E3
Paddocks Clo 17 C2
Pennyfield 17 A1
Pine Walk 17 D2
Pipers Clo 17 D3
Plough La 17 B4
Pony Chase 17 F1
Portsmouth Rd 17 A2
Queens Court Ride 17 A1
Ravenswood Clo 17 D3
River Hill 17 B3
River La 17 E4
Riverview Gdns 17 A1
Ross Rd 17 C1
St Andrews Gdns 17 C1
St Andrews Walk 17 B3
Sandy Ct 17 F1
Sandy La 17 F1
Spencer Rd 17 B3
Station Rd 17 E4
Stoke Clo 17 F4
Stoke Rd 17 C3
Summerhays 17 D2
Tartar Hill 17 B1
Tartar Rd 17 C1
The Barton 17 C1
The Bowsprit 17 C3
The Drive 17 E2
The Garth 17 E1
The Laurels 17 E3
The Stables 17 F3
Tilt Clo 17 E4
Tilt Meadow 17 E4
Tilt Rd 17 C3
Towngate 17 A1
Trafalgar Ct 17 A1
Tudor Clo 17 F1
Vincent Rd 17 E4
Warblers Grn 17 F2
Water La 17 F2
Winstanley Clo 17 B2
Winston Dri 17 E4
Woodend Pk 17 D3
Worlds End 17 A2
Wyndham Av 17 A1

CRANLEIGH

Acres Platt 18 D1
Ash Trees 18 C3
Aven Clo 18 C3
Avenue Rd 18 D3
Bank Buildings Rd 18 B2
Barber Dri 18 C1
Barnfield 18 C2
Barnhatch Rd 18 D1
Bax Clo 18 C3
Beaumont Sq 18 D2
Bishops Sq 18 D2
Bloggs Way 18 B2
Bloxham Rd 18 E2
Bookhurst Rd 18 E1
Bridge Rd 18 C2
Broad Walk 18 D3
Brookmead Ct 18 C2
Brookside 18 C4
Butt Clo 18 C1
Cameron Clo 18 C4
Charts Clo 18 C3
Church Path 18 B2
Coatham Pl 18 D2
Collingdon 18 D4
Common Rd 18 A1
Copse Edge 18 D1
Cranleigh Mead 18 D3
Cromwell Pl 18 D4
Dewlands Clo 18 C2
Dewlands La 18 C2
Dover Ct 18 E2
Drakes Clo 18 D3
Dukes Clo 18 D3
Durnsford Way 18 D3
East View La 18 A2
Edgefield Clo 18 A1
Ellery Clo 18 C4
Ewhurst Rd 18 C2
Fawley Clo 18 D3
Fettes Rd 18 E2
Fortune Dri 18 C4
Gingers Clo 18 D3
Glebe Rd 18 B1
Grange Pk 18 D2
Greenbush La 18 D4
Grove Clo 18 D4
Grove Rd 18 D4
Guildford Rd 18 A2
Hailey Pl 18 D1
Harrier Clo 18 C1
Harrowdene 18 C1
Heron Shaw 18 C3
High St 18 B2
Hitherwood 18 C3
Homestead 18 D1
Homewood 18 E2
Homewood Ct 18 C3
Horseshoe La 18 A1
Horsham Rd 18 C3
John Wiskar Dri 18 B2
Killicks 18 C1
Kiln Copse 18 C1
Kingsmead 18 C2
Kings Rd 18 C3
Knowle La 18 B3
Little Manor Gdns 18 B2
Littlewood 18 D2
Longpoles Rd 18 D3
Loretto Clo 18 D2
Mead Clo 18 C2
Mead Rd 18 C2
Mount Rd 18 C3
Mower Pl 18 C1
Napper Pl 18 C4
New Park Rd 18 C2
Nightingales 18 C4
Northdowns 18 C3
Nuthurst Av 18 C2
Oaklands 18 B3
Orchard Gdns 18 D3
Overford Clo 18 C3
Overford Dri 18 C3
Park Dri 18 D1
Parsonage Rd 18 B2
Peregrine Clo 18 C1
Queensway 18 D3
Redcroft Walk 18 C3
Rowland Rd 18 B2
Ryde Lands 18 D1
St James's 18 A2
St Nicolas Av 18 C1
St Nicolas Clo 18 C1
Sapt Clo 18 E2
Seltops Clo 18 D3
Sherrydon 18 D1
Slip of Wood 18 D1
Southwood Chase 18 D4
Stocklund Sq 18 B2
Strudwicke Fields 18 D1
Summerlands 18 C1
Sylvaways 18 E2
Taylors Cres 18 D1
The Drive 18 C3
The Malt Houses 18 C2
The Mount 18 C3
The Precinct 18 C1
The Ridgeway 18 C2
The Ridings 18 C1
Thistley La 18 C1
Thurlow Walk 18 C4
Trelawne Dri 18 C3
Victoria Rd 18 B2
Waldy Rise 18 C1
Wanborough La 18 E1
Waverleigh Rd 18 C3
Wellwynds Rd 18 C3
Wildwood Clo 18 D4
Woodland Av 18 D2
Woodland Clo 18 D2
Woodstock Clo 18 D4
Wyphurst Rd 18 B1

CROYDON

Abbey Rd 19 B4
Aberdeen Rd 19 D6
Addington Rd 19 B2
Ainsworth Rd 19 C3
Albion St 19 B3
Allen Rd 19 A2
Alton Rd 19 A5
Ampere Way 19 A3
Arundel Clo 19 B5
Arundel Rd 19 D1
Ashby Walk 19 C1
Ashley La 19 C5
*Baines Clo
 Cliffe Rd 19 D6
Barclay Rd 19 D4
Barham Rd 19 C6
Bartlett St 19 D6
Beddington Fm Rd 19 A4
Bedford Rd 19 D3
Bedford Pl 19 D3
Beech House Rd 19 D5
Bensham La 19 B1
Benson Rd 19 B5
Berney Walk 19 D1
Beulah Gro 19 C1
Birdhurst Av 19 D6
Bishops Rd 19 B2
Blunt Rd 19 D6
Booth St 19 B4
Borough Hill 19 B5
Boston Rd 19 A1
Bourne St 19 B4
Brafferton Rd 19 C5
Bramley Ct 19 C6
Bramley Hill 19 C6
Brighton Rd 19 D6
Broad Grn Av 19 B1
Broadfield Clo 19 A4
Burdett Rd 19 D1
Bute Rd 19 B3
Caironew Rd 19 C4
Cameron Rd 19 B1
Campbell Rd 19 B1
Canterbury Rd 19 A1
Cavendish Rd 19 B2
Chapel Walk 19 C3
Chapman Rd 19 A2
Charles St 19 C4
Charrington Rd 19 C3
Chartwell Clo 19 D2
Chatfield Rd 19 B2
Chatsworth Rd 19 D5
Cherry Hill Gdns 19 A6
Church Alley 19 B2
Church Path 19 C3
Church Rd 19 C4
Church St 19 C4
Clarence Rd 19 D1
Clarendon Rd 19 C3
Cliffe Rd 19 D6
*Cobblestone Pl,
 Oakfield Rd 19 C3
Coldharbour Rd 19 A6
College Rd 19 D4
Commerce Way 19 A4
Constance Rd 19 B1
Coombe Rd 19 D5
Cooper Rd 19 B6
Cornwall Rd 19 B4
Court Dri 19 A5
Courtney Av 19 A5
Courtney Pl 19 B5
Cranmer Rd 19 C4
Crawley Cres 19 B6
Croham Rd 19 D6
Cromwell Rd 19 D1
Crossland Rd 19 B1
Crown Hill 19 C4
Croydon Gro 19 B2
Croydon Rd 19 A5
Cuthbert Rd 19 B4
Davenant Rd 19 C5
Dean Rd 19 D6
Denmead Rd 19 B3
Dennett Rd 19 B2
Denning Av 19 A6
Derby Rd 19 C3
Dering Rd 19 C6
Dering Rd 19 C6
Devonshire Rd 19 D1
Dingwall Av 19 C3
Dingwall Rd 19 D3
Donald Rd 19 A1
Drake Rd 19 A2
Drayton Rd 19 C4
Drummond Pl 19 C4
Drummond Rd 19 C4
Drury Cres 19 A3
Duneved Rd Sth 19 B1
Duneved Rd West 19 A1
Duppas Av 19 B6
Duppas Hill La 19 C5
Duppas Hill Rd 19 B5
Duppas Hill Ter 19 C5
Duppas Rd 19 B5
Eastney Rd 19 B2
Eden Rd 19 D5
Edridge Rd 19 D5
Effingham Rd 19 A2
Eland Rd 19 B4
Elmwood Rd 19 B2
*Englefield Clo,
 Queens Rd 19 C1
Enterprise Clo 19 A3
Epsom Rd 19 A5
Euston Rd 19 A3
Factory La 19 A3
Fairfield Rd 19 D4
Fairholme Rd 19 B2
Fairmead Rd 19 A2
Faraday Way 19 A2
Farquharson Rd 19 C2
Fawcett Rd 19 C5
Fell Rd 19 D4
Fernleigh Clo 19 A6
Five Acre Clo 19 B1
Forster Rd 19 C1
Francis Rd 19 B1
Friends Rd 19 D4
Frith Rd 19 C4
Furtherfield Clo 19 A1
Galloway Path 19 D6
Galvani Way 19 A3
Gardners Rd 19 B3
George St 19 D4
Gladstone Rd 19 D2
Glen Gdns 19 B5
Godalming Av 19 A6
Godson Rd 19 A5
Gosedge Cres 19 B6
Grace Rd 19 C1
Grafton Rd 19 B3
Greenside Rd 19 B2
Greenwood Rd 19 C1
Grenaby Av 19 D2
Grenaby Rd 19 D2
Grindall Clo 19 B6
Gurney Cres 19 A3
Hampton Rd 19 D1
Handcroft Rd 19 B2
Hanover St 19 C5
Harcourt Rd 19 A1
Harrison Rise 19 B4
Hartley Rd 19 C1
Hathaway Rd 19 C1
Hatton Rd 19 B2
Headley Av 19 A6
Heathfield Rd 19 D5
Heighton Gdns 19 B6
High St 19 C4
Hillside Rd 19 B6
Hoga.th Cres 19 C2
Hood Clo 19 C3
Howley Rd 19 C4
*Hughes Walk,
 St Saviours Rd 19 C1
Hurst Rd 19 D6
Hyrstdene 19 C6
INDUSTRIAL ESTATES:
 Croydon Business
  Centre 19 A3
 Mill La Trading Est 19 A4
 Purley Way Centre 19 A3
 Wandle Park Ind Est 19 B3
Innes Yd 19 C5
Jennett Rd 19 A4
Johnson Rd 19 D1
Katharine St 19
Keeley Rd 19
Keens Rd 19
Kelling Gdns 19
Kemble Rd 19 B3
Kemp Gdns 19
Kidderminster Rd 19
King Gdns 19
Kingsley Rd 19 A
Lambeth Rd 19 B
Lancing Rd 19 A
Lansdowne Rd 19 D
Latimer Rd 19 E
Laud St 19 C
Lawdon Gdns 19 C
Layton Cres 19 B
Ledbury Pl 19 C
Ledbury Rd 19 D
Leighton St 19 B
Lennard Rd 19 C
Lennox Gdns 19 C
Limes Av 19 A
Limes Pl 19 D
Limes Rd 19 D
Lodge Av 19 A
Lodge Rd 19 C
London Rd 19 B
Longley Rd 19 B
Lower Coombe St 19 C
Ludford Clo 19 B
Lynton Rd 19 A
Lynwood Gdns 19 A
Marden Cres 19 A
Marden Rd 19 A
Martin Cres 19 A
Masons Av 19 D
Mayday Rd 19 B
Mead Pl 19 C
Merebank 19 A
Middle St 19 C
Midhurst Av 19 B
Mill La 19 A
Miller Rd 19 A
Milton Av 19 D2
Milton Rd 19 D2
Mint Walk 19 C4
Mitcham Rd 19 A2
Montague Rd 19 B2
Mulgrave Rd 19 D5
Nelson Clo 19 B3
Neville Rd 19 D1
Newgate 19 D2
North End 19 C3
Northcote Rd 19 D1
Nottingham Rd 19 C6
Nova Rd 19 C2
Oakfield Rd 19 C2
Oakwood Pl 19 A1
Oakwood Rd 19 A1
Old Palace Rd 19 C4
Old Town 19 C5
Onslow Rd 19 A2
*Otterbourne Rd,
 Ruskin Rd 19 C3
Overtons Yd 19 C3
Page Cres 19 B6
Park La 19 D5
Park St 19 D4
Parker Rd 19 C5
Parsons Mead 19 C3
Pemdevon Rd 19 B2
Penfold Clo 19 B5
Pitlake 19 C3
Poplar Walk 19 C3
*Prestwood Gdns,
 Windmill Gro 19 C1
Price Rd 19 B6
Princess Rd 19 C1
Priory Rd 19 A2
Progress Way 19 A4
Pump Pail Nth 19 C5
Pump Pail Sth 19 C5
Purley Way 19 A2
Queen St 19 C5
Queens Rd 19 C1
Raglan Ct 19 C6
Ravenswood Rd 19 B5
Rectory Gro 19 B4
Renown St 19 B3
Rigby Clo 19 C4
Robert St 19 C4
Rodney Clo 19 B3
Roman Way 19 B3
Ruskin Rd 19 C3
St Andrews Rd 19 C3
St Georges Walk 19 D4
St James's Pk 19 C2
St James's Rd 19 C2

Station Rd 22 B4
Stephen Clo 22 D5
Stoneylands Ct 22 B4
Stoneylands Rd 22 A4
Strode St 22 B3
Strodes College La 22 B4
Stroude Rd 22 B5
Sweeps La 22 A4
Tempest Rd 22 D5
The Avenue 22 C3
The Causeway 22 D3
The Crescent 22 A5
The Glanty 22 C3
The Grove 22 B4
The Lea 22 D6
Thirlmere Clo 22 D6
Thorpe Lea Rd 22 C6
Tinsey Clo 22 C4
Tite Hill 22 A4
Vicarage Av 22 C4
Vicarage Court 22 C5
Vicarage Cres 22 C4
Vicarage Rd 22 C4
Wards Pl 22 D5
Warwick Av 22 D6
Wavendene Av 22 D6
Wendover Pl 22 D4
Wendover Rd 22 D4
Wesley Dri 22 B5
Wetton Pl 22 B4
Whitehall La 22 A6
Wickham La 22 C6
Windermere Clo 22 C5
Windsor Rd 22 A2
Woodhaw 22 C3
Wraysbury Rd 22 C1
Yardmead 22 B2

EPSOM

Adelphi Rd 23 B2
Albert Rd 23 C3
Albert Villas 23 D4
Alexandra Rd 23 D3
Almond Rd 23 B1
Andrews Clo 23 C3
Ash Mews 23 C3
Ashdown Rd 23 D3
Ashley Av 23 B3
Ashley Ct 23 B3
Ashley Rd 23 B3
Aston Way 23 D5
Avenue Rd 23 B4
Axwood 23 A5
Barons Hurst 23 A6
Beaconsfield Pl 23 C2
Beech Rd 23 D5
Beech Walk 23 D1
Beechway 23 D5
Berkeley Pl 23 B5
Birches Clo 23 C4
Blenheim Rd 23 B1
Bridge Rd 23 D2
Bridle End 23 D3
Bridle Rd 23 D3
Burgh Heath Rd 23 C4
Burghfield 23 D5
Burnet Gro 23 A3
Carters Rd 23 D5
Cedar Clo 23 D3
Cedar Hill 23 A5
Chalk La 23 B5
Chalk Paddock 23 B5
Chantry Hurst 23 B5
Chartwell Pl 23 C4
Chase End 23 B2
Chase Rd 23 B2
Chelwood Clo 23 D2
Church Rd 23 C3
Church St 23 C3
Chuters Gro 23 C1
Clayton Pl 23 C2
Cleeves Ct 23 C2
College Av 23 D4
College Rd 23 C3
Conifer Park 23 C1
Copse Edge Av 23 D3
Court La 23 A2
Delaporte Clo 23 C2
Denham Rd 23 D2
Depot Rd 23 C3
Digdens Rise 23 A5
Dirdene Clo 23 D2
Dirdene Gdns 23 C2
Dirdene Gro 23 C2
Dorking Rd 23 A4
Dorling Dri 23 D2
Downs Av 23 C4
Downs Hill Rd 23 C4
Downs Rd 23 C4
Downs Way 23 C6
Downside 23 C3
Dudley Gro 23 A4
East St 23 C2
Eastway 23 A1
Elm Gro 23 A4
Elmslie Clo 23 A4
Epsom Rd 23 C1
Fairbriar Ct 23 B3
Fairview Rd 23 C1
Farriers Clo 23 C1
Farriers Rd 23 C1
Felstead Rd 23 B1
Gosfield Rd 23 B2
Grove Av 23 C3
Grove Rd 23 C3
Hadrian Walk 23 B4
Hambledon Hill 23 A6
Hambledon Vale 23 A6
Hamilton Clo 23 A1
Hampton Gro 23 D1
Hawthorne Pl 23 C2
Hazon Way 23 B2
Heathcote Rd 23 B3
Hereford Clo 23 B3
Hessle Gro 23 D1
High St 23 B3
Highridge Clo 23 C4
Hillcrest Clo 23 D5
Hook Rd 23 B1
Hookfield 23 A3
Horsley Clo 23 B2
Horton Gdns 23 A1
Horton Hill 23 A1
Hunters Clo 23 A3
Hurst Rd 23 B1
Hylands Clo 23 A5
Hylands Mews 23 A4
Hylands Rd 23 A5
INDUSTRIAL ESTATES:
Longmead Ind Est 23 B1
Nonsuch Ind Est 23 C1
Jackson Clo 23 B4
Kendor Av 23 A1
Kiln La 23 C1
King Shades Walk 23 B3
Kingsdown Rd 23 D3
Laburnum Rd 23 B3
Ladbroke Rd 23 B4
Langlands Rise 23 A3
Langton Av 23 D1
Leighton Way 23 B4
Leith Rd 23 C2
Linden Pl 23 C2
Lindsay Clo 23 A3
Links Rd 23 D3
Lintons La 23 C2
Little Orchards 23 C4
Longdown Rd 23 D3
Longmead Rd 23 B1
Lower Court Rd 23 A1
Lynwood Av 23 D4
Lynwood Rd 23 D4
Madans Walk 23 B4
Maidenshaw Rd 23 B2
Malvern Ct 23 B4
Manor Green Rd 23 A1
Manor House Ct 23 A3
Marshalls Clo 23 A3
Mathias Clo 23 A3
Meadow Ct 23 A3
Meadway 23 A2
Middle Clo 23 C2
Middle La 23 C2
Milburn Walk 23 C5
Miles Rd 23 B1
Mill Rd 23 C2
Milton Gdns 23 C4
Mospey Cres 23 D4
Norman Av 23 D2
Oak Hill 23 B6
Oak Leaf Clo 23 A2
Oakmead Grn 23 A5
Orchard Gdns 23 A4
Park Hill Rd 23 D1
Pikes Hill 23 C2
Pine Hill 23 B5
Pitt Pl 23 C3
Pitt Rd 23 C3
Portland Pl 23 C1
Pound La 23 B1
Prospect Pl 23 C2
Providence Pl 23 C2
Randolph Rd 23 C4
Richmond Clo 23 C3
Ridgeway 23 A2
Rosebank 23 A3
Rosebank West St 23 A3
Rosebury Av 23 C4
St Georges Gdns 23 D4
St James Clo 23 B3
St Johns Av 23 D2
St Martins Av 23 C4
St Martins Clo 23 C3
Sharon Clo 23 A2
Shaw Clo 23 D1
Sheraton Dri 23 A2
South St 23 B3
Spread Eagle Wk 23 B3
Squirrels Way 23 B4
Station App 23 B3
Station Way 23 B3
Stevens Clo 23 C2
Stones Rd 23 C1
Sunny Bank 23 A6
Sweet Briar La 23 B3
Temple Rd 23 B1
The Green 23 D1
The Grove 23 C3
The Oaks 23 C4
The Parade 23 B3
The Ridings 23 C5
The Spinney 23 B3
Tintagel Clo 23 C3
Treadwell Rd 23 C5
Tree Mount Ct 23 C3
Upper Court Rd 23 A1
Upper High St 23 C2
Vancouver Clo 23 A1
Victoria Pl 23 C2
Wallace Fields 23 D2
Walnut Clo 23 C5
Warren Hill 23 B6
Waterloo Rd 23 B2
West Hill 23 A3
West Hill Av 23 A2
West Lands Ct 23 A4
West St 23 A3
Weston Rd 23 C1
Wheelers La 23 A3
White Horse Dri 23 A4
Whitmores Clo 23 A5
Wilmerhatch La 23 A6
Wimborne Clo 23 C3
Windmill Av 23 D1
Windmill Clo 23 D2
Windmill End 23 D2
Windmill La 23 D1
Woodcote Clo 23 B4
Woodcote End 23 B5
Woodcote Green Rd 23 A5
Woodcote Hurst 23 A6
Woodcote Hurst Ct 23 B5
Woodcote Park Rd 23 A5
Woodcote Rd 23 B4
Wootton Clo 23 C5
Worlds End 23 B6
Worple Rd 23 B4
Wyeths Mews 23 C3
Wyeths Rd 23 C3
Yeomanry Clo 23 C2

ESHER

Acorns Way 24 C4
Arbrook La 24 D5
Arran Way 24 C1
Ashburnham Park 24 C3
Belvedere Clo 24 B4
Bracondale 24 C4
Brendon Clo 24 D5
Brendon Dri 24 D5
Brisson Clo 24 A4
Broom Clo 24 C4
Broomfields 24 D4
Carrick Gate 24 D2
Catos Hill 24 C3
Cedar Clo 24 A5
Chadworth Way 24 D4
Church St 24 C3
Clare Hill 24 B4
Claremont Av 24 A5
Claremont Dri 24 B5
Claremont End 24 C5
Claremont La 24 C3
Claremont Park Rd 24 B5
Clive Rd 24 B3
Compton Clo 24 D4
Copsem Dri 24 C5
Copsem La 24 C5
Copsem Way 24 C5
Courtlands Av 24 A5
Cranford Rise 24 C4
Dabernon Clo 24 B3
Dawes Ct 24 B3
Douglas Rd 24 B1
Drakes Clo 24 A3
Esher Clo 24 B4
Esher Grn 24 B3
Esher Park Av 24 C3
Esher Place Av 24 B3
Esher Rd 24 A3
Farm Rd 24 B1
Fir Tree Clo 24 C4
Hare La 24 D4
Hawkshill Clo 24 A5
Hawkshill Way 24 A5
Haymeads Dri 24 C5
Heati er Ct 14 B3
Heather Pl 24 B3
High Garth 24 C5
High St 24 B3
Hillbrow Rd 24 C3
Hillfield Ct 24 B4
Home Farm Clo 24 C5
Hunting Clo 24 B3
INDUSTRIAL ESTATES:
Sandown Ind Pk 24 A1
Joseph Locke Way 24 B1
Lakeside Dri 24 C5
Lammas La 24 A4
Latton Clo 24 B3
Little Mead 24 D3
Littleworth Av 24 D4
Littleworth Common Rd 24 D2
Littleworth La 24 D3
Littleworth Pl 24 D3
Littleworth Rd 24 D4
Lower Green Rd 24 B1
Lynne Walk 24 C4
Martineau Clo 24 D3
Meadway 24 B6
Milbourne La 24 C4
Milbrook 24 D5
Mill Rd 24 B1
More La 24 B1
Neville Clo 24 A5
New Rd 24 D2
Nightingale Rd 24 A4
Old Chestnut Av 24 B5
Orchard Way 24 C5
Orleans Clo 24 D1
Park Clo 24 A5
Park Rd 24 B3
Pelhams Clo 24 A3
Pelhams Walk 24 A2
Pemberton Pl 24 C2
Penates 24 D3
Portsmouth Rd 24 A6
Raleigh Dri 24 D4
Riverside Dri 24 A3
Rosebriars 24 D4
Sandown Av 24 C3
Sandown Gate 24 D1
Sandown Rd 24 C3
Station Rd 24 D1
Tellisford 24 B3
The Gardens 24 A3
The Mount 24 A5
Vincent Clo 24 B2
Warren Clo 24 C3
Wayneflete Tower Av 24 A2
West Acres 24 A5
West End Gdns 24 A4
West End La 24 A4
Westwood Clo 24 D2
Willowmere 24 C3
Winchester Clo 24 A2
Winterdown Rd 24 A5
Wolsey Gro 24 B3
Wolsey Rd 24 B3
Wood End 24 C1

EWELL

Aragon Av 25 C4
Arundel Av 25 D4
Banstead Rd 25 D5
Beaufort Way 25 C3
Beech Walk 25 C5
Beggars Hill 25 B2
Belfield Rd 25 A3
Bevan Park 25 B5
Blenheim Rd 25 A6
Bluegates 25 C2
Boleyn Av 25 C4
Bradford Dri 25 B
Bradstock Rd 25 C
Briarwood Rd 25 C
Bridleway Clo 25 D
Broadway 25 C
Brook Mead 25 A
Burford La 25 D
Calverley Rd 25 C
Carpenters Clo 25 B4
Castle Av 25 C4
Castle Par 25 C3
Castle Way 25 C4
Castlemaine Av 25 D3
Chadacre Rd 25 C1
Chatefield 25 C4
Cheam Rd 25 C4
Chelwood Clo 25 B6
Chessington Rd 25 A4
Chichester Ct 25 B3
Church St 25 C3
Chuters Gro 25 B6
Clandon Clo 25 B1
Cleves Av 25 D3
Conaways Clo 25 C4
Conifer Park 25 A6
Corbet Rd 25 A5
Courtlands Dri 25 A1
Cullerne Clo 25 B4
Cumberland Clo 25 A4
Cumnor Gdns 25 C2
Curvan Clo 25 B4
Dee Way 25 A4
Dell La 25 C1
Dell Rd 25 C1
Dirdene Clo 25 B6
Dirdene Gdns 25 B6
Dirdene Gro 25 A6
Dorling Dri 25 B6
East St 25 A6
Eastcroft Rd 25 A3
Elm Rd 25 B2
Elmstead Clo 25 A1
Elmwood Clo 25 C2
Elmwood Dri 25 C2
Epsom Rd 25 B5
Ernest Cotts 25 B3
Ewell By-Pass 25 C3
Ewell Court Av 25 A1
Ewell Downs Rd 25 C6
Ewell House Gro 25 B4
Ewell Park Way 25 C2
Fairfax Av 25 D4
Fairfield Way 25 A1
Fairview Rd 25 B6
Farriers Clo 25 A6
Farriers Rd 25 A6
Fennells Mead 25 B3
First Av 25 A3
Firswood Av 25 A1
Garbrand Walk 25 B4
Gayfere Rd 25 C1
Gibraltar Cres 25 A4
Glenwood Rd 25 C1
Glyn Clo 25 C4
Green Lanes 25 A3
Hampton Gro 25 B5
Hazel Mead 25 C4
Hessle Gro 25 B5
High St 25 B3
Highfield Dri 25 B2
Hillside Rd 25 D4
Hollymoor La 25 A3
Holman Ct 25 C3
Howard Av 25 C4
INDUSTRIAL ESTATES:
Nonsuch Ind Est 25 A5
Kenilworth Rd 25 B1
Kiln La 25 A6
Kingston Rd 25 A1
Kirby Clo 25 B1
Lakehurst Rd 25 A1
Lakeside 25 A1
Langton Av 25 B5
Larby Pl 25 A5
Leith Rd 25 A6
Lintons La 25 A6
London Rd 25 C2
Longmead Rd 25 A4
Lyncroft Gdns 25 B4
Manor Dri 25 A1
Marsh Av 25 A4
Masons Ct 25 B4
Meadow Walk 25 B2
Meadowview Rd 25 A3
Middle Clo 25 A6
Middle La 25 A6
Mill La 25 B3
Mill Rd 25 B6

ill View Clo	25 B3
ongers La	25 B5
ount Pleasant	25 B4
onsuch Court Av	25 C4
orthcroft Rd	25 A2
orthfields	25 A5
ursery Clo	25 A5
akland Way	25 A1
ld House Clo	25 B5
ld Schools La	25 B3
x La	25 C4
ark Av East	25 C2
ark Av West	25 C2
ark Hill Rd	25 B6
arr Av	25 D4
arry Clo	25 C2
etersfield Clo	25 B5
ortland Pl	25 A6
ortway	25 C4
ortway Cres	25 C4
reston Dri	25 A1
rimrose Walk	25 B2
urberry Gro	25 B5
Queensmead Av	25 D4
Reigate Rd	25 C5
River Way	25 A1
Riverholme Dri	25 A3
Rotherwyke Clo	25 C1
St James Av	25 B5
St Marys Clo	25 B3
St Normans Way	25 C5
Seaforth Gdns	25 B1
Seymour Av	25 D4
Shaw Clo	25 B5
Shere Av	25 D4
Shortcroft Rd	25 B2
Somerset Clo	25 A4
South Mead	25 A2
Spring Ct	25 B3
Spring Mews	25 D3
Spring St	25 B4
Springfield Rd	25 B4
Stane Way	25 B4
Station App, Ewell East	25 C5
Station App, Stoneleigh	25 B1
Station Av	25 A3
Stoneleigh Park Rd	25 B1
Stones Rd	25 A6
Sunnymede Av	25 A3
Tayles Hill	25 B2
The Drive	25 B2
The Glade	25 C1
The Green	25 C6
The Grove	25 B4
The Hawthorns	25 B2
The Headway	25 B4
The Kingsway	25 B5
The Mount	25 B5
The Orchard	25 B2
The Ridings	25 B3
The Rise	25 B4
Vicarage La	25 C3
Victoria Pl	25 A6
Village Gdns	25 B4
Walsingham Gdns	25 B1
Waverley Rd	25 C1
Welbeck Clo	25 C3
West Gdns	25 A5
West Mead	25 A2
West St	25 A4
Westmorland Clo	25 A4
Weston Rd	25 A5
Willow Way	25 A1
Windmill Av	25 B6
Windmill End	25 B6
Windmill La	25 B6
Woodland Clo	25 A2
Woodstone Av	25 C1
Yeomanry Clo	25 A6

FARNHAM

Abbey St	26 C3
Acheulian Clo	26 C6
Adams Park Rd	26 D1
Alfred Rd	26 C4
Arthur Clo	26 C4
Arthur Rd	26 C4
Aveley Clo	26 C6
Aveley La	26 C6
Avon Rd	26 B4
Babbs Mead	26 B4
Baldreys	26 B5
Bardsley Dri	26 A5
Bear La	26 C4
Beaufort Rd	26 C2
Beavers Clo	26 A3
Beavers Hill	26 A3
Beavers Rd	26 A3
Beldham Rd	26 A6
Bishops Mead	26 B3
*Borelli Mews Yd, Borough	26 C3
Borough	26 C3
Brambleton Av	26 B5
Bridgefield	26 D3
Brightwells Rd	26 C2
*Brookmead Ct, Pengilly Rd	26 B4
Broomleaf Corner	26 D3
Broomleaf Rd	26 D3
Byworth Rd	26 A3
Castle Field	26 B2
Castle Hill	26 B2
Castle St	26 B2
Cedarways	26 B6
Cherry Tree Clo	26 C2
Chestnut Av	26 A5
Cobbetts Way	26 A6
College Gdns	26 B3
Coxbridge Meadows	26 A4
Crondall La	26 A3
Crosby Way	26 B3
Darvills La	26 D3
Dogflud Way	26 C2
Dollis Dri	26 D2
Downing St	26 C3
East St	26 C2
Edward Rd	26 C6
Fairholm Gdns	26 C4
Falkner Rd	26 B3
Farnham By-Pass	26 A4
Fenns Yd	26 B3
*Ferns Mead, Pengilly Rd	26 B4
Firfield Rd	26 B6
Firgrove Ct	26 C4
Firgrove Hill	26 C4
Folly Hill	26 B1
Forge Clo	26 D2
Fox Rd	26 D6
Fox Yd	26 B3
Frensham Rd	26 D6
Garth Clo	26 D6
Great Austins Way	26 D5
Green La	26 A5
Greenfield Rd	26 A6
Greenhill Clo	26 A6
Greenhill Rd	26 D5
Greenhill Way	26 A0
Grove End Rd	26 B5
Guildford Rd	26 D2
Hale Rd	26 D2
Hazell Rd	26 A3
High Park Rd	26 C2
Highfield Clo	26 B6
Highlands Clo	26 B6
Hill View Rd	26 A3
Hillary Clo	26 B5
Hillary Rd	26 B6
Hookstile La	26 C4
INDUSTRIAL ESTATES:	
Farnham Bus. Pk	26 B4
Kimbers La	26 D2
Lancaster Av	26 D4
Langham Ct	26 C6
Lion & Lamb Yd	26 B3
Lion & Lamb Way	26 B3
Little Austin Rd	26 D5
Little Green La	26 A6
Long Bri	26 C3
*Long Garden Mews, Long Garden Walk E	26 B2
*Long Garden Pl, Long Garden Walk E	26 B2
Long Garden Walk	26 B3
Long Garden Walk E	26 B2
Long Garden Walk W	26 B3
Long Garden Way	26 B2
Longley Rd	26 D4
Lower Church La	26 C3
Lower South View	26 C2
Lynch Rd	26 D3
Lynton Clo	26 A6
Marston Rd	26 A3
Mavins Rd	26 D5
Mead La	26 B3
*Meadow Bank, Pengilly Rd	26 B4
Merlins Clo	26 C4
Middle Av	26 D5
Middle Bourne La	26 C6
Middlefield	26 C4
Mike Hawthorn Dri	26 C2
Morley Rd	26 C4
Mount Pleasant	26 A3
Oak Ct	26 C4
Old Church La	26 D6
Old Farnham La	26 D5
Old Park La	26 A1
Osborn Rd	26 D1
Parfitts Clo	26 A3
Park Rd	26 D1
Park Row	26 C2
Pengilly Rd	26 B4
Pilgrims Clo	26 B5
Potters Gate	26 B3
Red Lion La	26 B4
Ridgway Hill Rd	26 C5
Ridgway Rd	20 C5
Riverside Park	26 C2
Ryle Rd	26 B5
St Georges Rd	26 D4
St James Av	26 D2
St James Ter	26 C2
St Johns Rd	26 C5
Saxon Croft	26 C3
Searle Rd	26 C3
Sheephouse	26 C5
Shortheath Rd	26 B6
Snailslynch	26 D3
South St	26 C3
Southern Way	26 D4
Station Hill	26 C3
Station Rd	26 C4
Stephendale Rd	26 D1
Stoke Hills	26 C2
Stream Farm Clo	26 D6
Summer Rd	26 C2
Swingate Rd	26 D5
Talbot Rd	26 B3
The Buntings	26 A5
The Chantrys	26 A2
The Close	26 D4
The Cobbetts	26 A6
The Drive	26 C6
The Fairfield	26 D3
The Hart	26 B3
The Hatches	26 A5
The Lindens	26 D4
Thorold Rd	26 C2
Three Stiles La	26 A3
Thurbans Way	26 A6
Tilford Rd	26 D4
Timber Clo	26 B3
Tor Rd	26 A3
Trafalgar Ct	26 C4
Trebor Av	26 C6
Underhill La	26 C6
Union Rd	26 C3
Upper Church La	26 C3
Upper South Vw	26 C2
Upper Way	26 B5
Vicarage Clo	26 D6
Vicarage Hill	26 D6
Vicarage La	26 B3
Victoria Rd	26 C3
Waverley La	26 D3
Waynflete La	26 A3
Wessex Pl	26 C4
West End Gro	26 A3
West St	26 A4
Weybank Clo	26 C2
Weydon Hill Clo	26 B4
Weydon Hill Rd	26 C5
Weydon La	26 A5
Weydon Mill La	26 B4
Whitlet Clo	26 B4
Winton Rd	26 D1
Woolmead	26 C2
Wykeham Rd	26 C2
York Rd	26 C4

FRIMLEY

Abbetts La	27 A2
Albany Pk	27 A4
Alphington Av	27 D4
Alphington Grn	27 D4
Ansell Rd	27 C5
Apex Dri	27 B4
April Clo	27 A3
Armitage Dri	27 D4
Badgers Copse	27 C2
Badgerwood Dri	27 B3
Bailey Clo	27 B5
Bain Av	27 A3
Balmoral Dri	27 D5
Barnard Clo	27 C5
Barnes Rd	27 C5
Bassett Clo	27 D5
Bayfield Av	27 C3
Beech Av	27 C1
Beech Farm La	27 D1
Belmont Rd	27 A1
Belvoir Clo	27 D4
Bicknell Rd	27 C3
Birchfields	27 A1
Blackwater Valley Rd	27 A5
Blythwood Dri	27 C3
Bowling Green Ct	27 C6
Brackendale Clo	27 C2
Brackendale Rd	27 B1
Braemar Clo	27 D5
Bret Harte Rd	27 C4
Bridgemead	27 B5
Bristow Rd	27 A2
Broadlands	27 D5
Broughton Mews	27 D4
Buckingham Way	27 D4
Burleigh Rd	27 B5
Burrel Rd	27 B5
Caernarvon	27 D5
Campbell Pl	27 D2
Carisbrooke	27 D5
Caroline Way	27 D4
Castle Clo	27 D1
Castle Rd	27 D1
Cedar La	27 B5
Chantry Ct	27 B4
Chilham Clo	27 D5
Chillingham Way	27 A1
Chobham Rd	27 C3
Church Rd	27 B4
Coach Horse Clo	27 C2
Connop Way	27 D2
Conway Clo	27 D4
Coombe Clo	27 C5
Corfe Gdns	27 D4
Croft Way	27 D3
Cromwell Way	27 A6
Danebury Walk	27 D5
Dell Gro	27 D3
Denton Rd	27 C3
Donnington Clo	27 A1
Dunbar Rd	27 D6
Elgin Way	27 D5
Fairfax Rd	27 A6
Fairfield Dri	27 C2
Farm Rd	27 C3
Farnborough Rd	27 A6
Farrell Clo	27 A2
Felbridge Clo	27 D4
Ferniehurst	27 D1
Field La	27 C4
Forest Hills	27 A1
Frimley Green Rd	27 C6
Frimley Grove	27 C4
Frimley Grove Gdns	27 C4
Frimley High St	27 B5
Frimley Rd	27 A2
Garrick Way	27 C6
Gilbert Rd	27 B4
Glamis Clo	27 D6
Glynns Wood	27 D2
Goddards La	27 A2
Golf Dri	27 D1
Gordon Av	27 A1
Gordon Cres	27 A1
Gordon Rd	27 A1
Gorse Rd	27 C3
Greenbank Way	27 B3
Green Leas	27 C3
Grove Cross	27 B4
Grovefields Av	27 C4
Hale Way	27 B5
Hanover Clo	27 C4
Hawkswood Av	27 D3
Hawley La	27 A6
Hawthorn Rd	27 D3
Heatherdale Rd	27 B1
Heathermead	27 D3
Heenan Clo	27 C6
Henley Dri	27 C6
Hermitage Clo	27 D4
High Beeches	27 B3
Hillside Cres	27 D6
Holly Hedge Clo	27 C3
Holly Hedge Rd	27 C3
Holly Tree Gdns	27 B5
Holt Clo	27 A6
INDUSTRIAL ESTATES:	
Farnborough Gate Retail Park	27 A6
Frimley Business Pk	27 A5
Ingledell	27 C1
James Rd	27 A3
James Way	27 A3
Kenmore Clo	27 B5
Kenton Clo	27 D3
Kilmartin Gdns	27 D4
Kingsclear Pk	27 B1
Kingsley Av	27 B2
Lakeland Dri	27 C4
Lanark Clo	27 D3
Lancaster Way	27 A6
Latham Av	27 C3
Lauder Clo	27 C3
Laurel Clo	27 B1
Le Marchant Rd	27 D2
Lendore Rd	27 B5
Leonard Clo	27 B5
Linkway	27 A1
Longmeadow	27 D2
Longford	27 B1
Lyon Way	27 A4
Manbury Way	27 A2
Marston Clo	27 A6
Martin Way	27 C4
Maybury Clo	27 B5
Meadway	27 D3
Melville Av	27 D4
Merry Wood Pk	27 D1
Middlemoor Rd	27 C5
Middlemore Clo	27 D5
Montrose Clo	27 C3
Moor Rd	27 D5
Morton Clo	27 D6
Mulgrave Rd	27 D3
Murrells La	27 A2
Nairn Clo	27 C3
Newlands Rd	27 A4
Norwich Av	27 C2
Nursery Clo	27 D8
Oakway Dri	27 C4
Old Pasture Rd	27 D2
Old Pond Clo	27 A4
Oldbury Clo	27 D5
Oriel Hill	27 B1
Osbourne Clo	27 D6
Overdale Rise	27 C2
Pans Gdns	27 D1
Park Av	27 A1
Park Rd	27 A1
Parkstone Dri	27 A1
Parkway	27 A2
Parsonage Way	27 C4
Partridge Clo	27 C4
Petworth Clo	27 D6
Pine Av	27 B1
Pine Mount Rd	27 B1
Portsmouth Rd	27 B4
Prince Charles Cres	27 A5
Purley Way	27 C5
Raleigh Way	27 D2
Rideway Clo	27 A1
Ringwood Rd	27 A6
Robins Row	27 A1
Rudd Hall Rise	27 C2
Russett Gdns	27 C2
Saddlewood	27 A1
St Andrews Way	27 D6
St Catherines Rd	27 D4
St Peters Way	27 D6
Sandown Dri	27 C3
Sandringham Way	27 D6
Sayers Clo	27 C6
Scarlet Oaks Rd	27 C2
Shamrock Clo	27 C5
Sheridan Rd	27 B5
Sherwin Cres	27 A5
Stamford Av	27 D4
Station Rd	27 A5
Stirling Clo	27 C3
Stonehouse Rise	27 C4
Stoneleigh Ct	27 D4
Sturdee Clo	27 C4
Sycamore Clo	27 C4
Sycamore Dri	27 C4
Tekels Av	27 B1
Tekels Way	27 D2
The Cloisters	27 B4
The Close	27 B5
The Grove	27 C4
The Parade	27 B5
Tichborne Clo	27 D2
Tintagel Dri	27 D4
Tiverton Way	27 D4
Tomlins Av	27 D3
Trafford Rd	27 B5
Verran Rd	27 B2
Wandsyke Clo	27 D5
Warren Rise	27 D3
Watchetts Dri	27 C1
Watchetts Lake Clo	27 B2

Watchetts Rd	27 A2
Waverley Clo	27 D1
Ways End	27 C1
Well Clo	27 A1
Whims Clo	27 A1
Wilderness Rd	27 C3
Wilders Clo	27 C3
Wilmot Way	27 D2
Wilton Rd	27 A3
Windsor Way	27 D5
Winterbourne Walk	27 D5
Wood Rd	27 A4
Worsley Rd	27 D6
Yewtree Walk	27 D4

GODALMING

Aarons Hill	28 A3
Allden Cotts	28 B3
Alvernia Clo	28 C5
Angel Ct	28 C5
Ashtead La	28 C6
Badgers Hollow	28 C1
Ball Field Rd	28 C1
Bargate Rise	28 B3
Beech Way	28 D4
Birchanger	28 D4
Borough Rd	28 C3
Braemar Clo	28 C4
Briarpatch	28 C1
Bridge Rd	28 D3
Bridge St	28 D3
Brighton Rd	28 D3
Busbridge La	28 D4
Butts La	28 C4
Carlos St	28 D3
Catteshall La	28 D5
Chalk Rd	28 C2
Charterhouse Clo	28 D4
Charterhouse Rd	28 B1
Church St	28 C3
Cliffe Rise	28 B5
Cliffe Road	28 B5
College Hill	28 B5
Coopers Rise	28 B4
Cow La	28 C3
Croft Rd	28 C3
Crownpits La	28 D5
Dean Rd	28 C1
Deanery Rd	28 C2
Dormers Clo	28 C1
Duncombe Rd	28 C5
Eashing La	28 A4
Farncombe St	28 D1
Fernden Rise	28 D1
Filmer Gro	28 D2
Flambards Way	28 C3
Foxdene	28 B5
Franklyn Rd	28 A4
Frith Hill Rd	28 C1
Great George St	28 D3
Greenhill Clo	28 C4
Grosvenor Rd	28 D4
Grove Rd	28 B4
Harvest Hill	28 C3
Hawthorn Rd	28 A5
Heathfield Clo	28 C5
High Ridge	28 C5
High St	28 C3
Holloway Hill	28 C4
Holly La	28 B4
Huntsman La	28 C5
Ivybank	28 D1
Jubilee St	28 D3
Knoll Quarry	28 D1
Knoll Rd	28 C1
Ladywell Hill	28 C6
Latimer Rd	28 D3
Little Tumners Ct	28 D1
Lower Manor Rd	28 D1
Manor Gdns	28 D1
Maple Hatch Clo	28 D5
Marshall Rd	28 D1
Mary Vale	28 C5
May Clo	28 A5
Mill La	28 C3
Miltons Cres	28 A5
Minster Rd	28 C6
Mint St	28 C3
Monteagle	28 C4
Moss La	28 C3
New Way	28 C3
Nightingale Rd	28 D2
North St	28 D1
Oakdene Rd	28 C5
Ockford Ct	28 B4

Ockford Ridge	28 A4
Ockford Road	28 B4
Old Barn View	28 B4
Old Lodge Clo	28 A4
Old Station Way	28 D2
Orford Dri	28 B4
Ormonde Rd	28 D1
Park Chase	28 D6
Park Rd	28 C5
Parkfield	28 D5
Peperharow Rd	28 B2
Phillips Clo	28 C5
*Phillips Cotts,	
Aarons Hill	28 B3
Portsmouth Rd	28 A6
Pound Clo	28 D3
Pound Rd	28 D3
Primrose Ridge	28 A5
Pullman Way	28 B5
Quarry Hill	28 A4
Quarter Mile Rd	28 D6
Queen St	28 C3
Ramsden Rd	28 C4
Richmond Rd	28 D1
Sandy La	28 C1
Sellars Hill	28 C1
Seymour Rd	28 A4
Shackstead La	28 B4
Shadyhanger Rd	28 D1
Simmonds Cotts	28 A3
South Hill	28 D3
South St	28 C3
Station App	28 C3
Station Rd	28 C3
Stonepit Clo	28 B3
Summerhill	28 C1
Summerhouse Clo	28 C4
Summerhouse Rd	28 C4
The Avenue	28 D5
The Brambles	28 C1
The Burys	28 D3
The Drive	28 D5
The Horseshoe	28 B4
The Mint	28 C3
The Paddock	28 D5
Tottenham Rd	28 D1
Town End St	28 D3
Tuesley Corner	28 C5
Tuesley La	28 C4
Twycross Rd	28 C1
Underhill Clo	28 D4
Upper Manor Rd	28 D1
Valley Vw	28 C4
Vicarage Way	28 C3
Victoria Rd	28 D3
Walnut Tree Gdns	28 D1
Waterside La	28 B4
Westbrook Rd	28 B2
Weston Ct	28 D1
Wharf St	28 D3
Windy Wood	28 C5
Wolseley Rd	28 D2
Woolsack Way	28 D3

GODSTONE

Bakers Mead	29 C2
Bay Path	29 C4
Bell Meadow	29 B5
Bletchingley Rd	29 A4
Bullbeggars La	29 C5
Church La	29 C4
Court Rd	29 C4
Crowhurst Mead	29 C3
Dewlands	29 C3
Eastbourne Rd	29 C5
Enterdent Rd	29 C6
Evelyn Gdns	29 C3
Flower La	29 D3
Fosterdown	29 B1
Gangers Hill	29 D1
Godstone By-Pass	29 C2
Godstone Hill	29 B1
Hickmans Clo	29 B5
High St	29 B3
Hillbrow Cotts	29 C5
Ivy Mill Clo	29 B5
Ivy Mill La	29 A5
Leigh Place La	29 D5
Lindley Rd	29 C3
Love La	29 C5
North Park La	29 A4
Ockleys Mead	29 C3
Oxted Rd	29 C3
Quarry Rd	29 B1
Riders Way	29 C4

Rogers Mead	29 B5
Salisbury Rd	29 B3
Selbourne Sq	29 C2
The Green	29 B4
The Priory	29 B4
Tilburston Hill Rd	29 C5
Tylers Clo	29 B3
Waterhouse La	29 A5
Willow Way	29 B5

GREAT BOOKHAM/ LITTLE BOOKHAM

Admirals Rd	30 E4
Allen Rd	30 D3
Amey Dri	30 E2
Ashdale	30 E3
Ashley Clo	30 B3
Ashwood Pk	30 E1
Atwood	30 A1
Barn Meadow La	30 B1
Barrett Rd	30 F2
Beales Rd	30 D4
Beattie Clo	30 B1
Beckley Par	30 E3
Bennetts Farm Pl	30 B2
Blackthorne Rd	30 E3
Bookham Gro	30 D3
Bracken Clo	30 B1
Brodrick Gro	30 C3
Browning Rd	30 F2
Burney Rd	30 E2
Burnhams Rd	30 A1
Burrows Clo	30 B1
Camilla Clo	30 D2
Candy Croft	30 D3
Childs Hall Clo	30 B3
Childs Hall Dri	30 B2
Childs Hall Rd	30 B2
Chilmans Dri	30 D3
Christy La	30 D3
Church Rd	30 B1
Crabtree Clo	30 E3
Crabtree La	30 E3
Dawnay Rd	30 E3
Dean Walk	30 D3
Dorking Rd	30 D3
Dowlans Clo	30 C4
Dowlans Rd	30 D4
Downs View Rd	30 E4
Downs Way	30 E3
Durleston Park Dri	30 E2
East St	30 D3
Eastwick Dri	30 D1
Eastwick Park Av	30 D2
Eastwick Rd	30 B1
Edenside Rd	30 B1
Edgeley	30 A1
Elmswood	30 B1
Fairfield Cotts	30 D3
Fairlawn	30 B2
Fernlea	30 D1
Fife Way	30 C2
Fiona Clo	30 C1
Flint Clo	30 E3
Fox Covert	30 F2
Fox La	30 B2
Gardeners Walk	30 D4
Gilmais	30 E3
Glebe Clo	30 C3
Greathurst End	30 C1
Greenacres	30 C1
Greenway	30 D1
Greville Ct	30 D2
Griffin Way	30 C3
Groveside	30 C4
Groveside Clo	30 C4
Guildford Rd	30 B4
Halepit Rd	30 E3
Hales Oak	30 E3
Harecroft	30 E1
Hawkwood Dell	30 C3
Hawkwood Rise	30 C3
Hazel Way	30 E1
High St	30 D3
Highfields	30 F1
Hilltop Rise	30 E3
Howard Rd	30 E4
Huntsmans Clo	30 F2
INDUSTRIAL ESTATES:	
Bookham Ind Est	30 B1
Kennel Clo	30 E1
Kennel La	30 E1
Keswick Rd	30 E2
Kidborough Down	30 C4
Lang Clo	30 D1

Leatherhead Rd	30 E3
Lime Tree Clo	30 C1
Little Bookham St	30 B1
Long Copse Clo	30 D1
Long Meadow	30 B3
Longheath Dri	30 A2
Lower Rd	30 A3
Lower Shott	30 C3
Maddox La	30 A1
Maddox Pk	30 A1
Manor House La	30 A4
Maplehurst	30 F1
Mead Cres	30 C2
Meadowside	30 C1
Medefield	30 F1
Merrylands Rd	30 B1
Middlemead Clo	30 C3
Middlemead Rd	30 B2
Mill Clo	30 C2
Milton Way	30 C1
Murrelles Walk	30 C1
Newenham Rd	30 C3
Norbury Way	30 E3
Oakbank	30 F1
Oakdene Clo	30 E4
Oakdene Rd	30 B2
Oaklands	30 F1
Orchard End	30 E2
Oveton Way	30 D3
Park Clo	30 F1
Park Grn	30 C1
Park Vw	30 C2
Park Way	30 C1
Parklands	30 C1
Pelham Way	30 E3
Pine Dean	30 D2
Pine Walk	30 D1
Polesden View	30 D4
Post House La	30 C2
Priors Mead	30 E2
Proctor Gdns	30 D3
Rectory La	30 B3
Richmond Clo	30 E1
Richmond Way	30 E1
Ridgelands	30 F1
Roger Simmons Clo	30 E3
St Nicholas Av	30 D2
Sayers Clo	30 E1
Sharon Clo	30 C1
Sheri Jans Rd	30 E3
Sole Farm Av	30 B2
Sole Farm Clo	30 B2
Sole Farm Rd	30 B2
Solecote	30 C2
South End	30 E3
Southey Ct	30 D1
Spring Gro	30 D1
Squirrels Grn	30 C1
Stone Hill Clo	30 C3
Styles End	30 D4
Sumner Clo	30 F2
Swanns Meadow	30 C3
Ten Acres	30 F2
Ten Acres Clo	30 F2
The Approach	30 B1
The Blackburn	30 B2
The Garstons	30 B1
The Green	30 F2
The Lorne	30 B2
The Paddocks	30 D3
The Park	30 C1
The Ridge	30 F1
The Ridgeway	30 F1
The Spinney	30 D2
Timber Clo	30 E4
Townshott Clo	30 C3
Tudor Clo	30 C2
Turville Clo	30 D3
Twelve Acre Clo	30 B1
Vicarage Clo	30 D1
Vincent Clo	30 D1
Water La	30 A3
Wells Clo	30 E2
West Down	30 D4
White Way	30 D3

GUILDFORD

Abbot Rd	31 C5
Acacia Rd	31 C2
Addison Rd	31 D4
Agraria Rd	31 A4
Alexandra Pl	31 D4
Alexandra Ter	31 D4
Angel Gate	31 C4
Annandale Rd	31 A5

Ardmore Av	31 A
Ardmore Ho	31 A
Ardmore Way	31 A
Artillery Rd	31 B
Artillery Ter	31 C
Artington Walk	31 B
Avington Clo	31 D
Baillie Rd	31 D
Bedford Rd	31 B
Beech La	31 B
Beech Lawn	31 D
Berkeley Ct	31 D
Bray Rd	31 A
Bridge St	31 B
Bright Hill	31 C
Brodie Rd	31 D
Bury Fields	31 B
Bury Mews	31 B
Bury St	31 B
Castle Hill	31 C
Castle Sq	31 C
Castle St	31 C
Cathedral Clo	31 A3
Caxton Gdns	31 A
Chantry View Rd	31 C6
Chapel St	31 C
*Charlotte Ct,	
Addison Rd	31 D5
Chertsey St	31 C4
Cheselden Rd	31 D4
Chesham Mews	31 D4
Chesham Rd	31 D4
Chestnut Av	31 B6
Chestnut Rd	31 C2
Chevremont	31 D4
Church Rd	31 B3
Churchill Rd	31 D3
Clandon Rd	31 D3
*Clifford Manor Rd,	
Pilgrims Way	31 D6
Cline Rd	31 D4
College Rd	31 C4
Commercial Rd	31 B4
Cooper Rd	31 D4
Cross Lanes	31 D3
Crown Heights	31 C6
Dapdune Ct	31 B3
Dapdune Rd	31 B3
Deerbarn Rd	31 A1
Dene Rd	31 C3
Denmark Rd	31 C3
Denzil Rd	31 A4
Devon Bank	31 B5
Drummond Rd	31 B3
Dunsdon Av	31 A4
Eagle Rd	31 C3
Eastgate Gdns	31 C4
Echo Pit Rd	31 D6
Ennismore Av	31 D3
Epsom Rd	31 D4
Europa Park Rd	31 B1
Falcon Rd	31 C3
Farnham Rd	31 A5
Ferry La	31 B6
Finch Rd	31 C3
Flower Walk	31 B5
Fort Rd	31 C5
Foxenden Rd	31 C3
Friary Br	31 B4
Friary St	31 B4
Friary Vw	31 B3
Gardner Rd	31 B3
Genyn Rd	31 A4
George Rd	31 C3
Glebe Ct	31 D3
Great Quarry	31 C5
Guildford Park Av	31 A4
Guildford Park Rd	31 A4
Guildown Av	31 A6
Guildown Rd	31 A6
Hamilton Gordon Ct	31 B2
Hanover Ct	31 C1
Harvey Rd	31 C4
Haydon Pl	31 C4
Heather Clo	31 A1
High Pewley	31 D5
High St	31 C4
Hillside Ct	31 C4
Hitherbury Clo	31 B6
Hunter Rd	31 D4
Hurst Croft	31 D6
INDUSTRIAL ESTATES:	
Guildford Business Pk	31 A2
Ladymead Retail	
Centre	31 B1
Riverside Business	
Centre	31 B3
Iveagh Rd	31 A4

enner Rd 31 D4
osephs Rd 31 B2
ernel Ct 31 B3
ings Rd 31 C3
adymead 31 B2
angley Clo 31 B2
aundry Rd 31 B4
awn Rd 31 B5
eapale La 31 C4
eapale Rd 31 C4
eas Rd 31 B3
ido Rd 31 C2
inden Rd 31 B2
ondon Rd 31 D4
ondon Sq 31 D3
udlow Rd 31 A4
ynwood 31 A4
Madrid Rd 31 A4
Manor Cres 31 A1
Manor Gdns 31 A1
Manor Rd 31 A1
Maple Gro 31 C1
Mareschal Rd 31 B5
Margaret Rd 31 B3
Markenfield Rd 31 B3
Market St 31 C4
Martyr Rd 31 C4
Mary Rd 31 B3
Mathion Ct 19 H3
Melville Ct 31 B6
Middleton Ind Est Rd 31 A2
Middleton Rd 31 A2
*Milkhouse Gate, Sydenham Rd 31 C4
Mill La 31 C4
Millbrook 31 B4
Millmead 31 B5
Millmead Ter 31 B5
Minster Gdns 31 C3
Mount Pl 31 B4
Mount Pleasant 31 B5
Mountside 31 A6
Nethermount 31 A5
Nettles Ter 31 C3
Nightingale Rd 31 C3
North St 31 B4
Northdown La 31 D6
Old Palace Rd 31 A4
Onslow Rd 31 C3
Onslow St 31 B4
Oxford Rd 31 C4
Oxford Ter 31 C4
Pannells Ct 31 C4
Park Chase 31 D3
Park Rd 31 C3
Park St 31 B4
Parkhurst Rd 31 A1
Parkway 31 C2
Percy Rd 31 A1
Pewley Bank 31 D4
Pewley Hill 31 C5
Pewley Point 31 D5
Pewley Way 31 D4
Phoenix Ct 31 B4
Pilgrims Way 31 C6
Poltimore Rd 31 A4
Portsmouth Rd 31 B6
Poundfield 31 C2
Poyle Rd 31 C5
Priory Ct 31 B6
Quarry St 31 C4
Queens Rd 31 C3
Recreation Rd 31 B2
Ridgemount 31 A3
Rivermount Gdns 31 B6
Riverside 31 C1
Riverview 31 B2
Riverwood Gdns 31 B1
Rookwood Ct 31 B5
Rupert Rd 31 A4
St Catherines Dri 31 A6
*St Saviours Pl, Leas Rd 31 B3
Sandalwood 31 A4
Sandfield Ter 31 C4
Sandy La 31 B6
Semaphore Rd 31 D5
Shalford Rd 31 C5
South Hill 31 C5
Springfield Rd 31 C3
Springside Ct 31 B2
Station App 31 D3
Stocton Clo 31 B2
Stocton Rd 31 B2
Stoke Fields 31 C3
Stoke Gro 31 C3
Stoke Mews 31 C3
Stoke Park Ct 31 C3
Stoke Rd 31 C2
Stoughton Rd 31 B1
Stratford Pl 31 C6
Swan La 31 C4
Sycamore Ct 31 D4
Sycamore Rd 31 C2
Sydenham Rd 31 C4
Testard Rd 31 B4
The Bars 31 C4
The Friary 31 B4
The Meadows 31 B6
The Mews 31 B3
The Mount 31 A5
The Piccards 31 B6
*The Shambles, Quarry St 31 C4
*Tilehouse Rd, Pilgrims Way 31 D6
Turnham Clo 31 B6
Tunsgate 31 C4
Tunsgate Sq 31 C4
Upper Guildown Rd 31 A6
Upperton Rd 31 A4
Victoria Rd 31 D3
Walnut Tree Clo 31 B3
Walnut Tree Park 31 B3
Ward St 31 C4
Warren Rd 31 D4
Warwicks Bench 31 C5
Warwicks Bench La 31 D6
Warwicks Bench Rd 31 D6
Waterden Clo 31 D3
Waterden Rd 31 D3
Waterside Mews 31 B1
Wendy Cres 31 A1
West Mount 31 B5
West Rd 31 D4
Weston Rd 31 A2
Wey View Ct 31 B5
Weyside Gdns 31 B1
Weyside Rd 31 A1
Wharf Rd 31 B3
Wherwell Rd 31 B4
William Rd 31 B3
Wodeland Av 31 A5
Woking Rd 31 C1
Woodbridge Hill 31 A1
Woodbridge Mdws 31 B2
Woodbridge Rd 31 B2
Woodcote 31 A6
Worplesdon Rd 31 A1
Wych Elm Rise 31 D5
York Rd 31 C3

HASLEMERE

Azalea Dri 32 B1
Bartholomew Clo 32 E1
Beaufield Gate 32 F2
Beech Rd 32 E2
Border Rd 32 A3
Braeside Clo 32 B1
Bridge Rd 32 E2
Buffbeards La 32 A2
Bunch La 32 C2
Bunch Way 32 C2
Camelsdale Rd 32 A4
Cedar Ct 32 D3
Chatsworth Av 32 E1
Cherrimans Orchard 32 A3
Cherry Tree Av 32 B2
Chestnut Av 32 E2
Chilcroft Rd 32 B2
Chiltern Clo 32 D4
Church La 32 E2
Church Rd, Haslemere 32 E2
Church Rd, Shottermill 32 B3
Cobden La 32 E2
Collards La 32 E3
College Hill 32 E3
College Hill Ter 32 E3
Courts Hill Rd 32 D3
Courts Mount Rd 32 D3
Critchmere Hill 32 A2
Critchmere La 32 A3
Critchmere Vale 32 A3
Dale Vw 32 B3
Deepdene 32 A3
Dell Clo 32 C2
Denbigh Rd 32 F4
Dene Clo 32 E3
Derby Rd 32 D2
Dolphin Clo 32 A2
Eliots Dri 32 A3
Farnham La 32 B1
Field Path 32 E2
Field Way 32 E2
Fox Rd 32 A3
George Denyer Clo 32 E2
Grayswood Rd 32 F2
Hales Field 32 E3
Halfmoon Hill 32 E3
Haste Hill 32 F4
Hazel Dri 32 D3
Hedgehog La 32 C3
Herondale 32 A3
High La 32 D1
High St 32 E3
Highbury Gro 32 E1
Higher Combe Rd 32 F2
Hill Ct 32 D3
Hill Rd 32 E3
Hillside Rd 32 B4
Hindhead Rd 32 A2
Holly Ridge 32 D3
INDUSTRIAL ESTATES:
Weydown Ind Est 32 D2
Junction Pl 32 B3
Kemnal Pk 32 F2
Kiln Fields 32 E1
Kings Rd 32 B3
Linchmere Rd 32 A4
Lion Clo 32 B2
Lion Grn 32 B3
Lion La 32 B2
Lion Mead 32 B3
Liphook Rd 32 A3
Longdene Rd 32 C3
Lower St 32 D3
Lucas Field 32 A3
Mallard Clo 32 A3
Manor Clo 32 A3
Manor Cres 32 A3
Manor Lea 32 A3
Marley Combe Rd 32 B4
Marley La 32 A4
Mead Way 32 B3
Meadow Vale 32 C3
Midhurst Rd 32 C4
Mill Clo 32 A3
Moorfield Rd 32 B4
Museum Hill 32 E3
New Rd 32 B4
Nutcombe 32 A1
Oaklands 32 E2
Old Haslemere Rd 32 E4
Orchard Clo 32 B4
Park Rd 32 E3
Parsons Clo 32 E1
Parsons Grn 32 E1
Pathfields Clo 32 E2
Penwith Dri 32 A4
Peperham Rd 32 E1
Petworth Rd 32 E3
Pine View Clo 32 E1
Pitfold Clo 32 A3
Polecat Hill 32 B1
Polecat Valley 32 B1
Popes Mead 32 E2
Priors Wood 32 B3
Puckshott Way 32 E1
Roe Deer Copse 32 A3
Rosemary Ct 32 E2
St Christophers Grn 32 C3
St Christophers Rd 32 C3
St Stephens Clo, Haslemere 32 E2
St Stephens Clo, Shottermill 32 B3
Sandrock 32 D3
School Rd 32 B4
Scotlands Clo 32 D4
Scotlands Hill 32 E4
Scotlands La 32 D4
Shepherds Hill 32 E3
Shottermill Rd 32 A3
Sickle Mill Rd 32 B3
Sickle Rd 32 B3
Springfarm Rd 32 A4
Station App 32 D3
Stile Gdns 32 B3
Stoatley Hollow 32 C1
Stoatley Rise 32 C1
Sturt Av 32 B4
Sturt Rd 32 B3
Sun Brow 32 B3
Swanbarn Rd 32 F3
Tanners La 32 E2
Tennysons La 32 F4
The Avenue 32 B2
The Meads 32 B3
The Millstream 32 A3
The Paddock 32 C1
The Spinney 32 E1
Three Gates La 32 F2
Timber Mill Ct 32 B3
Trout Rd 32 A3
Underwood Rd 32 B2
Uplands Clo 32 F1
Vicarage La 32 B3
Well La 32 E2
West St 32 E2
Wey Hill 32 C3
Weycombe Rd 32 E1
Weydown Rd 32 D2
Weysprings 32 C2
Whitfield Clo 32 E1
Whitfield Rd 32 E1
Woodlands La 32 B2

HORLEY

*Abinger Keep, Langshott La 33 D2
Airport Way 33 B6
Albert Rd 33 C2
*Albury Keep, Langshott La 33 D2
Arne Gro 33 A1
Ashleigh Clo 33 B3
Aurom Clo 33 D4
Avenue Gdns 33 D4
Avondale Clo 33 B1
Baden Dri 33 A2
Bakehouse Rd 33 B1
Balcombe Gdns 33 D4
Balcombe Rd 33 C2
Barleymead 33 D2
Bay Clo 33 A1
Bayfield Rd 33 A2
Bayhorne La 33 D5
Benhams Clo 33 C1
Benhams Dri 33 C1
Birchwood Clo 33 D2
Blundell Av 33 A2
Bolters Rd 33 B1
Bolters Rd Sth 33 B1
Bonehurst Rd 33 C1
Brackenside 33 D2
Bremner Av 33 A2
Briarswood 33 D2
Brighton Rd 33 A4
*Brockham Keep, Langshott La 33 D2
Brookwood 33 D2
Burton Clo 33 C4
Carters Meade Clo 33 D2
Castle Dri 33 D4
Chaffinch Way 33 A2
Chantry Clo 33 B2
Charlesfield Rd 33 B2
Chatelet Clo 33 C2
Chequers Clo 33 B2
Chequers Dri 33 B2
Chesters 33 A1
Chestnut Rd 33 C1
Cheyne Walk 33 B5
Church Rd 33 B4
Church Walk 33 B4
Churchview Clo 33 A4
Collingwood Clo 33 D1
Consort Way 33 C3
Court Lodge Rd 33 A2
Cranbourne Clo 33 C1
Crescent Way 33 B5
Crewdson Rd 33 D3
Crossway 33 B6
Darenth Way 33 B1
Deepfields 33 B1
Delta Dri 33 C5
Dene Clo 33 A1
Downe Clo 33 A1
Drake Rd 33 A3
Elizabeth Ct 33 C3
Elmtree Clo 33 C2
Emlyn Rd 33 A2
Ewelands 33 D2
Fairfield Av 33 C4
Fairlawns 33 D4
Fairstone Ct 33 D2
Fallowfield Way 33 D2
Ferndown 33 B1
Fieldview 33 D2
Firlands 33 D2
Fishers 33 D2
Furlong Way 33 B6
Gatwick Way 33 B6
Gower Rd 33 A3
Granary Clo 33 B1
Grassmere 33 D2
Greatlake Ct 33 C2
Greenfields Clo 33 A1
Greenfields Rd 33 A1
Grendon Clo 33 B1
Grove Rd 33 A2
Hardy Clo 33 A3
Harrowsley Ct 33 D2
Harvestside 33 D2
Hatchgate 33 B4
Hayfields 33 D2
Heatherlands 33 D2
*Hedingham Clo, Langshott La 33 D2
Heritage Lawn 33 D2
Heronswood Ct 33 C2
Hevers Av 33 B2
High St 33 C3
*Holmbury Keep, Langshott La 33 D2
Homefield Clo 33 C2
Horley Row 33 B2
Hurst Rd 33 A2
Hutchins Farm 33 B1
Hutchins Way 33 B1
Hyperion Walk 33 C5
Kelsby Clo 33 B3
Kidworth Clo 33 B1
Kiln La 33 B1
Kimberley Clo 33 A3
Kings Rd 33 C3
Kingsley Clo 33 B1
Kingsley Rd 33 A1
Ladbroke Rd 33 C1
Lake La 33 D1
Landen Pk 33 A1
Langshott La 33 D2
Le May Clo 33 C2
Lechford Rd 33 B4
Lee St 33 A2
Limes Av 33 D4
Lincoln Clo 33 B4
London Rd 33 A5
Longbridge Gate 33 A6
Longbridge Rd 33 B5
Longbridge Walk 33 B5
Lumley Ct 33 C2
Lumley Rd 33 C2
Manor Clo 33 B3
Manor Dri 33 D3
Massetts Rd 33 B4
Mazecroft 33 D2
Meadow Croft Clo 33 D6
Meadowside 33 D2
Meathgreen Av 33 A1
Meathgreen La 33 A1
Michael Cres 33 C5
Mill Clo 33 A2
Mosford Clo 33 B1
Newland Clo 33 B1
Norfolk Clo 33 B4
North Way 33 A6
Northgate Rd 33 B6
Oakwood Rd 33 C2
Oatlands 33 D2
Oldfield Clo 33 B4
Oldfield Rd 33 B4
Orchard Clo 33 B2
Park Lawn Av 33 D1
Park View 33 B3
Park Way 33 B3
Parkhurst Gro 33 A2
Parkhurst Rd 33 A2
Parsons Clo 33 A2
Perimeter Rd 33 C6
Perimeter Rd North 33 A5
Pine Gdns 33 B4
Povey Cross Rd 33 A5
Powell Clo 33 A2
Poynes Rd 33 A1
Primrose Av 33 C5
Priory Clo 33 B2
Queens Rd 33 B3
Racecourse Way 33 B6
Ramsey Clo 33 A3
*Raymer Walk, Langshott La 33 D2
Reigate Rd 33 A4
Rickwood 33 D2
Ringley Av 33 B3
Riverside 33 B5
Roffey Clo 33 B3
Rosemary Ct 33 A2
Rosemary La 33 D3
*Rudgwick Keep, Langshott La 33 D2
Russell Cres 33 C4
Rutherwick Clo 33 A3
Ryelands 33 D2

St Georges Rd	33 D3	Berkeley Clo	34 B1
St Hildas Clo	33 C2	Berrylands	34 D6
Sangers Dri	33 B3	Birkenhead Av	34 C2
Sarel Way	33 C1	Bishops Hall	34 A3
Saxley	33 D2	Bloomfield Rd	34 B4
Silverlea Gdns	33 D4	Bonner Hill Rd	34 C3
Skipton Way	33 C1	Borough Rd	34 D1
Smallfield Rd	33 D3	Bridle Clo	34 B5
Smallmead	33 D3	Brook St	34 A1
Smithbarn Clo	33 C1	Broom Clo	34 A1
South Par	33 B2	Broom Park	34 A1
Southlands Av	33 B2	Brunswick Rd	34 D2
Spiers Way	33 C5	Buckingham Rd	34 C4
Staffords Pl	33 D4	Burnham St	34 D2
Station App	33 C3	Burritt Rd	34 D3
Station Rd	33 C3	Burton Rd	34 B1
Stockfield	33 D2	Cadogan Rd	34 A6
Stocks Clo	33 D4	Cambridge Gdns	34 D3
Stonecourt Clo	33 D3	Cambridge Grove Rd	34 D3
Suffolk Clo	33 B4	Cambridge Rd	34 C3
Tanyard Way	33 C1	Camm Gdns	34 C3
Tarham Clo	33 A1	Canbury Av	34 C1
Thatchers Clo	33 D1	Canbury Park Rd	34 B2
The Avenue	33 B4	Carlisle Clo	34 D1
The Coronet	33 D5	Castle St	34 B3
The Crescent	33 C5	Catherine Rd	34 A5
The Dell	33 C2	Caversham Rd	34 D3
The Drive	33 C5	Chatham Rd	34 D3
The Fieldings	33 D2	Cherry Wood Clo	34 C1
The Glebe	33 B3	Chesfield Rd	34 C1
The Grove	33 D4	Chesham Rd	34 D2
The Meadway	33 D3	Chesterton Ter	34 D3
The Ridgeway	33 C5	Chestnut Rd	34 B1
The Spinney	33 C1	Cheyne Hill	34 C5
Thornton Clo	33 A3	Chumleigh Walk	34 C5
Thornton Pl	33 A3	Church Gro	34 A2
Todds Clo	33 A1	Church Hill Rd	34 B6
Tower Clo	33 A3	Church Pass	34 B6
Upfield	33 C4	Church Rd	34 C3
Upfield Clo	33 C5	Church St	34 B3
Vicarage La	33 B2	Claremont Gdns	34 B5
Victoria Clo	33 B3	Claremont Rd	34 B6
Victoria Rd	33 B3	Clarence St	34 B3
Waltersville Way	33 D5	Clayhill	34 D5
Waterside	33 B1	Cleaveland Rd	34 A6
Wellington Way	33 B1	Clevedon Rd	34 D3
Wesley Clo	33 B1	Clifton Rd	34 C1
West Leas	33 A1	Cobham Rd	34 D3
*Westcott Keep,		Coombe Rd	34 D2
Langshott La	33 D2	Cowleaze Rd	34 C5
Wheatfield Way	33 D2	Cranes Dri	34 C5
Whitecroft	33 D2	Cranes Park	34 B5
Wickham Clo	33 B2	Cranes Park Av	34 C5
Willow Brean	33 A1	Cranes Park Cres	34 C5
Windmill Clo	33 D3	Craven Rd	34 C2
Wither Dale	33 A1	Crescent Rd	34 D1
Woolverton Clo	33 B5	Cromwell Rd	34 B2
Wolverton Gdns	33 B4	Cross Rd	34 C1
Woodcote	33 D2	Dagmar Rd	34 C1
Woodhayes	23 D2	Dawson Rd	34 C4
Woodroyd Av	33 B4	Deacon Rd	34 C2
Woodroyd Clo	33 B5	Denmark Rd	34 B4
attendon Rd	33 C3	Dolphin Clo	34 B6
Yewtree Clo	33 B1	Dolphin St	34 B2

KINGSTON UPON THAMES

		Downhall Rd	34 A2
		Dudley Rd	34 C3
		East La	34 A4
		East Rd	34 B2
		Eastbury Rd	34 D1
		Eaton Dri	34 D1
Acre Rd	34 B2	Eden St	34 B3
Addison Gdns	34 C5	Eden Walk	34 B3
Adelaide Rd	34 B6	Elm Cres	34 B2
Albert Rd	34 C3	Elm Gro	34 C2
Alexandra Rd	34 D1	Elm Rd	34 C2
Alfred Rd	34 C4	Elton Rd	34 D2
Alric Clo	34 D2	Eureka Rd	34 D3
Anglesea Rd	34 A5	Eversley Rd	34 C5
Archer Clo	34 B1	Ewell Rd	34 C6
Ardhay Gdns	34 B6	Excelsior Rd	34 D3
Arthur Rd	34 D1	Fairfield East	34 C3
Ashdown Rd	34 B3	Fairfield Nth	34 B3
Athelstan Rd	34 C4	Fairfield Pl	34 C4
Auckland Rd	34 C5	Fairfield Rd	34 B3
Avenue Elmers	34 B5	Fairfield Sth	34 B3
Avenue Rd	34 B4	Fairfield West	34 B3
Aycliffe Clo	34 D3	Fassett Rd	34 B4
Balmoral Rd	34 C4	Ferguson Av	34 C6
Bank La	34 B1	Fife Rd	34 B3
Bath Pass	34 B3	Florence Rd	34 C1
Bearfield Rd	34 B1	Franklin Clo	34 A3
Beaufort Rd	34 B5	Geneva Rd	34 C5
Beaumont Clo	34 D1	Gibbon Rd	34 B2
Becketts Pl	34 A2	Gladstone Rd	34 D4
Belgravia Mews	34 B5	Glamorgan Rd	34 A1
Bellevue Rd	34 C4	Glenthorne Rd	34 C4
Bennet Clo	34 A2	Glenville Rd	34 D1
Beresford Rd	34 C2	Gloucester Rd	34 D3

Gordon Rd	34 C2	School Rd	34 A2
Grange Rd	34 B3	Selsdon Clo	34 B6
Grove Clo	34 C5	Seymour Gdns	34 C6
Grove Cres	34 B4	Seymour Rd	34 A2
Grove La	34 B4	Shortlands Rd	34 C1
Grove Rd	34 A6	Skerne Rd	34 B2
Guildford Rd	34 C6	Somerset Rd	34 C3
Hampden Rd	34 D3	Sopwith Way	34 B2
Hampton Court Rd	34 A3	South La	34 A4
Hardman Rd	34 C2	Southsea Rd	34 B5
Hawks Rd	34 C3	Spring Cotts	34 A6
Haylett Gdns	34 B5	Springfield Rd	34 B4
Herbert Rd	34 C4	*Stapleford Clo,	
High St, Hampton Wick	34 A2	Vincent Rd	34 D3
High St, Kingston	34 A3	Station Rd,	
Hill Cres	34 C5	Hampton Wick	34 A2
Hillside Rd	34 D5	Station Rd,	
Home Park Walk	34 A5	Norbiton	34 D2
Horace Rd	34 C4	Staunton Rd	34 C1
Horsefair	34 A3	Steadfast Rd	34 A2
*Hugh Herland,		Surbiton Court	34 A6
Bellevue Rd	34 C4	Surbiton Cres	34 B5
Kent Rd	34 B4	Surbiton Hall Clo	34 B5
King Charles Rd	34 C6	Surbiton Hill Pk	34 C6
Kings Pass	34 A3	Surbiton Hill Rd	34 B5
Kings Rd	34 B1	Thames Side	34 A2
Kingsgate Rd	34 B2	Thames St	34 A3
Kingston Bri	34 A3	The Bittoms	34 B4
Kingston Hall Rd	34 A3	The Crescent	34 B6
Kingston Hill	34 D2	The Crest	34 D6
Knights Pk	34 B3	The Farthings	34 D1
Lady Booth Rd	34 B3	The Keep	34 C1
Lamberts Rd	34 C6	The Mall	34 A6
Linden Cres	34 C3	The Ridge	34 D6
Lingfield Av	34 B5	The Ridings	34 D6
London Rd	34 B3	Thorpe Rd	34 B1
Lovekyn Clo	34 B3	Tithe Barn Clo	34 C2
Lower Ham Rd	34 B1	Tudor Rd	34 D1
Lower Marsh Rd	34 C5	Union St	34 B3
Lower Teddington Rd	34 A1	Upper Teddington Rd	34 A2
Lowther Rd	34 C1	Uxbridge Rd	34 A5
Manorgate Rd	34 D2	Vicarage Rd	34 A2
Maple Rd	34 A6	Victoria Rd	34 C3
Maplehurst Clo	34 B5	Villiers Av	34 C6
Market Pl	34 A3	Villiers Clo	34 C5
Mill Pl	34 C3	Villiers Pth	34 C6
Mill St	34 C4	Villiers Rd	34 C5
Milner Rd	34 B4	Vincent Rd	34 D3
Minerva Rd	34 C4	Vine Clo	34 C6
Minniedale	34 C6	Waights Ct	34 B2
Minstrel Gdns	34 C5	Walter St	34 B2
Monmouth Av	34 A1	Washington Rd	34 D3
Neville Rd	34 D1	Water La	34 A2
New Rd	34 D1	*Watermans Clo,	
Norbiton Av	34 D3	Woodside Rd	34 B4
Normansfield Av	34 A1	Watersplash Clo	34 B4
Oaklea Pass	34 B4	Western Pk	34 B3
Old Bridge St	34 A2	Westfield Rd	34 A6
Orchard Rd	34 B3	Wheatfield Way	34 B3
Osborne Rd	34 B1	Willingham Way	34 D2
Palace Rd	34 A5	Willoughby Rd	34 C1
Palmer Cres	34 B3	Wimpole Clo	34 D3
Park Farm Rd	34 B1	Windsor Rd	34 B1
Park Rd,		Wolverton Av	34 D2
Hampton Wick	34 A2	Wood St	34 B2
Park Rd, Kingston	34 A2	Woodbines Av	34 A4
Park Rd, Surbiton	34 C6	Woodside Rd	34 B1
Parklands	34 C6	Wychelm Pass	34 C1
Penrhyn Rd	34 B5	Wyndham Rd	34 C1
Pine Walk	34 D6	York Rd	34 C1
Piper Rd	34 D3		
Portland Rd	34 B4		
Portman Rd	34 B2		

LEATHERHEAD

Pratts Pass	34 B3		
Princes Rd	34 D1		
Queen Elizabeth Rd	34 C3	Agates La	35 D1
Queens Rd	34 D1	Albany Park Rd	35 A1
Raeburn Clo	34 A1	Aperdele Rd	35 B1
Rayleigh Ct	34 D3	Barnett Clo	35 B1
Regent Rd	34 D6	Barnett Wood La	35 B2
Richmond Park Rd	34 B3	Beech Holt	35 C4
Richmond Rd	34 B1	Beechwood Park	35 C4
Riverside Clo	34 A5	Belmont Rd	35 A5
Riverside Walk	34 A3	Bilton Centre Pk	35 A2
Rose Wood Clo	34 D1	Blades Clo	35 D2
Rowlls Rd	34 B4	Boleyn Walk	35 A2
St Georges Rd	34 D1	Bourne Gro	35 D1
St James's Rd, Kingston	34 B3	Bridge St	35 A4
St James's Rd, Surbiton	34 A6	Bull Hill	35 B3
St Johns Rd	34 A2	Byron Pl	35 B4
St Leonards Rd	34 A6	Challenge Ct	35 B1
St Leonards Sq	34 A6	Chantry Clo	35 B4
St Lukes Pass	34 C1	Church Rd	35 B4
St Marks Hill	34 B6	Church St	35 B4
St Pauls Walk	34 D1	Clare Cres	35 B1
St Peters Rd	34 A3	Cleeve Rd	35 A2
School La	34 A2	Clements Mead	35 A1

Clinton Rd	35 C	Linden Gdns	35 B3
Cobham Rd	35 A	Linden Pit Path	35 B3
Copperfield Ct	35 B	Linden Rd	35 B3
Copthorne Rd	35 B	Longshaw	35 A1
Crabtree Dri	35 C	Magazine Pl	35 B4
Cressel Mead	35 C	Mayell Clo	35 C5
Cressel Clo	35 C	Melvin Shaw	35 C3
Daymerslea Ridge	35 C	Middle Rd	35 B3
Dilston Rd	35 A	Mill La	35 A4
Dorking Rd	35 B	Minchin Clo	35 B4
Downs La	35 B	Mole Valley Pl	35 D1
Elm Clo	35 B	North St	35 B3
Elm Dri	35 B	Oak Rd	35 A1
Elm Rd	35 B	Oaks Clo	35 A3
Elmer Cotts	35 A5	Old Station App	35 A3
Elmer Mews	35 A	Orchard Dri	35 D2
Emlyn La	35 A4	Orchard Leigh	35 C4
Epsom Rd	35 C3	Ottways La	35 D1
Ermyn Way	35 D	Owen Pl	35 B4
Fairfield Rd	35 B3	Park Clo	35 B4
Fairfield Walk	35 B3	Park Rise	35 B3
Fairs Rd	35 A1	Parr Clo	35 B4
Firtree Clo	35 D5		
Fir Tree Rd	35 C5		
Fortyfoot Rd	35 C3		
Garden Clo	35 C6		
Garlands Rd	35 C3		
Gaveston Rd	35 A2		
Gimcrack Hill	35 B4		
Glenheadon Clo	35 D5		
Glenheadon Rise	35 D5		
Grange Clo	35 D2		
Grange Mt	35 D2		
Grange Rd	35 D2		
Green La	35 D3		
Guildford Rd	35 A5		
Harriots Clo	35 D2		
Harriotts La	35 C1		
Hatherwood	35 D3		
Hawks Hill	35 A5		
Hawks Hill Clo	35 A5		
Hazelmere Clo	35 B1		
Headley Rd	35 D4		
Heymede	35 C5		
High St	35 B4		
Highfields	35 D1		
Highlands Av	35 C4		
Highlands Clo	35 C4		
Highlands Pk	35 D5		
Highlands Rd	35 C4		
Highwoods	35 C3		
Hilltop Clo	35 C5		
Holly Ct	35 A4		
Homefield Clo	35 C3		
Homelands	35 C3		
Howard Clo	35 C5		
Hulton Clo	35 C5		
INDUSTRIAL ESTATES:			
*Business Pk			
Hazelmere Clo	35 B1		
Business Pk,			
Kingston Rd	35 B2		
Mole Business Pk	35 A3		
Research Area	35 A2		
Kelvin Av	35 A2		
Kingscroft Rd	35 B2		
Kingslea	35 B2		
Kingston Av	35 B3		
Kingston House Gdns	35 B3		
Kingston Rd	35 B1		
Leach Gro	35 C4		
Leatherhead By-Pass	35 C2		
Leatherhead Rd	35 D3		
Leret Way	35 B3		
Levett Rd	35 C2		
Linden Ct	35 B3		

oplar Av 35 C4
oplar Rd 35 C4
ueen Annes Gdns 35 B3
ueen Annes Ter 35 B3
andalls Cres 35 A2
andalls Farm La 35 B2
andalls Park Av 35 A2
andalls Park Dri 35 A3
andalls Rd 35 A2
Reigate Rd 35 D5
Russel Ct 35 B4
St Johns Av 35 B3
St Johns Clo 35 C2
St Johns Rd 35 C3
St Marys Rd 35 B4
St Nicholas Hill 35 B4
Salvation Pl 35 A6
Shires Clo 35 B1
South View Rd 35 D1
Station App 35 A3
Station Rd 35 A3
Summerfield 35 D1
Sunmead Clo 35 A4
Swan Ct 35 B3
Taleworth Clo 35 D2
Taleworth Pk 35 B2
Taleworth Rd 35 D2
Tanners Dean 35 D4
Tate Clo 35 C5
The Crescent 35 B4
The Driftway 35 C5
The Knoll 35 C3
The Murreys 35 D1
The Priors 35 D1
The Withies 35 C2
Thorncroft Dri 35 B5
Tregarthen Pl 35 C0
Tudor Walk 35 A2
Uplands 35 B3
Upper Fairfield Rd 35 B3
Vicarage La 35 B4
Wallis Mews 35 A4
Waterfields 35 B1
Waterway Rd 35 A4
Waverly Pl 35 B4
West Farm Av 35 D1
West Farm Clo 35 C1
West Farm Dri 35 D1
Windfield 35 C2
Windmill Dri 35 C5
Wood End 35 D6
Woodvill Rd 35 C5
Worple Rd 35 C5
Yarm Ct Rd 35 C5
Yarm Way 35 D6
Young St 35 A8

LINGFIELD

Ash Clo 36 C3
Bakers Clo 36 C2
Bakers La 36 C3
Blackberry La 36 B6
Camden Rd 36 C3
Church Rd 36 C3
College Clo 36 B3
Crowhurst Rd 36 B1
Deacons Ct 36 A3
Drivers Mead 36 B4
East Grinstead Rd 36 B4
Edenbrook 36 C3
Felcourt Rd 36 B6
Godstone Rd 36 A2
Green La 36 A4
Grove Rd 36 C2
Gunpit Rd 36 B3
Haxted Rd 36 C1
Haywardens 36 B2
Headland Way 36 B3
High St 36 B3
Jenners Clo 36 B3
Jenny La 36 B3
Lincolns Mead 36 C4
Lingfield Common Rd 36 A1
Little Lullenden 36 C2
Mount Pleasant Rd 36 A3
Newchapel Rd 36 A3
Orchard Mead 36 C2
Park La 36 C2
Pauls Mead 36 B3
Plaistow St 36 B3
Racecourse Rd 36 C4
Ray Clo 36 A2
Ray La 36 A1
Rushfords 36 C2
St Piers La 36 D4
Saxbys La 36 C3
Selbys 36 C2
Stanfords Pl 36 B4
Station Rd 36 C2
Talbot Rd 36 B4
The Square 36 A3
Town Hill 36 C3
Vicarage Clo 36 B3
Vicarage La 36 B3

MILFORD

Amberley Rd 37 B1
Badgers Cross 37 C2
Bannister Clo 37 C6
Busdens Clo 37 C3
Busdens La 37 C3
Busdens Way 37 C3
Chapel Clo 37 C1
Chapel La 37 C1
Cherry Tree Rd 37 B2
Chichester Clo 37 B6
Church Clo 37 C2
Church Rd 37 C2
Cramhurst La 37 B5
Croft Rd 37 B5
Dorlecote 37 B6
Eashing La 37 C1
Elmside 37 C2
Flitwick Grange 37 C2
Gasden Clo 37 A5
Gasden Copse 37 A5
Gasden La 37 A5
George Elliot Clo 37 C6
George Rd 37 C1
Green La 37 B3
Guildford & Godalming By-Pass 37 C2
Haslemere Rd 37 B2
Heath View Rd 37 B4
High Croft 37 C3
Hurst Farm Clo 37 C1
Keswick Rd 37 A5
Khartoum Rd 37 D5
Ladycross 37 C3
Leehurst 37 B2
Little London 37 B5
Lower Moushill La 37 A2
Lower Oak Tree Rd 37 C2
Malthouse Mead 37 C6
Manor Fields 37 B1
Manor Grn 37 B2
Manor Lea Clo 37 B1
Manor Lea Rd 37 B1
Martins Wood 37 B4
Meadow Clo 37 B2
Merryacres 37 B4
Middlemarch 37 B6
Middleton Clo 37 C1
Milford Heath Rd 37 B3
Milford Lodge 37 C3
Milford Rd 37 A1
Mill La 37 C6
Moushill La 37 B3
New Rd 37 B2
Ockfields 37 C2
Old Elstead Rd 37 B2
Oxted Grn 37 B4
Petworth Rd 37 C4
Portsmouth Rd 37 A4
Potters Clo 37 C1
Rake La 37 C4
Roke Clo 37 B6
Roke La 37 B6
Sandy La 37 C4
Springwood 37 D2
Station La 37 D2
Sunny Down 37 B6
Sunny Hill 37 B6
Swallow Clo 37 B4
The Cedars 37 C2
The Lawns 37 C2
The Manor 37 C2
Upper Manor Rd 37 C2
Webb Rd 37 A5
Wheeler La 37 B5
Wildcroft Wood 37 B5
Willow Mead 37 C6
Willow Mews 37 C6
Yew Tree La 37 A5

OXSHOTT

Arnewood Clo 38 B4
Beech Clo 38 A2
Beech Close Ct 38 A2
Beechwood Dri 38 A2
Birch Vale 38 B3
Birchwood La 38 D1
Birds Hill Dri 38 D4
Birds Hill Rise 38 D4
Birds Hill Road 38 D3
Blundel La 38 A6
Braeken Hill 38 B2
Briars Ct 38 D4
Broom Hall 38 B4
Broomfield Ride 38 D3
Burn Clo 38 D6
Canterbury Mews 38 C4
Charlwood Dri 38 D6
Chatsworth Pl 38 D3
Clockhouse Mead 38 B4
Copsem La 38 C1
Courtleas 38 A3
Danemead 38 A2
Danes Clo 38 C5
Danes Way 38 C5
Esher By-Pass 38 A1
Fairmile Park Rd 38 A4
Fairoak Clo 38 D2
Fairoak La 38 D5
Falconhurst 38 D5
Fernhill 38 D5
Furze Field 38 D3
Goldrings Rd 38 C4
Hardwicke Clo 38 C6
Hawkhurst 38 A3
Hawksview 38 A3
Heath Ridge Grn 38 A4
Heath Road 38 C2
Heathfield 38 A5
High Dri 38 D4
High St 38 D4
Highfield Clo 38 D2
Holtwood Rd 38 C4
Irene Rd 38 B5
Kimberley Ride 38 B4
Leatherhead Rd 38 D5
Lebanon Dri 38 A2
Leys Rd 38 D3
Links Green Way 38 A4
Littleheath La 38 A4
Lyfield 38 B5
Manor Way 38 C6
Meadway 38 B6
Midgarth Clo 38 C4
Moles Hill 38 D2
Montrose Gdns 38 D3
Northcote 38 C5
Oakshade Rd 38 C4
Old Farmhouse Dri 38 D5
Oxdowne Clo 38 B4
Parkfields 38 D1
Pond Piece 38 C5
Pony Chase 38 A4
Poundhill Way 38 B2
Queens Dri 38 C1
Randolph Clo 38 A6
Richards Rd 38 B5
Sandroyd Way 38 A3
Sandy Dri 38 A2
Sandy La 38 A2
Sandy Way 38 A2
Sheaths La 38 B4
Silverdale Av 38 C4
Somerville Rd 38 A4
Spicers Field 38 D3
Spinney Clo 38 A2
Spinneycroft 38 D6
Station App 38 C3
Steels La 38 B4
Stokesheath Rd 38 C1
The Chase 38 C6
The Gables 38 A4
The Heights 38 A4
The Knoll 38 A4
The Ridgeway 38 A5
The Ridings 38 A3
The Spinney 38 C4
The Starlings 38 C4
The Warren 38 A4
Torland Dri 38 D4
Tudor Clo 38 A4
Twinoaks 38 A4
Uplands Dri 38 D4
Warren La 38 C1
Waverley Rd 38 B5
Webster Clo 38 B5
Woodside Rd 38 B4
Woodsway 38 D4
Wrens Hill 38 C5

OXTED/LIMPSFIELD

Amy Rd 39 B2
Barnfield Way 39 D6
Barrow Green Rd 39 A1
Beadles La 39 A3
Beatrice Rd 39 B2
Blind La 39 B3
Bluehouse Gdns 39 C1
Bluehouse La 39 B2
Boulthurst Way 39 D5
Brassey Rd 39 C3
Broadham Green 39 A5
Bromford Clo 39 C6
Central Way 39 A1
Chalkpit La 39 A1
Chalkpit Wood 39 A1
Chestnut Copse 39 D6
Chichele Rd 39 B1
Church La 39 A3
Church Way 39 C5
Coldshott 39 C6
Comforts Farm Av 39 C6
Culver Dri 39 B3
Detillens La 39 D2
Downs Way 39 B1
East Hill 39 B3
East Hill Ct 39 C5
East Hill Rd 39 B3
Eastlands Wy 39 A1
Ellice Rd 39 B2
Farley Pk 39 A3
Field Ct 39 A6
Gibbs Brook La 39 A6
Gordons Way 39 A1
Granville Rd 39 C1
Green Acres 39 B1
Greenhurst La 39 C4
Gresham Clo 39 C2
Gresham Rd 39 C2
Hall Hill 39 A4
Hallsland Way 39 C6
Haywain 39 A3
Hazlewood Rd 39 D5
High St, Limpsfield 39 D1
High St, Oxted 39 A3
Holland Cres 39 D6
Holland La 39 D6
Holland Rd 39 D6
Home Park 39 D4
Hookwood Cnr 39 D2
Hoskins Rd 39 B3
Hoskins Way 39 B2
Hurst Green Clo 39 C5
Hurst Green Rd 39 C5
Hurstlands 39 C5
Icehouse Wood 39 B4

INDUSTRIAL ESTATES:
Fairview Ind Est 39 D6
Johnsdale 39 B2
Laurel Dri 39 C4
Master Clo 39 B2
Meadow Brook 39 C5
Meldrum Clo 39 C5
Mill La 39 C5
Mill Shaw 39 C5
Neb Rd 39 A4
New Lodge Dri 39 C2
New Rd 39 D3
Nonappleton Way 39 D6
Oak Shaw 39 A1
Oast Rd 39 B4
Old La 39 B3
Orchard Way 39 C6
Oxted By-Pass 39 A3
Padbrook 39 D2
Paddock Clo 39 C4
Paddock Way 39 C4
Park Rd 39 C1
Parklands 39 B4
Peter Av 39 B4
Pollards Oak Cres 39 D5
Pollards Oak Rd 39 D5
Pollards Wood Hill 39 D4
Pollards Wood Rd 39 D4
Popes La 39 A6
Priest Hill 39 D2
Quarry Clo 39 B4
Quarry Rd 39 B4
Rockfield Clo 39 C4
Rockfield Rd 39 C4
Roseacre 39 D6
Rosemary Clo 39 C6
St Clair Clo 39 A4
St Marys Clo 39 B2
Silkham Rd 39 A1
Snatts Hill 39 A6
Southlands La 39 A6
Spring La 39 A4
Springfield 39 A4
Stanhopes 39 D2
Station App 39 B2
Station Rd East 39 B2
Station Rd West 39 B2
Sylvans Clo 39 B2
Tanhouse Rd 39 A5
Testers Clo 39 B5
The Greenway 39 D6
The Hawthorns 39 D6
The Maltings 39 B4
The Waldrons 39 C5
Titsey Rd 39 D1
Uvedale Rd 39 C3
Water La 39 C5
West Hill 39 A3
West Hill Bank 39 A3
Westerham Rd 39 C2
Westlands Way 39 A1
Wheeler Av 39 A2
Wilderness Rd 39 A3
Wolfs Hill 39 D4
Wolfs Rd 39 D3
Wolfs Row 39 D3
Wolfs Wood 39 D5
Woodhurst La 39 D1
Woodhurst Park 39 B3
Woodland Ct 39 A1
Woodland Rise 39 B3
Wynnstow Park 39 C4

REIGATE/REDHILL

Abbotts Rise 41 H1
Abinger Rd 41 F6
Albany Clo 40 B1
Albert Rd North 40 A3
Albert Rd South 40 A3
Albion Rd 40 C4
Alders Rd 40 C2
Alexander Rd 40 B6
Allingham Rd 40 B6
Alma Rd 40 C2
Alpine Rd 41 H1
Althorne Rd 41 G5
Arbutus Clo 40 D6
Arbutus Rd 40 D6
Ardshiel Dri 41 F5
Ash Dri 41 H5
Bancroft Clo 40 C4
Bancroft Rd 40 B4
Batts Hill 41 F2
Baxter Av 41 F3
Beaufort Clo 40 A3
Beaufort Rd 40 A3
Beech Dri 41 E3
Beech Rd 40 B1
Bell St 40 B4
Belmont Rd 40 D5
Beverley Heights 40 C1
Birchway 41 H5
Birkheads Rd 40 B2
Blackborough Clo 40 D4
Blackborough Rd 40 D4
Blackstone Clo 41 E4
Blackstone Hill 41 E4
Blackthorn Clo 40 D6
Blackthorn Rd 40 D6
Blanford Rd 40 B4
Bramble Clo 41 H5
*Bramble Walk,
  Bramble Clo 41 H5
Brambletye Park Rd 41 G5
Bramley Clo 41 F6
Brightlands Rd 40 D2
Brighton Rd 41 G4
Broadhurst Gdns 40 C6
Brokes Cres 40 B2
Brokes Rd 40 B2
Brook Rd 41 G4
Brooklands Ct 40 C2

Brooklands Way 41 F2
Brownlow Rd 41 E3
Buckhurst Clo 41 F2
Budgen Dri 41 G1
Burnham Dri 40 B3
Bur Wood Clo 40 D4
Caberfeigh 41 E3
Canons Clo 40 A2
Carlton Green 41 E1
Carlton Rd 41 E1
Carrington Clo 41 F3
Cartmel Clo 41 E2
Castlefield Rd 40 B3
Cavendish Gdns 41 H3
Cavendish Rd 41 H3
Caxton Rise 41 H3
Cedar Clo 40 D6
Chaldon Clo 41 F6
Chanctonbury Chase 41 H4
Chapel Rd 41 G3
Charman Rd 41 F3
Chart La 40 C4
Chart Way 40 C3
Chartfield Rd 40 D5
Cherry Green Clo 41 H5
Chestnut Clo 41 H5
*Chestnut Mead, Oxford Rd 41 F3
Chipstead Clo 41 G5
Church Ct 40 C3
Church Rd, Redhill 41 F5
Church Rd, Reigate 40 B6
Church St 40 B3
Church Walk 40 C4
Churchfield Rd 40 A3
Clarence Rd 40 D6
Clarence Walk 41 E6
Clarendon Rd 41 G3
Clarendon Rd South 41 G2
Clayhall La 40 A6
*Cleeves Ct, St Annes Mnt 41 H2
Clyde Clo 41 H3
Cockshot Hill 40 C5
Cokshot Rd 40 C5
Colebrook Rd 41 F2
Colesmead Rd 41 G1
Colman Way 41 F1
Common Rd 41 F6
Conifer Clo 40 B2
Coniston Way 41 E2
Copley Clo 41 F1
Coppice La 40 A1
Copse Rd 40 D6
Cornfield Rd 40 D5
Cotland Acres 41 E6
Crakell Rd 40 D4
Cranston Clo 40 C5
Crescent Rd 40 B6
Cromwell Rd 41 G3
Cronks Hill 40 D5
Cronks Hill Clo 41 E6
Cronks Hill Rd 41 E5
Crossland Rd 41 H3
Croydon Rd 40 C3
Daneshill Clo 41 F2
Daneshill La 41 F2
Deerings Rd 40 C3
Dennis Clo 41 F1
Devon Cres 41 E4
*Diamond Ct, St Annes Way 41 H2
Dome Way 41 F3
Doods Park Rd 40 D3
Doods Rd 40 D3
Doods Way 41 E3
Doran Dri 40 E3
Douglas Rd 40 C3
Downswood 41 E1
Duncroft Clo 40 A3
Dunottar Clo 41 E6
Durfold Dri 40 D3
Earlsbrook Rd 41 G5
Earlswood Rd 41 F5
East Rd 40 A3
East Walk 40 C3
Eastnor Rd 40 B6
Effingham Rd 40 C4
Eldersley Clo 41 F1
Eldersley Gdns 41 F2
Elm Rd 41 F4
Emlyn Rd 41 G5
Eversfield Rd 40 C3
Evesham Clo 40 A3
Evesham Rd 40 A3
Evesham Rd Nth 40 A3
Fairfax Av 41 F3
Fairlawn Dri 41 E5
Fengates Rd 41 F3
Fenton Clo 41 G3
Fenton Rd 41 G3
Fir Tree Walk 40 D3
Flint Clo 41 F2
Fountain Rd 41 F5
Frenches Ct 41 G1
Frenches Dri 41 G1
Frenches Rd 41 G1
Friths Dri 40 C1
Fulbourne Clo 41 F1
Furze Clo 41 F3
Furze Hill 41 F3
Furzefield Cres 40 D5
Furzefield Rd 40 D5
*Gable Ct, St Annes Mnt 41 H2
Garibaldi Rd 41 F4
Garlands Rd 41 F4
Gatton Clo 40 D1
Gatton Park Rd 41 E1
Gatton Rd 40 D1
Gloucester Rd 41 G2
Glovers Rd 40 C5
Goodwood Rd 41 F2
Gordon Rd 41 H1
Green La, Redhill 41 F1
Green La, Reigate 40 A4
Green Way 41 F2
Greenhayes Clo 40 D3
Greystones Clo 40 D6
Greystones Dri 40 D1
Grovehill Rd 41 F3
Haigh Cres 41 H5
Hardwick Rd 40 D6
Hardwicke Rd 40 B3
Harewood Clo 40 D1
Harrison Clo 40 C5
Hartington Pl 40 B2
Hartspiece Rd 41 H5
Hatchlands Rd 41 E3
Hawthorn Way 41 H5
Hazel Clo 40 C6
Hazel Rd 40 D6
Hethersett Clo 40 D1
High St, Redhill 41 G3
High St, Reigate 40 B4
High Trees Rd 40 D5
Highlands Rd 41 E3
Hill House Dri 40 C6
Hillfield Clo 41 H3
Hillfield Rd 41 H3
Hilltor Rd 40 C5
Hillview Dri 41 H5
Hitherwood Clo 41 E1
Holland Clo 41 F3
Holly Rd 40 C6
Holmesdale Rd 40 B3
Holmethorpe Av 41 H1
Hooley La 41 G5
Horley Rd 41 F6
Hornbeam Rd 40 C6
Howard Rd 40 C4
Huntersfield Circle 40 C1
Huntingdon Rd 41 G3
Hurstleigh Clo 41 F2
Hurstleigh Dri 41 G2
Ifield Clo 41 F6
Ifold Rd 41 G5
Isbells Dri 40 C5
Juniper Clo 40 D6
Juniper Rd 40 D6
Keats Av 41 H2
Kendal Clo 41 E2
Kilmarnock Pk 40 C2
Kingfisher Dri 41 H1
Kings Av 41 F5
Knighton Rd 41 G5
Ladbroke Gro 41 G3
Ladbroke Rd 41 G2
Laglands Clo 40 D1
Lakeside 41 H1
Larch Clo 40 D6
Ledbury Rd 40 B3
*Lennox Ct, St Annes Rise 41 H3
Lesbourne Rd 40 C4
Lime Clo 40 C6
Linkfield Gdns 41 E3
Linkfield La 41 F2
Linkfield St 41 F3
Linnell Rd 41 H5
London Rd, Redhill 41 G2
London Rd, Reigate 40 B3
Lorian Dri 40 D3
Lower Bridge Rd 41 F3
Lower Rd 40 D6
Lymden Gdns 40 C5
Lynwood Rd 41 G2
Mackrells 40 D6
Madeira Walk 41 E3
Mallard Clo 41 H1
Manor Rd 40 A2
Mark St 40 C3
Marketfield Rd 41 G3
Marketfield Way 41 G3
Mead Clo 41 G1
Merrywood Park 40 C1
Mill St 41 F4
Mill Way 41 E4
Millview Clo 41 E1
Milton Rd 41 G4
Monks Walk 40 C4
Monson Rd 41 G1
Mostyn Ter 41 H5
Mount Dri 40 D1
Mount Rise 41 E6
Mountview Clo 41 E6
Mountview Dri 41 E6
Nash Dri 41 G2
Nash Gdns 41 G2
New North Rd 40 A6
*Nightingale Ct St Annes Mnt 41 H2
Nightwood Clo 40 B6
Noke Dri 41 H3
Norbury Rd 40 A3
North Rd 40 A6
North St 41 F2
Nutfield Rd 41 H4
Nutley Gro 40 B3
Nutley La 40 A2
Oak Rd 40 C2
Oak Way 41 E4
Oakdene Rd 41 F3
Oakfield Dri 40 B2
Oakhill Rd 40 C5
Oaklands Dri 41 H5
Oaks Rd 40 D2
Oakwood Clo 41 H4
Old Pottery Clo 40 C6
Old Redstone Dri 41 H5
Orchard Rd 40 C3
Orewell Gro 40 C5
Osborne Rd 41 H1
Oxford Rd 41 F3
Palmer Clo 41 H4
Park Hall Rd 40 B2
Park House Dri 40 A6
Park La 40 A5
Park La East 40 A6
Park Rd 41 F1
Parkgate Rd 40 C5
Pendleton Clo 41 F5
Pendleton Rd 41 E6
Penrith Clo 41 E2
Philanthropic Rd 41 H5
Pilgrims Pl 40 B2
Pilgrims Way 40 A2
Princes Rd 41 G6
Princess Way 41 G3
Priory Dri 40 B6
Priory Rd 40 B6
Quarry Hill Rd 40 C1
*Queens Ct, St Annes Way 41 H2
Queensway 41 G3
Radnor Ct 41 F4
Raglan Clo 40 D2
Raglan Rd 40 C1
Randal Cres 40 B6
Ranelagh Rd 41 F3
Ravens Clo 41 F2
Reading Arch Rd 41 G4
Redstone Hill 41 G3
Redstone Hollow 41 H4
Redstone Manor 41 G4
Redstone Park 41 H3
Redstone Rd 41 G5
Redwood Mt 40 B1
Regent Cres 41 G2
Reigate Hill 40 B2
Reigate Hill Clo 40 B1
Reigate Rd 40 C3
Rennie Ter 41 H5
Ridgegate Clo 41 E1
Ridgeway Ct 41 F4
Ridgeway Rd 41 F4
Ringley Park Av 41 E4
Ringley Park Rd 40 D3
Robin Gdns 41 H1
Roebuck Clo 40 B4
Rosemead Clo 41 E6
Rowan Clo 40 D6
Rural Way 41 H4
Rushworth Rd 40 B3
Rutland Clo 41 F2
St Albans Rd 40 B2
St Andrews Clo 40 C5
St Annes Dri 41 H2
St Annes Mnt 41 H2
St Annes Rise 41 H2
St Annes Way 41 H2
St Clair Clo 40 D3
St Davids Clo 40 D2
St Johns 41 F6
St Johns Rd 41 G5
St Johns Ter 41 G5
St Lawrences Way 40 B4
St Marys Rd 40 C5
St Matthews Rd 41 G3
Sandcross La 40 A6
Sandhills Rd 40 B5
Sandpit Rd 41 F4
Saxon Way 40 A3
Seale Hill 40 B6
Sheep Walk 40 A1
Sheldon Clo 40 C5
Shrewsbury Rd 41 E3
Silverstone Clo 41 F2
Sincots Rd 41 G3
Slipshoe St 40 B3
Smith Rd 40 B6
Smoke La 40 C5
Somers Clo 40 B2
Somers Rd 40 B2
Somerset Rd 41 E6
South Rd 40 C4
South Walk 40 C3
Southmead Rd 41 G1
Sparrows Mead 41 H1
Springcopse Rd 40 C5
Station App 41 G6
Station Rd, Earlswood 41 G6
Station Rd, Redhill 41 F3
Summerly Av 40 B3
Sussex Clo 41 E4
Sycamore Wk 40 C6
Sylvan Way 41 H4
Talbat Clo 40 C5
The Belfry 41 F3
The Bield 40 B5
The Cedars 40 D3
The Chase 41 E4
The Clears 40 A1
The Close 40 C4
The Crescent, Earlswood 41 E6
The Crescent, Reigate 40 C3
The Cutting 41 F5
The Dell 40 B2
The Frenches 41 G1
The Mews 40 C3
The Ridings 41 E1
The Way 41 E2
Timperley Gdns 41 F1
Tree Way 40 C1
Trehaven Parade 40 C6
Trentham Rd 41 G6
Tunnel Rd 40 B3
Underhill Park Rd 40 B1
Upper Bridge Rd 41 F4
Upper West St 40 A3
Utterton Way 41 E6
Vandyke Clo 41 F1
Victoria Rd 41 G5
Vogan Clo 40 C6
Warren Rd 40 C2
Warwick Rd 41 G2
Washington Clo 40 B1
Waterlow Rd 40 D5
Waterslade 41 F3
Wesley Clo 40 A4
West Rd 40 C4
West St 40 A3
Westfield 40 C1
Westview Clo 41 F6
Whitebeam Dri 40 C6
Whitepost Hill 41 E4
Wiggie La 41 H1
Willow Rd 40 D6
Willow Walk 41 H6
Wilmots Clo 40 D3
Windemere Way 41 E2
Windmill Clo 41 E2
Windmill Dri 41 E2
Windmill Way 41 E1
Woodcrest Walk 41 E1
Woodfield Clo 41 F2
Woodfield Way 41 F2
Woodlands Av 41 G5
Woodlands Rd 41 F5
Woodside Way 41 H4
Worcester Rd 40 B3
Wordsworth Mead 41 H
Wray Common Rd 40 D
Wray La 41 E
Wray Park Rd 40 C
Wrayfield Av 40 D
Wrayfield Pl 40 C
Wrayland Dri 41 E
Yardley Clo 40 C
Yeats Clo 40 D
Yew Tree La 40 C
Yorke Gdns 40 B
Yorke Rd 40 B

RICHMOND

Adelaide Rd 42 D2
Albany Pass 42 C3
Albany Rd 42 C3
Albert Rd 42 C3
Alexandra Rd 42 A4
Alton Rd 42 C2
Arlington Clo 42 A4
Arlington Rd 42 A4
Ashley Rd 42 C1
Audley Rd 42 C3
Austin Clo 42 A3
Bardolph Rd 42 D2
Beatrice Rd 42 C3
Beaufort Rd 42 A5
Beaulieu Clo 42 B5
Beaumont Av 42 C2
*Benns Wk, Kew Rd 42 C2
Beresford Av 42 A4
Braddon Rd 42 D1
Brewers La 42 B3
Bridge St 42 B4
Broadhurst Clo 42 D4
Budds Alley 42 A3
Burdett Rd 42 D1
Calvert Ct 42 D2
Cambrian Rd 42 C4
Cambridge Pk 42 A5
Cambridge Pk Ct 42 A5
Cambridge Rd 42 B4
Caplan Ct 42 D4
Cardigan Rd 42 C4
Carrington Rd 42 D2
Castle Yd 42 B3
Castlegate 42 D1
Catherine Dri 42 C2
Cedar Heights 42 C6
Cedar Ter 42 C2
Charlotte Sq 42 D4
Charmouth Ct 42 D3
Chester Av 42 C4
Chilton Rd 42 D1
Chisholm Rd 42 C5
Chislehurst Rd 42 C4
Cholmondeley Walk 42 A3
Church Ct 42 B3
Church Rd 42 C2
Church Walk 42 B3
Clarence St 42 B2
Clevedon Rd 42 B4
Compass Hill 42 B4
Connaught Rd 42 C3
Courtlands 42 D3
Cresswell Rd 42 B4
Crofton Ter 42 C2
Crown Ter 42 D2
Dancer Rd 42 D1
Darell Rd 42 D1
Dee Rd 42 D2
Denbigh Gdns 42 D3
Denton Rd 42 B4
Downe Ter 42 C5
Drummond Pl 42 B3
Ducks Walk 42 A3
Duke St 42 B3
Duncan Rd 42 C2
Dunstable Rd 42 C2
Dynevor Rd 42 C3
Ellerker Gdns 42 B4
Ellesmere Rd 42 A4
Eton St 42 B3
Evelyn Gdns 42 C2
Evelyn Rd 42 C2
Evelyn Ter 42 C1
Fairlawns 42 A4
Fitzwilliam Av 42 D1
Friars La 42 A3
Friars Stile Pl 42 C4
Friars Stile Rd 42 C4
Gainsborough Rd 42 D1
Garrick Clo 42 A3
Gaston Bell Clo 42 C1

orge St	42 B3
Iden Ct	42 B3
rdon Rd	42 D1
eenside	42 B3
ena Gdns	42 D2
ena Rd	42 D2
eville Rd	42 D4
osvenor Av	42 C3
osvenor Rd	42 C3
ove Rd	42 D4
lford Rd	42 B3
aversham Clo	42 B5
eron Sq	42 B3
ll Rise	42 B4
ll St	42 B3
bart Pl	42 C6
oublon Rd	42 C3
owson Ter	42 B4
yde Rd	42 C3
ocelyn Rd	42 C1
ones Walk	42 D4
ew Foot Rd	42 B2
ew Rd	42 C2
ng George Sq	42 D4
ng St	42 B3
ings Farm Rd	42 D2
ings Mead	42 D4
ings Rd	42 C3
ancaster Pk	42 B4
arkfield Rd	42 C2
enton Rise	42 B1
ewis Rd	42 B3
chfield Gdns	42 C3
ime Rd	42 D2
ion Gate Gdns	42 C1
orne Rd	42 C3
ower George St	42 B3
ower Grove Rd	42 D4
ower Mortlake Rd	42 C2
ower Richmond Rd	42 D1
Maid of Honour Row	42 B3
Manning Pl	42 D4
Manor Gdns	42 D2
Manor Gro	42 D2
Manor Pk	42 D2
Manor Rd	42 D2
Marchmont Rd	42 C3
Marlborough Rd	42 C4
Meadow Clo	42 B6
Michels Row	42 B2
Montague Rd	42 C4
Morley Rd	42 A4
Mount Ararat Rd	42 C3
Nightingale La	42 C5
North Rd	42 D1
Northumberland Pl	42 B4
Old Deer Park Gdns	42 C1
Old House Gdns	42 A4
Old Palace La	42 A3
Old Palace Yd	42 A3
Onslow Av	42 C4
Onslow Rd	42 C4
Orchard Rd	42 D1
Orleans Rd	42 A6
Ormond Av	42 B3
Ormond Rd	42 B3
Pagoda Av	42 C1
Paradise Rd	42 B3
Park House Gdns	42 A3
Park La	42 B2
Park Rd, Richmond	42 C4
Park Rd, St Margarets	42 A4
Parkshot	42 B2
Patten Alley	42 B3
Paved Ct	42 B3
Peldon Av	42 D3
Peldon Pass	42 D3
Pembroke Villas	42 B3
*Perseverance Pl, Kew	42 C2
Petersham Rd	42 B4
Portland Ter	42 B3
Powers Ct	42 B5
Preston Pl	42 C3
Princes Rd	42 C3
Princes St	42 C3
Pyrland Rd	42 D4
Quadrant Rd	42 B3
Queensberry Pl	42 A3
Queens Court	42 D4
Queens Cres	42 D3
Queens Keep	42 A4
Queens Rise	42 D4
Queens Road	42 C5
Raleigh Rd	42 D1
Ravensbourne Rd	42 A4
Red Lion St	42 B3
Retreat Rd	42 B3

Reynolds Pl	42 C5
Richmond Bri	42 B4
Richmond Hill	42 B4
Richmond Hill Ct	42 C4
Richmond Rd	42 A5
River La	42 B6
Riverdale Gdns	42 A4
Riverdale Rd	42 A4
Riverside	42 A6
Rosedale Rd	42 C2
Roseleigh Clo	42 B5
Rosemont Rd	42 C4
Rosslyn Rd	42 B3
Royston Rd	42 C3
Russell Walk	42 D4
Rutland Dri	42 B6
Ryde Pl	42 A4
St George St	42 D2
St John's Gro	42 B2
St John's Rd	42 C2
St Margaret's Rd	42 A4
St Mary's Gro	42 D2
St Paul's Rd	42 C1
St Stephen's Gdns	42 A5
St Stephen's Pass	42 A5
Salisbury Rd	42 C2
Sandycombe Rd, N. Sheen	42 D1
Sandycombe Rd, St Margarets	42 D5
Sawyers Hill	42 D5
Sayers Walk	42 C5
Selwyn Av	42 C2
Shaftesbury Rd	42 C2
Sheen Pk	42 C2
Sheen Rd	42 C3
Sheendale Rd	42 C2
Spring Gro Rd	42 D3
Stafford Mews	42 C5
Stanmore Gdns	42 D1
Stanmore Rd	42 C1
Star & Garter Hill	42 C6
Sun Alley	42 B2
Sydney Rd	42 C2
Temple Rd	42 D1
Terrace La	42 C4
The Avenue	42 A3
The Green	42 B3
The Hermitage	42 B3
The Quadrant	42 B3
The Square	42 B3
The Vineyard	42 B4
The Wardrobe	42 A3
Topiary Sq	42 C1
Tower Rise	42 C1
Townshend Rd	42 C2
Townshend Ter	42 C2
Tree Clo	42 B6
Trinity Rd	42 D2
Twickenham Br	42 A3
Twickenham Rd	42 A2
Victoria Villas	42 D2
Vineyard Pass	42 B3
Vivienne Clo	42 A5
Wakefield Rd	42 B3
Warren Ftpth	42 B5
Warrington Rd	42 B3
Water La	42 B3
Waterloo Pl	42 B3
Wayside Ct	42 A4
West Sheen Vale	42 C2
Whittaker Av	42 B3
Willoughby Rd	42 A4
Wilton Av	42 D2
Windham Rd	42 D3
Winter Box Walk	42 D3
Worple Way	42 C3
York Rd	42 C3

STAINES

Allyn Clo	43 C5
Annie Brookes Clo	43 A2
Argosy Gdns	43 C5
Aspen Clo	43 C2
Augur Clo	43 C4
Avenue Rd	43 A4
Avondale Av	43 A6
Baden Clo	43 D6
Barons Way	43 A5
Beehive Rd	43 D6
Berkeley Clo	43 A1
Billet Rd	43 D2
Birch Grn	43 C3
Bishops Way	43 A5
Boleyn Clo	43 B4

Bowes Rd	43 B4
Bremer Rd	43 D2
Bridge St	43 B3
Broad Acre	43 D4
Budebury Rd	43 C4
Bundys Way	43 B5
Burges Way	43 D4
Carlyle Rd	43 C6
Chandos Rd	43 A4
Cherry Orchard	43 C4
Chertsey La	43 B4
Chestnut Manor Clo	43 D4
Church St	43 A3
Claremont Rd	43 A4
Clarence St	43 B3
Colnbridge Ct	43 B4
Commercial Rd	43 C5
Coopers Clo	43 B4
Cornwall Way	43 B5
Cotswold Clo	43 D4
Crooked Billet	43 D3
Crossways	43 A5
Cumberland St	43 A4
Devils La	43 A6
Dolphin Ct	43 D2
Drakes Av	43 C4
Edgell Rd	43 C4
Egham Roundabout	43 A4
Eton Ct	43 C4
Factory Path	43 C3
Fairfield Av	43 C3
Farm Clo	43 B4
Farm Rd	43 D5
Farmers Rd	43 B4
Farnoll Rd	43 D2
Ferry Av	43 B6
Florence Gdns	43 D0
Garrick Clo	43 C6
George St	43 B3
Georgian Clo	43 D3
Gloucester Dri	43 A2
Goodman Pl	43 B3
Gordon Clo	43 D6
Goring Rd	43 A4
Gorings Sq	43 B3
Grange Clo	43 D4
Green Pk	43 B2
Greenlands Rd	43 D3
Gresham Rd	43 C4
Grosvenor Rd	43 D6
Grovebarns	43 C5
Guildford St	43 C6
Hale St	43 B3
Hawks Way	43 C2
High St	43 B3
Huntingfield Way	43 A6
Hythe Park Rd	43 A5
Hythe Rd	43 A4
Hythefield Av	43 A5

INDUSTRIAL ESTATES:

Butts Business Pk	43 B4
Island Clo	43 A3
Jamnagar Clo	43 C5
Kestrel Av	43 C2
Kingfisher Dri	43 C3
Kingsbury Cres	43 A3
Kingston Rd	43 C3
Knights Clo	43 A5
Knightsbridge Cres	43 D5
Knowle Grn	43 D4
Knowle Park Av	43 D4
Lacey Clo	43 A6
Laleham Rd	43 C4
Langley Rd	43 A5
Langton Way	43 A4
Lansdowne Rd	43 D6
Lark Av	43 C2
Leacroft	43 D3
Leacroft Clo	43 D3
London Rd	43 C3
Manor Pl	43 D4
Market Sq	43 B4
Matthews La	43 C3
Mayfield Gdns	43 B5
Meadow Ct	43 B2
Meadow Gdns	43 A4
Meadway	43 C3
Meadway Clo	43 C6
Millmead	43 B3
Monsell Gdns	43 B4
Moor La	43 A1
Moormede Cres	43 C2
Murdoch Clo	43 C3
Mustard Mill Rd	43 B3
New St	43 C3
Norris Rd	43 B3
Nursery Gdns	43 D6
Octavia Way	43 D5

Park Av	43 C5
Penton Hook Rd	43 C6
Penton Rd	43 C6
Pine Wood Dri	43 D4
Plover Clo	43 C2
Priory Grn	43 D4
Prospect Pl	43 C5
Railway Ter	43 A4
Raleigh Ct	43 D3
Richmond Cres	43 C4
Richmond Rd	43 D4
River Park Av	43 A3
Riverfield Rd	43 C5
Riverside Rd	43 B4
Robin Way	43 C2
Rochester Way	43 Ab
Rosefield Rd	43 D3
Ruskin Rd	43 C5
St Olaves Clo	43 C6
St Pauls Rd	43 A4
St Peters Clo	43 C5
Sidney Rd	43 C3
Silverdale Ct	43 D3
Simmons Pl	43 B4
South St	43 C4
Staines Bridge	43 B3
Staines By Pass	43 A2
Stanwell Moor Rd	43 D2
Stanwell New Rd	43 C3
Station Path	43 C3
Swallow Clo	43 C3
Thames St	43 B4
The Causeway	43 A3
The Fernery	43 B4
The Hythe	43 B4
Thorpe Lea Rd	43 A6
Thorpe Rd	43 A4
Tilly's La	43 B3
Timsway	43 D4
Vicarage Rd	43 A2
Victoria Rd	43 B2
Wapshott Rd	43 B4
Waters Dri	43 B2
Wendover La	43 A4
Wendover Rd	43 A4
Westbourne Rd	43 D6
Westbrook Rd	43 C4
Wheatsheaf La	43 C6
Witheygate Av	43 D5
Wraysbury Rd	43 A2
Wyatt Rd	43 C4
Yeoveney Clo	43 A1

SUNBURY

INDUSTRIAL ESTATES:

Allen Clo	44 D4
Allen Rd	44 D4
Annett Clo	44 A6
Anvil Rd	44 C6
Aragon Clo	44 A2
Ashridge Way	44 B1
Avon Rd	44 A2
Barnard Clo	44 C2
Batavia Clo	44 D4
Batavia Rd	44 C3
Beauclere Ct	44 A1
Beechwood Av	44 B1
Beechwood Ct	44 C1
Belgrave Cres	44 D3
Belgrave Rd	44 D3
Benwell Ct	44 B3
Beverley Rd	44 B4
Bingley Rd	44 B2
Bracken Clo	44 A1
Brackenwood	44 C3
Bridgefoot	44 B3
Bridle Clo	44 C6
Broad Oak	44 A1
Brook Dri	44 A1
Brooklands Clo	44 A3
Broomfield	44 C3
Bryan Rd	44 B2
Bryony Way	44 A1
Burgoyne Rd	44 A1
Cadbury Clo	44 A2
Cadbury Rd	44 A2
Camilla Clo	44 A2
Cardinals Walk	44 A2
Carlton Rd	44 B2
Castle Clo	44 A2
*Castle Walk, Elizabeth Gdns	44 D5
Catherine Dri	44 A2
Cavendish Clo	44 B1
Cavendish Ct	44 A1

Cavendish Rd	44 A1
Cedar Way	44 A2
Chaplin Cres	44 A1
Chertsey Rd	44 A1
Chestnut Clo	44 A1
Churchill Way	44 C1
Church St	44 C6
Claremont Av	44 D4
Cleeves Way	44 A1
Crayonne Clo	44 A3
Croysdale Av	44 C5
Cumberland Rd	44 C6
Dale Rd	44 A2
Downside	44 B3
Elizabeth Gdns	44 D5
Elm Dri	44 D4
Elmbrook Clo	44 C3
Evelyn Cres	44 B4
Evelyn Way	44 B4
Fairlawns	44 B5
Falcon Way	44 A4
Farrier Clo	44 C6
Fordbridge Rd	44 C6
Forest Dri	44 B3
Forge La	44 C5
Freeman Dri	44 A6
French St	44 D4
Furzewood	44 C3
Grangewood Dri	44 B3
Green La	44 B2
Green Leas	44 B2
Green St	44 B3
Green Way	44 B6
Griffin Way	44 C4
Halliford Rd	44 B6
Hamilton Pl	44 C3
Hanworth Rd	44 C2
Harris Way	44 A3
Hawkewood Rd	44 C5
Heath Gro	44 B2
Heathcroft Av	44 B2
Heatherlands	44 B1
Heathlands Clo	44 B4
Helgiford Gdns	44 A2
Holmebank Dri	44 A6
Homewaters Av	44 B3
Howard Clo	44 A2
Ilex Clo	44 D4

INDUSTRIAL ESTATES:

Dolphin Ind Est	44 A3
Windmill Business Village	44 A3
Kelly Clo	44 A4
Kempton Av	44 D2
Kempton Ct	44 D2
Kenyngton Dri	44 B1
Keywood Dri	44 C1
Kings Av	44 B1
Kingsmead Av	44 D5
Laburnam Cres	44 C3
Laytons La	44 A4
Lime Crest	44 D4
Loudwater Clo	44 C6
Lyndhurst Av	44 B5
Manor Rd	44 B4
Manor Gdns	44 B4
Manor La	44 C4
Martingale Clo	44 B6
Maryland Way	44 C4
Meadows End	44 B3
Mill Farm Av	44 A3
Minsterley Av	44 A6
Montford Rd	44 C6
Nursery Gdns	44 B4
Nursery Rd	44 A4
Oak Gro	44 C2
Oakington Dri	44 D4
Old Orchard	44 D5
Orchard Rd	44 C2
Park Rd	44 C2
Parke Rd	44 C6
Parkwood Gro	44 B5
Percy Bryant Rd	44 A3
Peregrine Rd	44 A4
Pinewood	44 C3
Priory Clo	44 C3
Queensway	44 C4
Ravendale Rd	44 B4
Ravenscourt	44 B4
Rooksmead Rd	44 B5
Rope Walk	44 D5
Saddlebrook Pk	44 A2
St Marys Clo	44 B6
Salix Clo	44 C2
Saxonbury Av	44 D5
Scotts Av	44 A2
Scotts Way	44 A2
Seymour Way	44 A2

Shire Ct 44 C5
Silverdale Dri 44 C4
Spelthorne Gro 44 A3
Springfield Gro 44 B3
Staines Rd East 44 C3
Staines Rd West 44 A2
Station App 44 C3
Station Rd 44 B3
Stile Path 44 C6
Stratton Rd 44 B4
Summer Trees 44 C3
Sunbury Cross 44 B3
Sunmead Rd 44 B5
Sunna Gdns 44 D4
Sutherland Av 44 B4
Sutherland Gdns 44 B4
Thames St 44 C6
The Avenue 44 C3
The Chase 44 D3
The Crofts 44 A6
The Green 44 A6
The Parade 44 B2
The Pines 44 C5
The Ridings 44 B3
The Rowans 44 B1
The Spinney 44 C3
The Vale 44 C1
The Vineyards 44 C5
Upper Halliford Grn 44 A6
Upper Halliford Rd 44 A5
Vereker Dri 44 C5
Vicarage Rd 44 B1
Wychwood Clo 44 B2
Windmill Rd 44 A3
Windmill Rd West 44 A4
Windsor Ct 44 B2
Windsor Rd 44 B2
Wolsey Rd 44 B2
Woodberry Clo 44 C2

SUTTON

Albany Mews 45 A4
Albert Rd 45 D4
Albion Rd 45 D6
Albury Ct 45 C3
Alexandra Av 45 A2
Alfred Rd 45 D4
All Saints Rd 45 C1
Ambleside Gdns 45 D5
Angel Hill 45 B1
Angel Hill Dri 45 C1
Anton Cres 45 A1
Ashton Clo 45 A3
Avon Clo 45 D3
Avondale Ct 45 C1
Banbury Ct 45 B6
Beauchamp Rd 45 A3
Bedford Ter 45 D5
Beech Tree Pl 45 B4
Beggars Roost La 45 A5
Belsize Gdns 45 C2
Benfleet Clo 45 D1
Benhill Av 45 C3
Benhill Rd 45 D1
Benhill Wood Rd 45 C1
Benhilton Gdns 45 B1
Beulah Rd 45 A3
Bishops Clo 45 B1
Blackbush Clo 45 C6
Blackwater Rd 45 B3
Blenheim Rd 45 B1
Bletchworth Clo 45 D3
Bramley Rd 45 D4
Brandon Rd 45 B3
Brandy Way 45 A6
Bridge Rd 45 B5
Bridgefield Rd 45 A5
Brighton Rd 45 C5
Brunswick Ct 45 C2
Brunswick Rd 45 C3
Bryanstone Ct 45 C2
Burgess Rd 45 B3
Burnell Rd 45 B2
Bushey La 45 B2
Bushey Rd 45 B2
Cadogan Ct 45 B5
Calthorpe Gdns 45 C1
Camborne Rd 45 B6
Camden Gdns 45 B4
Camden Rd 45 B4
Carshalton Rd 45 C4
Cavendish Rd 45 C6
Cedar Gdns 45 C5
Cedar Rd 45 C5
Chalcot Clo 45 A6
Chalk Pit Way 45 C4
Chaucer Gdns 45 A2
Chaucer Rd 45 A2
Cheam Rd 45 A5
Chilworth Gdns 45 C1
Christchurch Pk 45 C6
Chudleigh Gdns 45 D1
Clarence Rd 45 B3
*Cliff Walk,
Greyhound Rd 45 D4
Clowser Clo 45 D4
Clyde Rd 45 B3
Collingwood Rd 45 A1
Compton Ct 45 C2
Coniston Gdns 45 D5
Constance Rd 45 D3
Coombe Walk 45 B1
Copse Hill 45 C6
Cranford Ct 45 C2
Cressingham Gro 45 C2
Crown Rd 45 B3
Cumnor Rd 45 D5
Deans Rd 45 B2
Devonshire Rd 45 D6
Dibdin Clo 45 A1
Dibdin Rd 45 A1
Dovercourt La 45 C2
Duke St 45 D2
Eaton Rd 45 D5
Elgin Rd 45 D1
Elm Gro 45 B3
Erskine Rd 45 D2
Evesham Clo 45 A6
Falcourt Clo 45 B4
Ferndown Clo 45 D5
Forest Dene Ct 45 C5
Frampton Clo 45 A6
Gibson Rd 45 B4
Glena Mt 45 C2
Godsens Clo 45 D4
Godstone Rd 45 D2
Grange Rd 45 A6
Grange Vale 45 C6
Greenford Rd 45 B3
Grennell Rd 45 D1
Greyhound Rd 45 C4
Grove Av 45 A5
Grove Rd 45 A5
Haddon Rd 45 B3
Hallmead Rd 45 B1
Heather Gdns 45 A6
Henry Hatch Walk 45 C6
High St 45 B2
Hill Rd 45 C4
Hillcroome Rd 45 D5
Hillview Rd 45 D1
Homefield Park 45 B5
Hope Clo 45 D3
Hunting Gate Mews 45 C1
Ivydene Clo 45 C3
Jengar Clo 45 C2
Keswick Clo 45 C2
Landseer Rd 45 A5
Langley Park Rd 45 D4
Langley Rd 45 D5
Lavender Rd 45 D2
Lenham Rd 45 C3
Leslie Gdns 45 B6
Lewis Rd 45 B2
Lind Rd 45 D3
Litchfield Rd 45 C3
Lodge Pl 45 C3
Lower Rd 45 D3
Magnolia Ct 45 B6
Manor Ct 45 C3
Manor La 45 C3
Manor Park Rd 45 C4
Manor Pl 45 C3
Marian Ct 45 B4
Marlins Clo 45 D4
Marshalls Rd 45 B3
Mayfield Rd 45 D5
Milestone Clo 45 D6
Milford Gro 45 C2
Milton Rd 45 A2
Mitre Clo 45 D6
Monksdene Gdns 45 C1
Montpelier Rd 45 D3
Montrose Gdns 45 C1
Morland Rd 45 D4
Mulgrave Rd 45 A6
Myrtle Rd 45 D3
Norman Rd 45 A3
Northspur Rd 45 A1
Nursery Rd 45 C3
Oakhill Rd 45 C2
Oakwood Ct 45 C2
Oldfields Rd 45 A1
Oliver Rd 45 D3
Orchard Gdns 45 A3
Orchard Rd 45 A3
Osbourne Clo 45 D4
Overton Rd 45 A6
Palmerston Rd 45 D3
Parkhurst Rd 45 D2
Petersham Clo 45 A4
Princess St 45 D3
Pylbrock Rd 45 B1
Reading Rd 45 D4
Rectory Rd 45 B2
Ripley Gdns 45 C3
Robin Hood La 45 A4
Rose Hill 45 B1
Roseberry Gdns 45 C2
Russell Clo 45 B4
Rutherford Clo 45 D5
St Barnabas Rd 45 D4
St James Av 45 A3
St James Rd 45 A3
St Nicholas Centre 45 B3
St Nicholas Rd 45 C4
St Nicholas Way 45 B3
Sherwood Park Rd 45 B4
Shott Clo 45 D4
Sidney Rd 45 A3
Sorrento Rd 45 B1
Stanley Rd 45 B6
Stanmore Gdns 45 C2
Stayton Rd 45 A1
Strathearne Rd 45 B3
Sunnyhurst Clo 45 A1
Sutton Arcade 45 C4
Sutton Common Rd 45 B1
Sutton Court Rd 45 C5
Sutton Park Rd 45 B4
Tapestry Clo 45 B6
Tate Rd 45 A4
The Green 45 B2
The Quadrant 45 C5
Thicket Cres 45 D3
Thicket Rd 45 D3
Thorncroft Rd 45 B3
Throwley Rd 45 C4
Throwley Way 45 C3
Times 2 45 C4
Tormead Clo 45 A5
Town Sq 45 C4
Turnpike La 45 D4
Upper Vernon Rd 45 D4
Upton Dene 45 B6
Vale Rd 45 B2
Vermont Rd 45 B1
Vernon Rd 45 D4
Vicarage Rd 45 B2
Victoria Rd 45 D4
Village Row 45 A6
Vine Clo 45 C1
Walnut Mews 45 C6
Warwick Rd 45 C3
Waterloo Rd 45 D3
Wellesley 45 C5
West St 45 B4
Western Rd 45 A4
Weymouth Ct 45 B6
White Lodge Clo 45 D6
Wilcox Rd 45 B3
William Rd 45 D3
Wings Clo 45 A3
Woodend 45 C1
Woodside Rd 45 C2
Worcester Rd 45 A6
York Rd 45 A5

TADWORTH/ BURGH HEATH

Acres Gdns 46 C3
Alcocks Clo 46 D3
Alcocks La 46 D4
Allum Gro 46 A4
Ashcombe Ter 46 A4
Avenue Clo 46 A5
Ballards Grn 46 D2
Bayeux 46 C5
Beechdene 46 A5
Bidhams Cres 46 B4
Birchgate Mews 46 B4
Bonsor Dri 46 D5
Brier Rd 46 A2
Brighton Rd 46 D4
Broad Walk 46 C2
Broadfield Clo 46 B3
Campion Dri 46 A2
Cann Hatch 46 D2
Canons La 46 D2
Cedar Walk 46 D4
Chapel Gro 46 B2
Chapel Rd 46 B6
Chapel Way 46 B2
Cheam Clo 46 B4
Chetwode Dri 46 C2
Chetwode Rd 46 B2
Christopher Ct 46 B6
Church La 46 C1
Copleigh Dri 46 D3
Copley Way 46 C3
Copt Hill La 46 D4
Coxdean 46 B2
Croffets 46 C4
Cross Rd 46 B5
Cuddington Clo 46 C3
Delves 46 C5
Derby Clo 46 A2
Dorking Rd 46 C6
Downland Clo 46 A1
Downland Gdns 46 A1
Downland Way 46 A1
Downs Clo 46 A4
Downs View 46 A4
Downs Way 46 A4
Duncan Rd 46 D2
Egmont Way 46 D2
Elm Gdns 46 B2
Epsom La 46 A1
Epsom La South 46 B5
Fairacres 46 B4
Ferriers Way 46 C2
Fleetwood Clo 46 C4
Glen Clo 46 D6
Gorse Clo 46 A3
Great Tattenhams 46 A1
Harendon 46 B5
Harpurs 46 C5
Hatch Gdns 46 C3
Hawes Rd 46 C3
Headley Dri 46 A2
Headley Gro 46 B3
Heath Clo 46 D5
Heathcote 46 C5
Heathdene 46 D2
Heathlands 46 C5
Heathside Ct 46 B6
Henbit Clo 46 A2
Hewers Way 46 B3
High St 46 B6
Hill La 46 D4
Hillview 46 B4
Home Farm Clo 46 C1
Homefield Gdns 46 B3
Hudsons 46 C4
Kilasser Ct 46 B6
Kings Ct 46 B5
Kingsdene 46 A5
Kingswood Rd 46 A4
Kipings 46 C5
Long Walk 46 C2
Longfield Cres 46 C3
Longmere Gdns 46 C2
Lordsgrove Clo 46 A3
Lothian Wood 46 A6
Lywood Clo 46 B5
*Mabbotts, Harendon 46 B5
Mallow Clo 46 A2
Marbles Way 46 C2
Maybury Clo 46 D2
Meadow Way 46 D1
Meare Clo 46 B6
Meon Clo 46 A5
Merefield Gdns 46 C3
Merland Grn 46 B3
Merland Rise 46 B2
Merton Gdns 46 C3
Michelham Gdns 46 B4
Mill Rd 46 C6
Milstead Clo 46 A6
Morden Clo 46 C3
Morston Clo 46 A3
Morton 46 C4
Motts Hill La 46 A6
New Rd 46 B6
North Ashurst Rd 46 A4
Oakdene 46 D3
Oaklands Way 46 B5
Oaks Way 46 A2
Oatfield Rd 46 A4
Oatlands Rd 46 D2
Parthia Clo 46 B2
Pit Wood Grn 46 B3
Preston La 46 B4
Prossers 46 C4
Radolphs 46 C5
Reigate Rd 46 C1
Royal Dri 46
Ruffetts Way 46
Russells 46
St Leonards Rd 46
St Marks Rd 46
Saxons 46
Shawley Cres 46
Shawley Way 46
Shelvers Grn 46
Shelvers Hill 46
Shelvers Spur 46
Shelvers Way 46
Somerfield Clo 46
Spindlewood 46
Staithes Way 46
Station App Rd 46
Stewarts 46
Stokes Ridings 46
Summerlay Clo 46
Tadorne Rd 46
Tadworth St 46
Tangier Way 46 D
Tangier Wood 46 D
Tattenham Cres 46 A
Tattenham Gro 46 A
Tattenham Way 46 C
The Avenue 46 A
The Dell 46 B
The Green 46 D
The Hoppetty 46 C
The Knowle 46 B
The Lye 46 B
The Ridings 46 D
The Rise 46 B
The Spinney 46 A
The Walled Garden 46 C
The Warren 46 D
Thurnham Way 46 C
Tower Rd 46 B
Trittons 46 C
Troy Clo 46 A
Tulyar Clo 46 A
Upland Way 46 B1
Vernon Walk 46 C
Waterer Gdns 46 D1
Waterfield 46 A
Waterfield Grn 46 A4
Waterhouse La 46 D4
Watermead 46 A4
Watts La 46 C5
Watts Mead 46 C6
Wessels 46 C4
West Dri 46 C1
Whitebeam Way 46 A4
Whitegate Way 46 A3
Wilsons 46 C5
Woodland Way 46 D6

VIRGINIA WATER

Abbey Rd 47 E2
Abbots Dri 47 C2
Badgers Hill 47 D2
Beechmont Av 47 E3
Blacknest Rd 47 A1
Bourne Rd 47 E3
Bourneside 47 B4
Bridge La 47 F3
Brockway 47 D2
Cabrera Av 47 D3
Cabrera Clo 47 D3
Callow Hill 47 C1
Chapel Sq 47 F1
Chestnut Av 47 A2
Christchurch Rd 47 B1
*Connolly Ct,
Holloway Dri 47 F2
*Crossland Ho,
Holloway Dri 47 F2
Crown La 47 E4
Crown Rd 47 D4
East Dri 47 B4
Edgell Clo 47 F1
Friars Rd 47 E2
Furnival Clo 47 E4
*Gillespie Ho,
Holloway Dri 47 F2
Gorse Hill La 47 E2
Gorse Hill Rd 47 E2
Harpesford Av 47 C3
Heath Clo 47 E1
Heath Rise 47 E2
Heatherside Dri 47 B4
Hillside 47 D3
Hollow La 47 D1

Meadows Leigh Clo 50 C2
Melrose Rd 50 B3
Minorca Rd 50 B2
Molyneux Rd 50 B3
Montrose Walk 50 B1
Monument Grn 50 B2
Monument Hill 50 C2
Monument Rd 50 C2
Mount Pleasant 50 B1
Mulberry Clo 50 C2
New Rd 50 C3
North Common 50 C3
Northfield Pl 50 B5
Oakdale Rd 50 B2
Oakfield Glade 50 D2
Oatlands Av 50 D3
Oatlands Clo 50 D3
Oatlands Dri 50 C2
Old Avenue 50 D5
Old Palace Rd 50 C2
Outram Pl 50 D4
Palace Dri 50 C2
*Palace Way, Palace Dri 50 C2
Park Dri 50 B4
Park Lawn Rd 50 C2
Park Way 50 D2
Pine Ct 50 D3
Pine Gro 50 C3
Pine Gro Mews 50 D3
Portmore Park Rd 50 A2
Portmore Quays 50 A2
Portmore Way 50 B2
Princes Rd 50 C3
Pyrcroft La 50 C3
Queens Rd 50 C3
Radnor Rd 50 B1
*Rede Ct, Palace Dri 50 C2
Round Oak Rd 50 A2
St Albans Av 50 B1
St Charles Pl 50 B3
St Georges Av 50 C4
St Georges Clo 50 D4
St Georges Lodge 50 D3
St James Mews 50 B3
St Michaels Ct 50 D3
Segrave Clo 50 B5
Sorbie Clo 50 D4
South Rd, Brooklands 50 C6
South Rd, Weybridge 50 D3
Southerland Clo 50 D2
Southfield Pl 50 C6
Spencer Av 50 B6
Springfield La 50 B2
Springfield Meadows 50 B2
Stoneleigh Pk 50 C4
Stroudwater Park 50 C4
*Stuart Ct, Palace Dri 50 C2
Thames St 50 B1
The Crescent 50 B2
The Meades 50 D4
The Square 50 D3
The Willows 50 B1
Towers Walk 50 C4
Trelawney Gro 50 B4
Tudor Walk 50 C1
Vaillant Rd 50 C2
Vale Clo 50 D1
Vale Rd 50 D1
Virginia Clo 50 D4
Warpole Park 50 B5
Warren Ct 50 B4
Warren Way 50 C4
Warreners La 50 D6
Waverley Rd 50 B3
West Palace Gdns 50 C1
West Rd 50 C6
Wey Rd 50 A2
Weybridge Pk 50 B3
Weybridge Rd 50 A2
White Knights Rd 50 D5
Windsor Walk 50 C3
Winterbourne Gro 50 D4
Wood La 50 D6
Woodland Way 50 D3
Woodsome Lodge 50 C4
York Rd 50 D3

WOKING

Abbey Rd 51 A3
Abbotsford Clo 51 E2
Achilles Pl 51 A2
Addison Rd 51 D2
Albert Dri 51 F1
Alpha Rd 51 F1
Andover Ct 51 B4
Arnold Rd 51 F1
Arthurs Bridge Rd 51 A3
Ashwood Park 51 D4
Ashwood Rd 51 D4
Avon Mead 51 A3
Azalea Ct 51 B4
Barrens Brae 51 E4
Barrens Clo 51 E4
Barrens Pk 51 E4
Beaufort Rd 51 F2
Beech Gdns 51 B1
Belgrave Manor 51 C4
Beta Rd 51 F1
Birch Clo 51 A4
Birch Hill 51 A4
Blackness La 51 C4
Blandford Clo 51 F3
Bluebell Ct 51 B4
Board School Rd 51 D2
Boundary Rd 51 D2
Boundary Way 51 E1
Bracken Clo 51 D3
Bradfield Clo 51 C3
Brambledene Clo 51 A3
Brewery Road 51 B2
Bridge Barn La 51 A3
Bridge Clo 51 A3
Bridge Mews 51 A3
Brooklyn Clo 51 C4
Brooklyn Rd 51 C4
Broomhall End 51 C2
Broomhall La 51 C2
Broomhall Rd 51 C2
Brynford Clo 51 C1
Bullbeggars La 51 A2
Bury Clo 51 A2
Bury La 51 A2
Butts Rd 51 C3
Bylands 51 D4
Calluna Ct 51 D3
Canewden Clo 51 C4
Cavendish Rd 51 B4
Cavenham Clo 51 C4
Cawsey Way 51 C3
Chapel St 51 C3
Cherry St 51 B3
Chertsey Rd 51 D2
Chobham Rd 51 C1
Chobham Rd Sth 51 D2
Church Clo 51 B1
Church Hill 51 B2
Church Path 51 D3
Church Rd 51 B1
Church St E 51 D2
Church St W 51 C3
Cleardown 51 F4
Clover Ct 51 B4
Coley Av 51 D3
College La 51 A4
College Rd 51 F2
Commercial Way 51 C3
Constitution Hill 51 C4
Courtenay Rd 51 E1
Crobars Av 51 A1
Cromar Ct 51 A1
Daneshill 51 E4
De Lara Way 51 B3
Delta Rd 51 E1
Dianthus Ct 51 B4
Dinsdale Clo 51 D3
Dorchester Ct 51 E2
Dorset Dri 51 F3
Downside Orchard 51 E3
Duke St 51 D2
East Hill 51 F2
Eastbrook Clo 51 E2
Effingham Ct 51 C4
Elm Clo 51 B1
Elm Rd 51 D1
Elm Rd, Mt Hermon 51 B4
Emmetts Clo 51 A2
Erica Ct 51 B4
Eve Rd 51 F1
Everlands Clo 51 C4
Fairmead 51 A3
Fairview Av 51 C4
Fairview Clo 51 C4
Fenns Way 51 C1
Ferndale Rd 51 C2
Fircroft Clo 51 D4
Forge End 51 C3
Foxglove Dri 51 D1
Foxhanger Gdns 51 E2
Foxhills 51 A3
Frailey Clo 51 F2
Frailey Hill 51 F2
Friars Rise 51 E4
Glendale Clo 51 A3
Goldsmiths Clo 51 A3
Goldsworth Rd 51 A3
Graylands Clo 51 C2
Greenham Walk 51 A4
Greenheys Pl 51 D3
Grove Rd 51 D2
Guildford Rd 51 C3
Hall Pl 51 E2
Hammond Clo 51 A1
Hammond Rd 51 A1
Harelands Clo 51 A3
Harelands La 51 A3
Heath Rd 51 D1
Heather Clo 51 A1
Heathfield Clo 51 E3
Heathfield Rd 51 E3
Heathside Cres 51 D3
Heathside Gdns 51 E3
Heathside Park Rd 51 D3
Heathside Rd 51 D3
Hedgerley Ct 51 A3
High St, Horsell 51 A1
High St, Woking 51 C3
Hill Clo 51 A1
Hill View 51 C4
Hill View Rd 51 C4
Hockering Gdns 51 E3
Hockering Rd 51 E3
Holbeck Pl 51 C3
Holyoake Av 51 A2
Holyoake Cres 51 A2
Hopfields 51 C2
Horsell Moor 51 B3
Horsell Park 51 B2
Horsell Park Clo 51 B2
Horsell Rise 51 B1
Horsell Rise Clo 51 B1
Horsell Vale 51 B1
Horsell Way 51 A1
Ivy La 51 F3
Janoway Hill La 51 A4
Japonica Clo 51 A3
Julian 51 A4
Kent Rd 51 F1
Kerry Ter 51 E1
Kettlewell Clo 51 C1
Kettlewell Hill 51 C1
Kilrush Ter 51 E1
Kings Rd 51 E1
Kingsway 51 A4
Kingsway Av 51 B3
Kirby Rd 51 A2
Knowl Hill 51 F4
Laleham Ct 51 C1
Lampeter Clo 51 C4
Lancaster Clo 51 E2
Langdale Clo 51 A2
Langley Walk 51 B4
Lavender Rd 51 F2
Lockfield Dri 51 A3
Lych Way 51 B2
Lyndhurst Clo 51 B1
Lytton Rd 51 E2
Mabel St 51 A3
Manor Rd 51 A2
Maple Ct 51 A2
Market Sq 51 C3
Marlborough Rd 51 D2
Maybury Hill 51 F2
Maybury Rd 51 D2
Mayhurst Av 51 F2
Meadway Dri 51 A1
Merrivale Gdns 51 A3
Midhope Clo 51 C4
Midhope Gdns 51 B4
Midhope Rd 51 B4
Montgomery Rd 51 C4
Monument Rd 51 E1
Monument Way E 51 F1
Monument Way W 51 E1
Moorholme 51 C4
Morton Clo 51 A1
Morton Rd 51 A1
Mount Hermon Clo 51 B4
Mount Hermon Rd 51 B4
North Rd 51 E2
Oak La 51 F2
Oakbank 51 C4
Oaks Rd 51 C3
Ockenden Clo 51 D4
Ockenden Rd 51 D4
Old Malt Way 51 B2
Old Woking Rd 51 F4
Omega Rd 51 E1
Onslow Clo 51 E2
Onslow Cres 51 E3
Orchard Clo 51 F2
Orchard Dri 51 C1
Oriental Clo 51 D2
Oriental Rd 51 D3
Ormonde Rd 51 A2
Pares Clo 51 B2
Park Dri 51 C4
Park Pl 51 D4
Park Rd 51 D3
Parley Dri 51 A3
Pembroke Gdns 51 E3
Pembroke Rd 51 E3
Pollard Rd 51 F1
Poolc Rd 51 B3
Poplar Gro 51 C4
Portugal Rd 51 D2
Princess Gdns 51 F1
Princess Rd 51 F1
Queen Mary Clo 51 F1
Radstone Ct 51 D4
Ravenswood Ct 51 D4
Ridgeway 51 B1
Ridgeway Gdns 51 B1
Roscoe Dri 51 E2
Rosehill Av 51 A2
Round Hill Clo 51 F4
Round Hill Dri 51 F4
Royal Oak Rd 51 A4
Russetts Clo 51 C1
St Andrews Clo 51 A2
St Fillans 51 F2
St Johns Rd 51 A4
St Marys Rd 51 A2
St Pauls Rd 51 E2
St Thomas Clo 51 A2
Sandy Clo 51 F3
Sandy La 51 F2
Sandy Way 51 F2
Selhurst Clo 51 D1
Shaftesbury Rd 51 E3
Sidcock Hill 51 A3
Silversmiths Way 51 A3
South Clo 51 A1
South Rd 51 A1
Southcote 51 B1
Southview 51 C4
Stanley Rd 51 D2
Station App 51 D3
Station Rd 51 C3
Sylvan Clo 51 F3
Tamerton Sq 51 C4
The Birches 51 D3
The Broadway 51 D3
The Dell 51 A4
The Furlogh 51 E2
The Grove 51 C2
The Mount 51 B4
The Peacocks 51 C3
The Ridge 51 F2
The Rowans 51 C4
Thornash Clo 51 A1
Thor-ash Rd 51 A1
Thornash Way 51 A1
Thorsden Clo 51 C4
Thorsden Ct 51 C4
Thurlton Ct 51 C1
Tintagel Way 51 E2
Tower Clo 51 B2
Town Sq 51 C2
Triggs Clo 51 A4
Triggs La 51 A4
Tudor Clo 51 E3
Vale Farm Rd 51 B3
Verralls 51 F3
Victoria Rd 51 C3
Victoria Way 51 C2
Waldens Park Rd 51 A2
Waldens Rd 51
Walton Ct 51
Walton Rd 51
Walton Ter 51
Waverley Ct 51
Well Clo 51
Well La 51
Wendela Clo 51
West Hill Rd 51
West St 51
Wheatsheaf Clo 51
White Rose La 51
Whopshott Av 51
Wilbury Rd 51
Wilders Clo 51
Wilfred St 51
Wilson Way 51
Winnington Way 51 A
Wolsey Walk 51 C
Woodham Rd 51 C
Woodlands Ct 51 C
Woodlands 51 C
Woodstock Clo 51 C
Wych Hill Pk 51 B
York Rd 51 B

WONERSH/ BRAMLEY

Barnett Clo 52 D
Barnett Hill 52 C
Barnett Rd 52 D
Barton Rd 52 B
Birtley Rise 52 B
Birtley Road 52 C
Blackheath La 52 D
Blunden Ct 52 B
Bracken Clo 52 C
Brambles Pk 52 B
Chestnut Way 52 C
Chinthurst La 52 B
Clockhouse La 52 A
Drodgers Clo 52 A
Eastwood Rd 52 A
Edencroft 52 B2
Firs Av 52 B2
Fisher Rowe Clo 52 B2
Garden Clo 52 F4
Grantley Av 52 D2
Guildford Rd 52 C2
Hall Rd 52 B2
High St 52 B2
Hill Clo 52 C2
Hill Meade 52 F4
Home Park Clo 52 A3
Horsham Rd 52 A1
Hullbrook La 52 F4
Linersh Dri 52 B2
Linersh Wood Clo 52 B2
Links Rd 52 A1
Lords Hill 52 E4
Mellersh Hill Rd Sth 52 D2
Mill La 52 A3
New Rd 52 D1
Norley Rd 52 E3
Northcote La 52 E3
Nursery Hill 52 E4
Old Rectory Clo 52 B2
Park Dri 52 A3
Ricardo Ct 52 B3
Riverside Dri 52 B1
Snowdenham La 52 A3
Station Rd 52 B2
Stonards Brow 52 E4
Sweetwater Clo 52 E4
Sweetwater La 52 E4
Tanyard Rd 52 A1
The Beeches 52 A2
The Close 52 C2
The Coombs 52 B3
The Drive 52 C3
The Farriers 52 B3
The Range 52 B4
Windrush Clo 52 B2
Wonersh Common Rd 52 C1
Woodhill La 52 F4
Woodrough Copse 52 B3
Woodyers Clo 52 C2